MY SOUL SHALL BE HEALED

THE NEW TRANSLATION OF THE MISSAL

Patrick Mullins OCarm

W/O

VERITAS

Published 2012 by
Veritas Publications
7–8 Lower Abbey Street
Dublin 1, Ireland
publications@veritas.ie
www.veritas.ie

ISBN 978 1 84730 406 3
Copyright © Patrick Mullins, 2012
10 9 8 7 6 5 4 3 2 1

A catalogue record for this book is available from the British Library.

Cover designed by Dara O'Connor, Veritas
Printed in the Republic of Ireland by Walsh Colour Print, Kerry

Veritas books are printed on paper made from the wood pulp of managed forests. For every tree felled, at least one tree is planted, thereby renewing natural resources.

CONTENTS

Introduction

Dictionaries are designed to help those unfamiliar with a particular word or language to discover the meaning of an unfamiliar word. That word may be in one's own language or in a language with which one is not familiar. The 1987 edition of *A Latin Dictionary* by Lewis and Short gives 'carrying or removing from one place to another' as the essential meaning of the word *translatio*. It notes the transfer of money from one place to another, the transplanting of plants and the pouring of a liquid into another vessel as the three literal uses of the word. It also lists the shifting of blame for a crime, translation into another language, transfer to a figurative signification and the transposition of letters or words as among its figurative meanings.[1] Noting the root meaning of transportation, Dr Johnson's *Dictionary of the English Language* described translation as 'changing into another language, retaining the sense',[2] and for Roguet and Sheppard the success of the translator 'can be measured by the amount of "sense"' that is retained.[3]

There are different kinds of translation. When we do not understand what someone is saying to us because we do not speak their language, a summary paraphrase that communicates the essential points is generally sufficient. A Spanish-English phrasebook that translates *playa* as 'beach', for example, can provide all the help that we need in following the signs to the sand and water where we plan to spend the day. When we are trying to communicate in a language in which we are not fluent, we must sometimes be satisfied with an approximate formulation that may not quite capture what we want to say. The subtitles provided in a DVD of a foreign-language film may not capture every nuance of every conversation but they are usually sufficient to enable us to follow the plot. Because of its importance in our lives, or because of the conflicting interpretations proposed concerning it, however, there are circumstances where we might not be satisfied with a perhaps inaccurate paraphrase. Were we to be arrested and charged with a serious crime in a country where we do not speak the language, we would probably want a detailed and faithful translation of the precise charges against us in order to mount a defence. When our only access to an important text in another language is by means of a particular translation, the quality of that translation, the degree to which it has faithfully carried over the meaning of the original into our own language, becomes a matter of particular concern.

'A translator must be like a pane of glass, that lets all the light through but is not seen itself' is a statement attributed to the teenage St Teresia Benedicta a Cruce (Edith Stein).[4] Her German edition of Alexandre Koyré's study on Descartes and the Scholastic Philosophers (1923) is described in the subtitle[5] and in one of Stein's letters[6] as having been 'translated (*Übersetzt*)' by Edith Stein and Hedwig Conrad-Martius. Stein seems to have come to recognise that a 'translation (*Übersetzung*)' in which the original work was perfectly reproduced was a rarely achieved ideal, however. Sarah Borden points out that she describes all her later work in translating the English writings of Blessed John Henry Newman and the Latin writings of St Thomas Aquinas as a 'paraphrase (*Übertragung*)'[7] rather than as a 'translation (*Übersetzung*)'.[8] In these works, she was not so much trying to recreate the original in a different language as guide the reader in appreciating the significance of the text from a particular point of view.

In liturgical translation, Roguet and Sheppard recognise that 'two very different courses can be adopted' and that these courses 'are suitable for different purposes and uses'. The first, 'the reproduction of the foreign text in English', was often used when translating 'sacred texts which were held to be verbally inspired, and therefore even the arrangement of the words in a sentence was respected as far as possible.'[9] The second course is to adopt the principle proposed by Ronald Knox,[10] quoting Hilaire Belloc, by trying to answer the question, 'What would an Englishman have said to express this?' In this case the purpose of the translation is 'to produce not a copy but a fresh creation, an English book of such limpidity of style and ease of reading that the reader has the impression of immediate contact with the original.'[11] There is always the danger that, in trying to make the translation intelligible, we lose touch with the sense of the original; indeed the Italians have a proverb to this effect: *Traduttore, traditore* (The translator [is a] traitor).

During the Second Vatican Council (1962–65), the normative 'Roman' Ordinary of the Mass celebrated all over the Catholic world was that of the 1962 Latin Missal,[12] which updated the Tridentine Missal (1570) of Pope Pius V. The first of the documents promulgated by the Second Vatican Council was the Constitution on the Sacred Liturgy, *Sacrosanctum Concilium* (1963). In keeping with the recognition in Pius XII's 1947 encyclical, *Mediator Dei*, of the Mass as 'the source and centre of Christian piety' (n. 201), it described the liturgy as 'the summit toward which the activity of the church is directed' and 'the source from which all its power flows' (n. 10). As well as laying the foundation for a general revision of the Latin Missal, it promoted the 'full, conscious, and active participation' of all the faithful in liturgical celebrations

(n. 14) and it approved an extended use of the vernacular (the language commonly used in a particular region) in the liturgy of the Mass (n. 36). Striking a balance between simplification and preserving and even restoring essential elements, it said that the rites of the Mass were 'to be simplified, due care being taken to preserve their substance' and that 'parts which were lost through the vicissitudes of history are to be restored according to the ancient tradition of the holy Fathers, as may seem appropriate or necessary' (n. 50). In his address to the Congress of Liturgical Translators in Rome in 1965, Pope Paul VI said that 'the language that translators must use for the passages taken from Scripture, which contains the word of God, differs from the language that they must adopt for collects and hymns'.[13] In 1969, he approved the new Latin 'typical edition' of the Missal on which all translations into vernacular languages were to be based and the Latin edition of the new Paul VI Missal was published on 26 March 1970.

The previous year, 1969, the commission entrusted with the implementation of *Sacrosanctum Concilium* had issued *Comme le prévoit*, an instruction 'on the translation of liturgical texts for celebrations with a congregation'. *Comme le prévoit* regarded the translation of a Latin liturgical text as a form of communication using language that was both 'worthy of expressing the highest realities' and in 'common' usage (n. 7, 15). Laying down specific norms for the translation of Eucharistic Prayers and certain other kinds of liturgical texts, it encouraged translators to focus on the meaning of each Latin word in the dynamic 'total context' of the passage under consideration, rather than on its fixed meaning in a dictionary (n. 6). The emphasis on finding the English equivalent that reflects the dynamic total context of a particular passage, rather than on focusing on the formal equivalent of each word to be translated, has since become known as 'dynamic' or 'functional' equivalence.[14] A good example of this approach, perhaps, is that of Roguet and Sheppard who argued in 1970 that, when translating the non-biblical texts that cease 'to be used as a translation' when they are 'endowed with a new dignity and … a sort of autonomy' as 'the liturgical text', there was no 'middle course' between being rigorously faithful to the original when translating texts from Scripture and producing, instead, an easily read version. In the non-biblical liturgical texts, it 'is no longer God who speaks' to the hearer but rather the hearer 'who speaks to God', and such texts 'cannot therefore be expressed in archaic or tortuous language which would give the impression of a fabrication or a faculty reconstruction'.[15] Some liturgical historians have described the liturgical experimentation of the 1960s and 1970s, 'with home masses, folk masses, home-grown Eucharistic Prayers, and even liturgical texts sung to the tune of Bob Dylan's "Blowin' in the Wind"',[16] as a time of 'complete liturgical anarchy'.[17] It was during this period that the International Commission on

English in the Liturgy (ICEL) produced an English translation of the 1970 Latin Missal in just three years, and the Jesuit liturgist Pecklers comments that 'few liturgical scholars would disagree' with the judgement that this translation has 'numerous flaws'.[18] The 'dynamic equivalence' approach seems to have been adopted somewhat uncritically and, using the terminology proposed by Robert Taft, the recipient language (English) seems to have taken precedence over the donor language (Latin) even when all other things were anything but equal.[19]

Approved in 1973, the new English translation is identical with the version of the new English Missal for Ireland that was published in 1974 except for the inclusion of 'My Lord and My God' as a memorial acclamation and the texts concerning Irish saints.[20] The 1973 translation was never intended to be the final and definitive translation and Comme le prévoit recognised (n. 1) that 'after sufficient experiment and passage of time, all translations will need review'. During the period 1973 to 2011, different viewpoints on the strengths and weakness of the 1973 translation emerged. Although many expressed their appreciation for the way in which the 'dynamic equivalence' approach of ICEL had translated the original Latin of the 1970 'typical edition', there was a growing unease among others because of what had been lost in that translation. Liturgical experts debated the relative merits of the 'dynamic equivalence' approach adopted in the 1973 translation and of a more word-for-word 'formal equivalence' or 'formal correspondence' approach. In 1982, ICEL initiated a consultation process with the different English-speaking Conferences of Bishops with a view to preparing a revised English translation. Work on the preparation of the Revised Sacramentary, as it was known, began in 1987 and the first of eight different segments was issued in 1992. When the Revised Sacramentary was completed in 1998, it was approved by the eleven English-speaking Bishops' Conferences involved, but the Congregation for Divine Worship was not happy with the text and refused to grant the required approval or recognitio. Such a situation had been envisaged in 1969, when Comme le prévoit had established that any translations prepared and approved by Episcopal Conferences could only be promulgated 'after approval, that is, confirmation by the Holy See' (n. 2).

In effect, the Congregation for Divine Worship had moved away somewhat from the 'dynamic equivalence' approach that had been the inspiration for the work of ICEL in drawing up the Revised Sacramentary towards a greater emphasis on word-for-word 'formal equivalence'. In 2001, the Vatican's Congregation for Divine Worship and the Discipline of the Sacraments issued an instruction, Liturgiam authenticam, with the subtitle, 'On the Use of Vernacular Languages in the Publication of the Books of the Roman Liturgy'. This instruction established an approach that put greater emphasis on 'formal equivalence' as the new norm for the translation of liturgical texts. In effect, it asked translators to follow the wording and structure of the original Latin more closely, to highlight any implicit references to the language and images used in the Bible, and to restore some of the theological vocabulary in the Latin text that had been lost.

In 2002, Pope John Paul II promulgated a new typical edition of the Paul VI Missal[21] and the process of drawing up a new translation of the Missal for use in English-speaking countries began that same year. New statutes for ICEL were approved in 2003, and between 2004 and 2009 ICEL prepared and issued a new draft English Missal in twelve segments that were approved by the Irish Bishops' Conference before being submitted to the Congregation for Divine Worship and the Discipline of the Sacraments for review.[22] Having incorporated the various comments and suggestions received, the new translation received the required approval or *recognitio* in 2010. A more detailed description of the norms for the translation of liturgical texts into English, the *Ratio translationis for the English Language*,[23] was issued by the Congregation for Divine Worship and the Discipline of the Sacraments in 2007 and these norms are reflected in the final drafts.

In his post-synodal apostolic exhortation, *Sacramentum Caritatis* (2007), Pope Benedict XVI noted that the words of the dismissal, *Ite, missa est,* implied a missionary dimension:[24]

> After the blessing, the deacon or the priest dismisses the people with the words: *Ite, missa est*. These words help us to grasp the relationship between the Mass just celebrated and the mission of Christians in the world. In antiquity, *missa* simply meant 'dismissal'. However in Christian usage it gradually took on a deeper meaning. The word 'dismissal' has come to imply a 'mission.' These few words succinctly express the missionary nature of the Church. The People of God might be helped to understand more clearly this essential dimension of the Church's life, taking the dismissal as a starting-point. In this context, it might also be helpful to provide new texts, duly approved, for the prayer over the people and the final blessing, in order to make this connection clear.[25]

In 2008, having sought and received seventy-two proposals for implementing the change that had been suggested by the Synod of Bishops on the Eucharist in 2005, nine were chosen for presentation to Pope Benedict XVI, who eventually approved three new alternative versions of the Dismissal:[26]

> Go and announce the Gospel of the Lord (*Ite ad Evangelium Domini nuntiandum*).

> Go in peace, glorifying the Lord by your life (*Ite in pace, glorificando vita vestra Dominum*).
> Go in peace (*Ite in pace*).

In its review of the new translations that would be used in the various anglophone countries of the world, the Congregation for Divine Worship and the Discipline of the Sacraments was assisted by Vox Clara, a committee of senior bishops that includes Bishop Philip Boyce of Raphoe. Like the majority of its equivalents throughout the English-speaking world, the new translation of the Missal for Ireland was published in 2011,[27] and from Advent 2011 these approved new translations became mandatory in the regions for which they had been written.

Drawn up on the basis of the directives in *Liturgiam authenticam* and in the *Ratio translationis for the English Language*, the new translation is somewhat 'more formal' and 'in parts, more complex'[28] than the older translation. Among the changes in the people's parts, the response 'And also with you' has become 'And with your spirit', and there are new translations of the 'I Confess', the 'Glory to God in the highest', the Creeds, the acclamations in the Eucharistic Prayers, the 'Lord, I am not worthy' and a number of other prayers and responses. Writing in 2009, Pecklers suggested that the 'rationale' for the linguistic shift from the old to the new translation of the Missal has 'not always been articulated' as clearly as it might. Had the principles adopted in the new translation been adopted by 'the English-language world' when it originally translated the Latin text, 'we would not be the position we are in today' where, having grown accustomed to the old translation, 'lay people understandably feel that something is being taken from them' and where 'many read a conservative agenda into such a shift.'[29] The Benedictine liturgist, Anscar Chupungco, has described the translation of liturgical texts as 'perhaps the most delicate and complex matter arising from the Church's decision to shift from Latin to the vernacular languages.'[30] While Chupungco recognises that the 'dynamic equivalence' approach to translation proposed in *Comme le prévoit* is considered 'dated' after the publication of *Liturgiam authenticam* in 2001, he recognises that 'its value as a guideline for liturgical translation stands on solid scientific grounds.' While 'due respect should always be given to the grammar, lexicon and syntax of both the source and receptor languages', he continues to maintain that, in order to 'help today's liturgical assembly to grasp the meaning of what was originally communicated, the message should be reexpressed using the linguistic patterns proper to the receptor language.'[31]

This book is designed to address some of these issues by helping people to understand the principles that were used in the drawing up of the 1973 and 2011 translations and by trying to evaluate both the older and the more recent translation in the light of the principles of translation that had been adopted. In order to facilitate readers who may not be familiar with the technical aspects of Latin translation, the use of Latin words and the details concerning particular translations and paraphrases have been confined to the notes as far as possible. The first chapter describes the approach that was adopted in the first English translation in 1973 based on *Comme le prévoit* (1969). The second chapter outlines the changes to the most commonly used sections of the Missal that have been introduced in the 2011 translation based on *Liturgiam authenticam* (2001) and the *Ratio translationis for the English Language* (2007). It focuses particularly on the way in which the language used in the Bible to describe the human person's relationship with God, which had been lost in the 1973 English translation, has been reintroduced. The third chapter explores the way in which key anthropological terms such as soul (*anima*), body (*corpus*) and spirit (*spiritus*) have been translated in the 1973 and 2011 translations. Based on the preceding chapters, the conclusion outlines the main strengths and weaknesses of both translations.

If this book makes even a modest contribution towards helping people to engage in liturgical prayer based on the new translation of the Missal, its author will be more than satisfied. Whatever positive qualities it may have reflect his many debts to his teachers, his colleagues, his students, his confreres and his friends but he takes full responsibility for its shortcomings and will consider it a kindness if these are pointed out to him.

CHAPTER I

Comme le prévoit and the 1973 Translation

The Consilium for implementing Vatican II's Constitution on the Sacred Liturgy issued the document *Comme le prévoit* in January 1969. Its French title reflects the fact that it was originally drafted in French and it was given the subtitle *On the Translation of Liturgical Texts for Celebrations with a Congregation*. In this chapter, we begin by outlining the principles of translation given in *Comme le prévoit*. We will then analyse the way in which those principles have been used in the 1973 English translation of the Missal.

Comme le prévoit (1969)

The instruction encouraged the presidents of the different Episcopal Conferences to appoint international commissions so that one text might be prepared for all the countries where a common language was spoken (n. 2). Recognising that translations 'are the responsibility of the competent territorial authority of each country' (n. 3) and that translations could only be promulgated when they had been confirmed by the Holy See (n. 2), it tried 'to lay down, in common and non-technical terms, some of the more important theoretical and practical principles for the guidance of all who are called upon to prepare, to approve, or to confirm liturgical translations' (n. 4).

Under the heading 'General Principles', *Comme le prévoit* recognised that a liturgical text 'is a medium of spoken communication' that is 'received by the senses' but also that 'to believers who celebrate the sacred rites a word is itself a "mystery"' by means of which 'Christ himself speaks to his people and the people, through the Spirit in the Church, answer their Lord' (n. 5). From this perspective, the 'purpose of liturgical translations is to proclaim the message of salvation to believers and to express the prayer of the Church to the Lord' (n. 6) with the result that

> ... it is not sufficient that a liturgical translation merely reproduce the expressions and ideas of the original text. Rather it must faithfully communicate to a given people, and in their own language, that which the Church by means of this given text originally intended to communicate to another people in another time. A faithful translation, therefore, cannot be judged on the basis of individual words: the total

context of this specific act of communication must be kept in mind, as
well as the literary form proper to the respective language.

Translations 'must be faithful to the art of communication in all its various
aspects, but especially in regard to the message itself, in regard to the
audience for which it is intended, and in regard to the manner of expression'
(n. 7). The translator 'should give first consideration to the meaning of the
communication' (n. 8).

The translator 'must follow the scientific methods of textual study as used
by experts' to discover 'the true meaning of a text' (n. 9). Latin terms 'must
be considered in the light of their uses – historical or cultural, Christian or
liturgical' and, in an English liturgical text, the Latin word *oratio*, for example,
does not mean 'an oration (one of its senses in classical Latin) but a prayer' (n.
11). The Latin *caro* 'is inadequately rendered in English as "flesh"'; *servus* and
famula 'are inadequately rendered in English by "slave, servant, handmaid"';
and the 'force of an image or metaphor must also be considered, whether
it is rare or common, living or worn out' (n. 11). Article 12 points out that
the '"unit of meaning" is not the individual word but the whole passage'
and the importance of particular phrases should not be exaggerated so that
'it obscures or weakens the meaning of the whole'. The 'piling up' of Latin
adjectives 'may increase the sense of invocation' but, in other languages, a
'succession of adjectives', 'the too casual use of superlatives' or 'the routine
addition' of Saint or Blessed to a saint's name 'may actually weaken the force
of the prayer'. In English, understatement 'is sometimes the more effective
means of emphasis'. To ensure that words and expressions 'keep the correct
signification', they 'must be used in their proper historical, social, and ritual
meanings' (n. 13). Many of 'the phrases of approach to the Almighty', such as
'*Quaesumus, dignare, clementissime, maiestas*, and the like', were 'originally
adapted from forms of address to the Sovereign in the courts of Byzantium
and Rome' and it is now 'necessary to study how far an attempt should be
made to offer equivalents in modern English' (n. 13).

Comme le prévoit says that the 'accuracy and value of a translation can
only be assessed in terms of the purpose of the communication' (n. 14) and, in
order to 'serve the particular congregations who will use it', translators should
ensure that the 'language chosen should be that in "common" usage, that
is, suited to the greater number of the faithful who speak it in everyday use,
even "children and persons of small education"' (n. 15). The language 'should
not be "common" in the bad sense', however, but 'worthy of expressing
the highest realities' and, although 'liturgical texts must sometimes possess
a truly poetic quality … this does not imply the use of specifically "poetic
diction"' (n. 15). Sometimes 'the everyday common meaning' of words and

phrases 'taken from the so-called sacral vocabulary now in use' can 'carry a pre-Christian, quasi-Christian, Christian, or even anti-Christian meaning' and the translation 'should also consider whether such words can convey the exact Christian liturgical action and manifestation of faith' (n. 17). For example, the 'proper meaning' of the word *misericordia* in biblical Latin 'is not accurately expressed in English by "mercy" or "pity"' (n. 17). Because there is often 'no word in common use that exactly corresponds to the biblical or liturgical sense of the term to be translated', the 'nearest suitable word must then be chosen', as when the Latin *gloria* is used to translate the Hebrew *kabod* (n. 18). The translation of *hominibus bonae voluntatis* as 'men of good will' or 'good will to men' will be 'misleading', *venerabilis* in *venerabiles manus* cannot 'be translated as "venerable"' and 'there is no exact equivalent of *mysterium*' in English because '"mystery" means something which cannot be readily explained or else a type of drama or fiction' (n. 18). Because the prayer of the Church 'is always the prayer of some actual community, assembled here and now', it is 'not sufficient that a formula handed down from some other time or region be translated verbatim, even if accurately, for liturgical use' (n. 20).

Sometimes, as in 'heaven and earth are full of your glory (*pleni sunt caeli et terra gloria tua*)', 'a text can be translated word for word and keep the same meaning as the original' but, at other times, 'the metaphors must be changed to keep the true sense, as in *locum refrigerii*[1] in northern regions' (nn. 22–23). Because a 'particular form of expression and speech is required for spoken communication' (n. 25), translators should remember that the 'literary genre of every liturgical text depends first of all on the nature of the ritual act signified in the words – acclamation or supplication, proclamation or praying, reading or singing. Every action requires its proper form of expression' (n. 26). Recognising that some elements are 'secondary and subsidiary', the 'essential elements, so far as is possible, should be preserved in translation, sometimes intact, sometimes in equivalent terms' (n. 28). If 'any particular kind of quality is regarded as essential to a literary genre (for example, intelligibility of prayers when said aloud), this may take precedence over another quality less significant for communication (for example, verbal fidelity)' (n. 29).

Under the heading 'Some Particular Considerations', *Comme le prévoit* outlines particular norms for some blessing and sacramental formularies:

> Some euchological and sacramental formularies like the consecratory prayers, the anaphoras, prefaces, exorcisms, and those prayers which accompany an action, such as the imposition of hands, the anointing, the signs of the cross, etc., should be translated integrally and faithfully, without variations, omissions, or insertions. These texts, whether ancient or modern, have a precise and studied theological

elaboration. If the text is ancient, certain Latin terms present difficulties of interpretation because of their use and meaning, which are much different from their corresponding terms in modern language. The translation will therefore demand an astute handling and sometimes a paraphrasing, in order to render accurately the original pregnant meaning. If the text is a more recent one, the difficulty will be reduced considerably, given the use of terms and a style of language which are closer to modern concepts. (n. 33)

It also describes how the Presidential Prayers are to be translated:

The prayers (opening prayer, prayer over the gifts, prayer after communion, and prayer over the people) from the ancient Roman tradition are succinct and abstract. In translation they may need to be rendered somewhat more freely while conserving the original ideas. This can be done by moderately amplifying them or, if necessary, paraphrasing expressions in order to concretize them for the celebration and the needs of today. In every case pompous and superfluous language should be avoided. (n. 34)

All texts that 'are intended to be said aloud', and especially 'the acclamations where the act of acclaiming by voice is an essential element', should 'follow the laws proper to their delivery and, in the case of written texts, their literary genre' in the sense that it is 'insufficient to translate the exact meaning of an idea unless the text can also be expressed by sound and rhythm' (n. 35). When they 'become part of the liturgy', the 'responses (versicles, responsories) and antiphons' that 'come from Scripture … enter into a new literary form' so that, in 'translating them, it is possible to give them a verbal form which, while preserving their full meaning, is more suitable for singing and harmonises them with the liturgical season or a special feast' (n. 35.c).

Having outlined the principles of translation given in *Comme le prévoit*, we will now analyse how these principles were implemented in the 1973 translation of some of the most frequently used texts of the Missal. The original Latin and the 1973 English translation of these texts are given in the Appendix.

The 1973 Translation of the Ordinary of the Mass
Because of the particular norms in *Comme le prévoit* n. 33 concerning the anaphoras (Eucharistic Prayers), I will consider these Prayers in a separate section from the Introductory Rites, the Liturgy of the Word, the Liturgy of the Eucharist and the Communion and Concluding Rites. Here I will analyse the

1973 translation of the texts other than the Eucharistic Prayers in terms of its readability, its omission of any of the words in the Latin text, its additions to the words in the Latin text, its options for a paraphrase rather than a direct translation of the Latin text, its approach to the translation of gendered words, its use of punctuation and its use of capitalisation.

The Irish Jesuit theologian, Raymond Moloney, has recognised that, although it 'corresponds to the scriptural meaning of the phrase (cf. 2 Tm 4:22)', the translation 'And also with you (*et cum spiritu tuo*)' does not reflect the 'deeper meaning' of the word 'spirit' in liturgy and is out of line with the explicit reference to 'spirit' in the translations used by other modern languages.[2] Recognising that it may have been 'in consonance with the modern holistic view of the human person' that *spiritu tuo* was not translated literally, Chupungco nevertheless agrees that the translation given 'fails to convey the full sense of the original formula'.[3]

The 1973 text did not translate certain words or phrases of the Latin text of the Introductory, Communion and Concluding Rites or of the Liturgies of the Word and of the Eucharist. In the *Confiteor*, it seems to have overlooked the implicit reference to King David's 'I have greatly sinned (*peccavi nimis*)' (1 Chr 21:8) when it did not translate the adverb *nimis*. It also omitted both the gesture of beating one's breast and the accompanying words, *mea culpa, mea culpa, mea maxima culpa*.[4] It is difficult to see how a translation with such omissions could 'faithfully communicate … that which the Church by means of this given text originally intended to communicate to another people in another time', as *Comme le prévoit* n. 6 intended. There are a number of other omissions in the Introductory Rites where the implied Scripture reference makes the omission questionable.[5] As well as other omissions,[6] a significant number of adverbial and adjectival qualifiers[7] and some whole phrases[8] are also omitted in the Introductory Rites, the Liturgy of the Word, the Liturgy of the Eucharist and the Communion and Concluding Rites.

On occasion, the 1973 translation added certain words (in English italics in what follows) that are not found in the Latin text: In the Introductory Rites, for example, the 1973 text translated *misericordiam* as 'mercy *and love*' rather than as 'mercy'[9] and there are similar additions in the Liturgy of the Word, the Liturgy of the Eucharist and the Communion and Concluding Rites.[10]

Comme le prévoit n. 33 recognised that 'an astute handling and sometimes a paraphrasing' might be necessary when translating an ancient text such as the Gloria or the Creed because 'certain Latin terms present difficulties of interpretation because of their use and meaning, which are much different from their corresponding terms in modern language'. There are, in fact, a significant number of paraphrases in the 1973 text and, although the number of paraphrases identified depends to some extent on the number of words seen as constituting the paraphrase, the approximate number per 100 Latin words is least[11] in the Liturgy of the Word and greatest[12] in the Communion and Concluding Rites. The density for the other two sectors is slightly less than that for the Communion and Concluding Rites but it is greater in the Introductory Rites[13] than in the Liturgy of the Eucharist.[14] The best-known example is probably the translation of *Et cum spirito tuo* as 'And also with you'.[15] This English translation, the Irish translation, *Agus leat féin*, and the Brazilian Portuguese translation, *Ele esta no meio de nos* (literally, 'He is in our midst'), were among a small minority that did not translate the phrase, *Et cum spiritu tuo*, literally. Like the earliest versions of the Book of Common Prayer, which translated *Et cum spirito tuo* as 'And with thy spirit',[16] the majority opted for a literal translation.[17] Although it did not take account of the New Testament roots of the phrase, the translation 'And also with you' was recognised in some traditions as the true significance of the phrase as it was originally used in Hebrew culture[18] and some more recent translations of the Book of Common Prayer have 'And also with you'.[19] In 1948, Ronald Knox interpreted the dialogue that includes this phrase as follows:

> And then, just to make sure that he is carrying the congregation with him, he says, 'The Lord be with you'. And the server answers, 'And with you likewise' (that is all 'And with thy spirit' means). Priest and people are going about this great business of theirs shoulder to shoulder.[20]

In addition to the re-allocation of the words to be said by the priest and by the people during the Penitential Rite,[21] *mea culpa, mea culpa, mea maxima culpa* was paraphrased as 'through my own fault'[22] and there are other similar examples in the Introductory Rites.[23] There are a significant number of other paraphrases in the Liturgy of the Word,[24] the Liturgy of the Eucharist[25] and the Communion and Concluding Rites.[26] Rather than opting for a more modern or literal translation of the *Pater noster*,[27] the translators of the 1973 text chose a version that dates back, at least in part, to the early sixteenth century: 'Our Father, who art in heaven … .'[28] In some cases, the paraphrases in the 1973 text were not in keeping with the way a word or phrase was generally translated in similar contexts. Like the World English Bible, Young's Literal Translation, and the New American Standard (1995) Bibles, and like some English Translations of the Catechism of the Catholic Church, but unlike most other Bibles, the 1973 text translated the phrase *communicatio Sancti Spiritus* (see the *Nova Vulgata Editio* of 2 Cor 3:14) as 'the fellowship of the Holy Spirit'.[29] Leaving *vobis* untranslated and moving away from the syntax of both the original Greek greeting found in a number of the letters written by, or associated with, St Paul[30] and of the Latin translations of those greetings in the *Nova Vulgata Editio*, the 1973 text translated *Gratia vobis et pax a Deo Patre nostro et Domino Iesu Christo* as 'The grace and peace of God the Father and the Lord Jesus Christ be with you'.[31] There are a number of other examples in the Introductory Rites,[32] the Liturgy of the Word[33] and the Liturgy of the Eucharist[34] where the implicit citations of the *Nova Vulgata Editio* make the paraphrases chosen somewhat questionable.

In terms of how gendered words were translated, the 1973 text translated *homo* as 'man' and used the corresponding masculine pronoun, but it implicitly recognised the gender-inclusive nature of this Latin word (and of its then generally accepted English equivalent, 'men') when it translated *propter nos homines* in the Nicene-Constantinopolitan Creed as 'For us men'.[35] It translated *fratres* either as 'Brethren' or as 'brothers and sisters'.[36]

If we consider the punctuation in the 1973 text, we notice that it sometimes translated a single Latin sentence as two,[37] three[38] or even seven[39] sentences. On five occasions, it combines two Latin sentences into a single English sentence.[40] Of the sixteen full colons found in the Latin text of these sections of the Missal, six are translated by a full stop,[41] four are translated by a comma,[42] three are translated by a full colon[43] and three are translated by no punctuation.[44] In some places, a full colon is introduced where the Latin had a full stop or a comma.[45]

The 1973 text tends[46] to use a lowercase word to translate a word that is in uppercase in the Latin text, as can be seen in the translation of both *Corpus et Sanguinem* and *Corporis et Sanguinis* as 'body and blood'.[47] There are similar examples in the Introductory Rites,[48] in the Liturgy of the Word[49] and in the Liturgy of the Eucharist.[50] The 1973 text also translated the lowercase *domne* and *missa* as 'Father' and 'Mass'[51] and, possibly a typographical error, it translated *omnipotentem* as 'Almighty'.[52]

The 1973 Translation of the Eucharistic Prayers

As before, this section will analyse the 1973 translation of the Eucharistic Prayers in terms of its readability, its omissions or additions, its use of paraphrase, its approach to the translation of gendered words and its use of punctuation and capitalisation.

Recognising that it is not always possible to distinguish clearly between form and content, we will consider here the ways in which four commentaries have assessed the readability in English of Eucharistic Prayers 1 to 4. We begin with Roguet and Sheppard, who are concerned exclusively with Eucharistic Prayer 1. We then consider Raymond Moloney's assessment of these prayers and we also outline how Nicholas King and Gilbert Ostdiek evaluate the 1973 translation in comparison to the 2011 translation.

Roguet and Sheppard describe the language of Eucharistic Prayer 1 as 'a noble, ceremonial Latin, given to repetition'. They approved the approach of the ICEL translation then in use that, like the later 1973 translation, did not translate all five adjectives that qualify our offering in the *Quam oblationem* because 'redundancy of this kind is cumbersome in English where it produces an unfortunate impression of thought that is pedestrian and of language that is full of padding'. They liked the way in which the English text did not translate *quaesumus, propitius, mereamur* and *digneris*, commenting that in 'most cases it will be the translator's duty to ignore' such 'linguistic adjuncts' as they are 'used far less for their precise meaning than because they endow the sentences with a pleasing rhythmic cadence.'[53] In order to avoid translations that were 'in old-fashioned or antiquated English which is outmoded and inaccurate' or that ascribed 'a religious or ritual meaning' to 'adjectives like "pure", "holy", "unspotted" in conjunction with "victim" or "host"', Roguet and Sheppard defended the translation of *hostiam sanctum, hostiam puram, hostiam immaculatam* as 'this holy and perfect sacrifice'. In order not to imply that Christ used 'a sacred vessel, a piece of gold plate, confined to the celebration of Mass' at the Last Supper, they argued that *calyx* should be translated as 'cup' rather than as 'chalice'.[54] Arguing for 'the suppression of qualifying adjectives that have no function according to English usage', they were positive about the translations 'the bread of life and the cup of eternal salvation (*panem sanctum vitae aeternae et calicem salutis perpetuae*)', 'we pray that your angel may take (*per manus sancti angeli tui*)' and 'with every grace and blessing (*omni benedictione caelesti et gratia*)'. Roguet and Sheppard also approved of the translation of *communicantes* as 'in union with' rather than 'in communion with' because 'it might popularly be supposed to refer to Eucharistic communion in the limited sense'.[55]

For Moloney, there are both positive and negative aspects to the 1973 translation of the Eucharistic Prayers. On Eucharistic Prayer 1, he notes that, '"We offer you this sacrifice of praise (*et omnium circumstantium ... offerunt hoc sacrificium laudis*)"', although not strictly a literal translation, 'rightly implies that this sacrifice of praise is offered by all the congregation, whom the prayer calls the "*circumstantes*"'. He is critical, however, of the translation 'In union with the whole Church (*Communicantes*)' because it presents the Church as 'honouring Mary' rather than 'the Church in union with Mary offering its worship to God'. Moloney is also critical of the translation 'The ever-virgin Mother' because it 'does not quite do justice' to Mary's title 'Mother of God' (*Theotokos*) and of 'He took the cup', which he regards as an example of the 'clear intention on the part of the English translators to reduce the ceremonial and sacred character of the original language' going 'too far'. He says that the implicit reference to 1 Corinthians 11:26 is 'clearer in the Latin' than in the translation 'Christ has died ... come again' and that the translation 'The bread of life and the cup of eternal salvation (*Panem sanctum vitae aeternae et Calicem salutis perpetuae*)' does not refute those who think the reference is to unconsecrated bread and wine 'as clearly as it might'. Moloney implies that the failure to translate the words *Sanctum sacrificium, immaculatam hostiam* in relation to Melchizedek, which were inserted into the text by Pope St Leo I, was a mistake, and he notes that the English translations omitted some 'very beautiful' lines from the commemoration of the dead.[56] On Eucharistic Prayer 2, he notes that the English translation 'misses a traditional metaphor for the descent of the Holy Spirit which is contained in the Latin version ... where it asks the Lord to sanctify our gifts by the dew of the Spirit.' He also comments that in 'Make us grow in love (*ut eam in caritate perficias*)' the translators 'have improved on the Latin', giving us 'a fine phrase ... to treasure in our prayer and in our preaching'.[57] On Eucharistic Prayer 3, Moloney says that the 'slow-moving rhythm of the lines in the English translation' of the *Vere Sanctus* 'captures well the required mood', and he describes 'a holy and living sacrifice (*hoc sacrificium vivum et sanctum*)' as 'a fine phrase'. He is critical of the translations 'And so Father (*Supplices ... deprecamur*)' for neglecting 'the note of humility and adoration with which this prayer opens in the original' and 'Eucharist (*haec mysteria*)' for playing down 'the sense of mystery in the liturgy'. He is also critical of the translations 'which has made our peace with you (*nostrae reconciliationis proficiat*)' because it implies 'that this offering has made our peace with God' when it is 'rather that it is in the process of bringing it about', and 'the prayers of the family you have gathered here (*Votis huius familiae*)' because 'the logic of the Latin' would suggest that the family referred to is 'the entire Church'.[58] On Eucharistic Prayer 4, he recognises the 'eloquence and content' of the opening *Vere dignum* but he is critical of the translation 'You alone are God (*unus es Deus vivus et verus*)' and of 'When the time came for him to be glorified (*cum hora venisset ut glorificatur*)' because it obscures the term 'hour' as used in John's Gospel. He also criticises the translation 'bread and wine (*hoc uno pane ... et calice*)' which he describes as 'both a mistranslation and an error of judgment'.[59]

Comparing the 1973 translation with the 2011 translation, Nicholas King says that translating some Latin sentences as two English sentences[60] made them easier to read.[61] In Eucharistic Prayer 1, parts of n. 84 were easier to pronounce and rearranging the order of the Latin in n. 92 made those paragraphs easier to pronounce.[62] In Eucharistic Prayer 3 he agreed with the decisions not to translate 'relatively unimportant words such as *igitur*' in the first stanza of n. 113 and to simplify the 'plethora of adjectives, taken lock, stock and barrel from the Latin'[63] describing Mary in the third stanza. He liked 'enable us' in the third stanza and 'advance the peace and salvation of all the world' and 'your pilgrim Church on earth' in the fourth stanza.[64] In Eucharistic Prayer 4, he preferred the translation 'by rising' in the 1973 text to 'rising' in the 2011 text.[65]

Ostdiek comments that, in keeping with *Comme le prévoit*, the 1973 translation 'adopted a restrained pastoral approach in translating' Eucharistic Prayer 1.[66]

Comme le prévoit n. 33 said that the Eucharistic Prayers 'should be translated integrally and faithfully, without … omissions, or insertions'. Despite this, a significant number of words and phrases were omitted in the translation given in the 1973 text of the Eucharistic Prayers. In Eucharistic Prayer 1, for example, an alternative phrase,[67] a long list of adjectives or adjectival phrases (in both the section up to and including the words of consecration[68] and in the remaining section),[69] a significant number of adverbs[70] and a number of other terms[71] were left untranslated. Recognising that *quaesumus* and some other terms had been adapted from secular courtly language, *Comme le prévoit* 13 had proposed that the question of translating such terms using modern English equivalents needed further study. Apparently concluding that all such language should be eliminated, the translators of the 1973 text did not translate the words *quaesumus* or *digneris* in any of the Eucharistic Prayers. *Comme le prévoit* 18 said that *venerabilis* in the phrase *sanctas et venerabiles manus* should not 'be translated as "venerable", which nowadays means elderly', and, despite the prohibition of omissions in *Comme le prévoit* 33, the 1973 text implemented this recommendation by omitting the phrase completely.[72] Eucharistic Prayer 2 also omitted some adjectives[73] and adverbs[74] as well as a smaller number of other terms.[75] Some adjectives[76] and adverbs[77] and a smaller number of other terms[78] were not translated in the 1973 text of Eucharistic Prayer 3. Eucharistic Prayer 4 also omitted some adjectives[79] and adverbs,[80] and a smaller number of other terms.[81] The number of untranslated words and phrases is higher, but perhaps not very significantly higher, in Eucharistic Prayer 1 than in the other three Eucharistic Prayers but the basic pattern of ignoring many of the adjectives and adverbs is found in each case. The words omitted do not seem to be included in the form of a paraphrase, except, perhaps, in the omission of some prepositions in the words of Consecration[82] and in a small number of vague allusions to the omitted words.[83] Despite being prohibited in *Comme le prévoit* n. 33, there were also some insertions in each of the Eucharistic Prayers. The number of insertions in Eucharistic Prayers 1[84] and 2[85] is relatively small but it is somewhat larger in Eucharistic Prayer 3[86] and the largest number of insertions is found in Eucharistic Prayer 4.[87]

Comme le prévoit n. 33 also said that the Eucharistic Prayers 'should be translated integrally and faithfully, without variations' and, recognising that ancient texts 'demand an astute handling and sometimes a paraphrasing, in order to render accurately the original pregnant meaning', it said that this difficulty 'will be reduced considerably' if the text is 'a more recent one'. Although it might not be immediately clear how *Comme le prévoit* distinguished between 'variations' and paraphrases, it seems that they probably refer to the translation of a word or phrase in a way that would be fundamentally different from the meaning of that word or phrase in its original context. The general context is that of translating the text 'integrally and faithfully' and variations are distinguished from 'omissions, or insertions' and from 'an astute handling and sometimes a paraphrasing'. It would seem, then, that reformulations that are fundamentally different in meaning are called 'variations' and that reformulations that are fundamentally similar in meaning are called 'paraphrases'.

If we consider the variations first, we notice, for example, that rather than translating the Latin literally, the 1973 text may have been influenced by Revelation 4:8 (*Sanctus, sanctus, sanctus Dominus, Deus omnipotens*) when it translated *Sabaoth*[88] in the *Sanctus* using the variation 'of Power and Might'.[89] There are a number of other texts common to the four Eucharistic Prayers where variations have been introduced because implicit citations of Scripture texts seem to have been ignored or because other texts of Scripture appear to have influenced the translation inappropriately.[90] Sometimes, the 1973 text introduced a variation by narrowing the meaning to a possible or probable application rather than translating the term as such. In all four Eucharistic Prayers, for example, the noun *Domine* is clearly used to address God the Father but, rather than translating it literally as 'Lord' or 'O Lord', the 1973 text sometimes translated it as 'Father'[91] or as 'Lord Jesus'.[92] In Eucharistic Prayer 1 the paraphrases 'we come ... with praise and thanksgiving' and 'we pray' do not reflect accurately the humble nature of the prayer implied in the Latin word *supplices*.[93] There are a number of other similarly problematic paraphrases in the section of Eucharistic Prayer 1 leading up to the Consecration,[94] in the texts of the Consecration itself,[95] and in the section after the Consecration.[96] There are similar 'variations' in Eucharistic Prayers 2,[97] 3[98] and 4.[99]

Comme le prévoit n. 33 recognised that 'a paraphrasing' or a translation that is fundamentally similar to that of the original Latin text[100] might sometimes be necessary 'in order to render accurately the original pregnant meaning' of ancient texts. Eucharistic Prayer 2, which is based on a text found in the Apostolic Tradition,[101] 'has the most ancient ancestry' and our present prayer probably came about when the 'Holy, Holy, Holy', the invocation of the Holy Spirit before the institution narrative, and some other intercessions[102] were added to that original third or fourth century text.[103] Although it was specifically designed following the Second Vatican Council to encompass the history of our salvation from beginning to end, Eucharistic Prayer 4, is based on the Alexandrine Anaphora composed or edited by St Basil of Caesarea in the fourth century,[104] making it the second oldest of the Eucharistic Prayers. It is now generally accepted that Eucharistic Prayer 1, the Roman Canon, 'was composed of a number of distinct prayers over the course of several centuries'[105] but its origins 'can be traced back to the fourth century' and, although it includes 'elements that are older still', it is regarded by many as probably slightly later than Eucharistic Prayer 4.[106] Eucharistic Prayer 3 is the most recent of the four and it was an original composition by the Benedictine monk, Cipriano Vagaggini, designed 'to reflect, in its own particular way, the theological interests of the Church of our day'.[107] In the light of *Comme le prévoit* n. 33, we might expect the number of paraphrases to be greater in the more ancient texts of Eucharistic Prayers 1, 2 and 4 than in the more recently composed Eucharistic Prayer 3. Although counting the number of paraphrases is not a very exact science, since the number can vary depending on the length of the phrase considered, the approximate number of paraphrases per 100 words of Latin[108] in the newly composed Eucharistic Prayer 3[109] is 5.27,[110] which, as *Comme le prévoit* n. 33 would have led us to expect, is less than the 5.94[111] for Eucharistic Prayer 2[112] and the 7.1[113] for Eucharistic Prayer 4.[114] Surprisingly, however, it is greater than the 4.13[115] for Eucharistic Prayer 1.[116] In some cases, the paraphrases used in the Eucharistic Prayers seem to have been influenced by particular biblical texts. Apparently using the borrowed phrase 'in spirit and in truth (*in Spiritu et veritate*)' from John 4:23 to translate *adscriptam, ratam, rationabilem*, for example, the 1973 text of Eucharistic Prayer 1 paraphrases *Quam oblationem tu, Deus, in omnibus, quaesumus, benedictam, adscriptam, ratam, rationabilem, acceptabilemque facere digneris* as 'Bless and approve our offering; make it acceptable to you, an offering in spirit and in truth.'[117] Although it seems to have acknowledged the implicit citation of Hebrews 4:15 (*per omnia ... absque peccato*) when it translated *per omnia absque peccato* as 'in all things but sin',[118] the 1973 text of Eucharistic Prayer 4 does not seem to have recognised the implicit reference to 2 Corinthians 5:15 (*sed ei, qui pro ipsis mortuus est et resurrexit*) when it paraphrased *sed sibi qui pro nobis mortuus est atque surrexit* as 'but for him'.[119] There are other similar examples of paraphrases that do not seem to have taken implicit biblical citations into account in Eucharistic Prayers 2,[120] 3[121] and 4.[122]

In the Eucharistic Prayers, the 1973 text tended to prefer the conventions of contemporary punctuation to those used in the Latin text and it sometimes translated a single Latin sentence as two,[123] three[124] or four[125] English sentences. There are also cases where it combined two Latin sentences into a single English sentence.[126] Of the thirty-five full colons in the Eucharistic Prayers, eighteen are translated by full colons,[127] nine by full-stops,[128] four by commas,[129] two by semi-colons,[130] one by a dash and one by no punctuation.[131] Apparently because the lack of a predicate and the stark simplicity of the Latin might make it difficult for people to appreciate, the 1973 text translated *Mysterium fidei* as 'Let us proclaim the mystery of faith'.[132] Before the reform of the Eucharistic liturgy after Vatican II, the Latin phrase *Mysterium fidei* had been part of the words of consecration in the Roman Canon[133] but it had come to be generally regarded as an addition to the biblical formula. In 1968, Pope Paul VI decided that it should be removed from that position and proclaimed by the celebrant after the consecration in all the Eucharistic Prayers. Its stark simplicity and its acclamation without predicate or amplification was intended to call attention to the profound nature of the mystery of faith.[134]

In a number of cases, the 1973 text translated words that were capitalised in Latin with lowercase words. In Eucharistic Prayer 1, for example, we find 'N. our Bishop', 'Mary, the ever-virgin mother' and 'apostles … martyrs … saints', 'body … blood', 'bread … cup', 'angel … body and blood' and 'apostles … martyrs … saints'.[135] There are similar examples in Eucharistic Prayers 2,[136] 3[137] and 4.[138]

The 1973 Translation of the Prefaces and Other Presidential Prayers

In this section, the 1973 translation of a selection of extracts from Prefaces and from the other Presidential Prayers (Opening Prayers, Prayers over the Offerings and Prayers after Communion for Sundays and Solemnities of the Lord)[139] will be analysed in terms of their readability, their omissions or additions, their use of paraphrase, their approach to the translation of gendered words and their use of punctuation and capitalisation. Like the Eucharistic Prayers, *Comme le prévoit* n. 33 said that the Prefaces 'should be translated integrally and faithfully, without … omissions, or insertions' but it recognised that 'an astute handling and sometimes a paraphrasing' might be needed if the text 'is ancient'. The following article (n. 34) said that the 'prayers (opening prayer, prayer over the gifts, prayer after communion, and prayer over the people) from the ancient Roman tradition are succinct and abstract' and that, in translation 'they may need to be rendered somewhat more freely while conserving the original ideas'. Noting that 'pompous and superfluous language should be avoided' in every case, it said that this can be achieved 'by moderately amplifying them or, if necessary, paraphrasing expressions in order to concretize them for the celebration and the needs of today'.

The encouragement given to translators to relax somewhat the emphasis on translating 'integrally and faithfully' (*Comme le prévoit* n. 33) and to develop a style of translation that would be less 'succinct and abstract' and more in keeping with 'the needs of today' (n. 34) is evident in the 1973 translations of the Opening Prayers, the Prayers over the Gifts, and the Prayers after Communion. If their weakness, at least in some cases, lies in the way in which they are sometimes translated too freely and in a way that does not faithfully conserve the original ideas, their strength probably lies in their simplicity and readability.

Generally speaking, the 1973 translation of the Prefaces is careful to translate 'integrally and faithfully, without … omissions' (*Comme le prévoit* n. 33) but some words and phrases are occasionally omitted.[140] Despite their greater simplicity and readability, there are also occasions when the omissions that the 1973 translation made in relation to the Latin text seem to go beyond the need to avoid 'pompous and superfluous language' or to paraphrase, where necessary, in order to 'concretize' the prayers 'for the celebration and the needs of today' (*Comme le prévoit* n. 34). The clearest example, perhaps, is the strange omission of the adjective 'one' before 'bread from heaven', which not only ignores the implied citations of John 6:32 and 1 Corinthians 10:17 but also undermines the parallel with becoming 'one in peace and love' on which the whole structure of the Prayer after Communion depends.[141] Given that a literal English translation of the prayer was already well-known as part of the Angelus, the omission of certain words[142] from the translation given for the Collect of the Fourth Sunday of Advent was also surprising. Some other omissions are equally problematic within the overall context of the prayer in which they are found[143] but there are a number of other examples where the omissions are less significant, although there seems to be no evident reason why the word or phrase was omitted.[144]

Similarly, although the Prefaces were to be translated 'integrally and faithfully, without … insertions' (*Comme le prévoit* n. 33), the 1973 translation introduced a number of additions.[145] The greater readability of the Presidential Prayers was sometimes achieved at the cost of additions that, while they might be defended as only 'moderately amplifying' the original text[146] or making it more concrete,[147] seem to have changed the original sense unnecessarily.

Comme le prévoit n. 33 said that the Prefaces 'should be translated integrally and faithfully' but also that 'an astute handling and sometimes a paraphrasing' might be needed if the text 'is ancient'. The 1973 translation, however, paraphrased texts that seem relatively straightforward[148] and some of its paraphrases altered[149] or over-interpreted[150] the original idea, upset the internal balance between elements of the prayer[151] or introduced a somewhat questionable understanding of liturgical participation.[152] *Comme le prévoit* n. 34 wanted the other Presidential Prayers to be translated 'somewhat more freely while conserving the original ideas' and, 'if necessary', using a paraphrase. While not exact, the translations of *Concede nobis … ut* as 'help us to' and *tota mente* as 'with all our hearts' were broadly in keeping with the original ideas but the 1973 translation can hardly be said to have conserved the original ideas when it paraphrased *veneremur* and *rationabili affectu* as 'love you' and 'as you love them'.[153] There are paraphrases that were based on a not dissimilar idea[154] but there are also some where another idea was substituted for the original idea in a way that unbalanced the structure of the prayer.[155] In the paraphrase 'revealed himself to us by becoming man',[156] for example, the parallel between the carnal and the spiritual in the implied intertextual reference to Tertullian[157] is lost because the word 'flesh (*carnis*)' is not translated as such. Similarly, in the paraphrase 'with the light of your Gospel',[158] the reference to St Ambrose[159] that is implicit in the phrase *gratiae tuae splendore* has been lost. A tendency to restrict or to specify the meaning more than the original Latin did is evident when, rather than always being translated as 'God',[160] *Deus* is interpreted in three places as denoting God the Father,[161] apparently 'to add warmth to the prayers and especially to make it plain that the prayer was directed to the first person of the Trinity',[162] and when it is interpreted on another occasion as denoting Jesus Christ.[163] This tendency is also evident when *Domine* is paraphrased on one occasion as 'Father' and on another as 'Lord Jesus Christ'.[164]

The 1973 translation of the Prefaces and other Presidential Prayers tended to avoid abstract terms like 'adoption', 'duty/care', 'faithful', 'flesh', and 'incarnation', in favour of what may have been seen as more concrete terms like 'sons and daughters', 'a Father's love', 'faithful people', 'man' and 'coming as man'.[165] Rather than recognising the often gender-inclusive meaning of the word *filii* ('sons' or 'children'), the 1973 translation opted for the circumlocution 'the image of your Son … within us', which obscured the link with being 'reborn' in the original,[166] or for the less specific word 'family', which obscured the link between being God's children and holding firm to the things that will endure eternally.[167] In one place, the word *homo* is translated by the gender-neutral word 'all'[168] in the singular, and the apparently gender-inclusive terms 'man'[169] and 'men'[170] are also used in the singular and plural, respectively.

The 1973 translation often breaks a single Latin sentence into two[171] or three[172] English sentences but, occasionally, it unites two Latin sentences into a single English sentence[173] or changes the way in which two Latin sentences are divided.[174] Of the two full colons used in the Latin texts, one is translated by a full-stop[175] and one by no punctuation.[176] There are a number of examples of uppercase Latin words being translated by lowercase English words.[177]

Evaluating the 1973 Translation

Nicholas King recognises that the 1973 translation is 'a much-loved one' but, somewhat tongue in cheek perhaps, he damns it with faint praise when he says that it 'has worked well that is to say, for solemn high occasions, and for

Masses for those with learning difficulties, and for informal celebrations with Oxbridge academics.'[178]

The distinction that *Comme le prévoit* (n. 33) makes between ancient and more recent texts, and the presumption that 'an astute handling and sometimes a paraphrasing' would be needed more frequently 'in order to render accurately the original pregnant meaning' of more ancient texts, would lead one to expect a greater density of paraphrases in the ancient texts of Eucharistic Prayers 1, 2 and 4 and a lesser density in more modern texts, such as Eucharistic Prayer 3. Although there is a lower density in Eucharistic Prayer 3 (5.27) compared with Eucharistic Prayers 2 (5.94) and 4 (7.1), the density in Eucharistic Prayer 1 (4.13) is less than in Eucharistic Prayer 3. By comparison, the number of paraphrases per 100 Latin words in the other texts from the Ordinary of the Mass[179] given in the Appendix is 5.7.[180]

The translations given in the 1973 text might, perhaps, be seen as an attempt to be 'faithful to the art of communication … in regard to the audience for which it is intended, and in regard to the manner of expression', as *Comme le prévoit* n. 7 recommended. In the light of the implicit biblical citations, however, they can hardly be seen as faithfully communicating 'the message itself' (n. 6), giving 'first consideration to the meaning of the communication' (*Comme le prévoit* n. 8), or following 'the scientific methods of textual study as used by experts' to discover 'the true meaning of a text' (n. 9). The paraphrase of *unigenitum* as 'only Son', for example, obscured the distinction between our adoption as the children of God the Father and the unique and eternal relationship of the 'only-begotten Son' to the Father that the original text was intended to communicate.

CHAPTER II

Liturgiam authenticam and the 2011 Translation

The English Missal of 1973 was a translation of Pope Paul VI's Roman Missal (1970), which was the first edition of the Vatican II Missal, and the English Missal of 2011 is a translation of the third edition of that Missal (2002) as amended in 2008. If we compare the new (2011) English translation of the Mass with the parallel texts in the older (1973) English translation with which we have become familiar,[1] we might get the initial impression that a somewhat old-fashioned text is replacing a text that embodied the liturgical reforms of the Second Vatican Council. We might even suspect that the third edition of Pope Paul VI's Missal (2002/2008) had reversed the changes that had been introduced when Pope Paul VI's Roman Missal of 1970 became the official text for the celebration of Mass. This is not the case, however, for although the 2011 English translation is very different from the 1973 translation, the Latin texts on which those translations are based are essentially identical. Although there are some additions in the Latin text of 2002 that are not found in the Latin text of 1970, including the alternative formulas for the dismissal and the proper prayers for the Saints who had since been canonised, the 2002 Latin text of the most commonly used texts of the Mass, given in sections A–F of the Appendix, is the same as the 1970 Latin text, with the result that the 1973 and 2011 texts are, in effect, translations of the same Latin text. The appendix of this book puts the two English translations into parallel columns underneath the Latin text on which both translations are based.

In this chapter I want to outline the nature of the changes that have been made and to identify the apparent reasons for those changes. We begin by outlining the approach to translating liturgical texts in the 2001 instruction, *Liturgiam authenticam*, and in the *Ratio translationis for the English Language* (2007), highlighting the difference in emphasis in comparison with the 1969 instruction *Comme le prévoit*. We will then outline the changes that the 2011 translation made in relation to the 1973 translation in the light of these two documents.

Liturgiam authenticam (2001)

The instruction on the use of vernacular languages in the publication of the books of the Roman liturgy, *Liturgiam authenticam* (2001),[2] shifted the emphasis in translation so that it leaned more in the direction of formal, word-for-word equivalence and less in the direction of dynamic equivalence. The approach of the Jesuit, Robert Taft, writing in 1988, might be regarded as representative of the dynamic equivalence approach. He held that all translations were necessarily interpretations and that the 'aim of a good translation is to be faithful to two languages, the donor and the recipient'. When there is some conflict between being faithful to both donor and recipient, however, Taft held that 'the recipient language takes precedence, all other things being equal.'[3] This, as we shall see, was not the approach recommended by *Liturgiam authenticam*.

Citing Vatican II's Constitution on the Sacred Liturgy, *Sacrosanctum Concilium*, it highlighted (n. 1) the need 'to preserve with care the authentic Liturgy, which flows forth from the Church's living and most ancient spiritual tradition, and to adapt it with pastoral wisdom to the genius of the various peoples.' Recognising that Vatican II asked that the traditions of those particular Churches that 'are distinguished by their venerable antiquity ... be preserved whole and intact' (n. 4), it pointed out that 'the same vigilance is required for the safeguarding and the authentic development of the liturgical traditions, and the discipline of the Latin Church, and in particular, of the Roman Rite' and for 'the translation of the liturgical texts into vernacular languages.' In preparing a translation of the liturgical books, it said (n. 5) that 'the greatest care is to be taken to maintain the identity and unitary expression of the Roman Rite, not as a sort of historical monument, but rather as a manifestation of the theological realities of ecclesial communion and unity.' It noted (n. 6) that the 'omissions or errors which affect certain existing vernacular translations – especially in the case of certain languages – have impeded the progress of inculturation that actually should have taken place' and had prevented the Church 'from laying the foundation for a fuller, healthier and more authentic renewal.'

The second section of *Liturgiam authenticam*, which outlined the general principles applicable to all translations, sought to correct certain misapprehensions about the nature of the liturgical text and about its translation into vernacular languages. Rather than being 'intended primarily to be a sort of mirror of the interior dispositions of the faithful', the words spoken in liturgical celebrations 'express truths that transcend time and space' because 'by means of these words God speaks continually with the Spouse of his beloved Son ... and the Church perpetuates and transmits all that she herself is and all that she believes' (n. 19). Article 20 outlines the need for fidelity in translating the original text:

The Latin liturgical texts of the Roman Rite, while drawing on centuries of ecclesial experience in transmitting the faith of the Church received from the Fathers, are themselves the fruit of the liturgical renewal, just recently brought forth. In order that such a rich patrimony may be preserved and passed on through the centuries, it is to be kept in mind from the beginning that the translation of the liturgical texts of the Roman Liturgy is not so much a work of creative innovation as it is of rendering the original texts faithfully and accurately into the vernacular language. While it is permissible to arrange the wording, the syntax and the style in such a way as to prepare a flowing vernacular text suitable to the rhythm of popular prayer, the original text, insofar as possible, must be translated integrally and in the most exact manner, without omissions or additions in terms of their content, and without paraphrases or glosses. Any adaptation to the characteristics or the nature of the various vernacular languages is to be sober and discreet.

For our purposes, the key phrase here is probably the following: 'the original text, insofar as possible, must be translated integrally and in the most exact manner, without omissions or additions in terms of their content, and without paraphrases or glosses.'

Any adaptations of the texts to meet the needs of particular cultures should be based on 'true cultural or pastoral necessity, and should not be proposed out of a mere desire for novelty or variety, nor as a way of supplementing or changing the theological content of the *editiones typicae*', the approved typical editions of the liturgical text (n. 22). Article 24 of *Liturgiam authenticam* outlines the norms for translating texts from Sacred Scripture as follows:

Furthermore, it is not permissible that the translations be produced from other translations already made into other languages; rather, the new translations must be made directly from the original texts, namely the Latin, as regards the texts of ecclesiastical composition, or the Hebrew, Aramaic, or Greek, as the case may be, as regards the texts of Sacred Scripture. Furthermore, in the preparation of these translations for liturgical use, the *Nova Vulgata Editio*, promulgated by the Apostolic See,[4] is normally to be consulted as an auxiliary tool, in a manner described elsewhere in this Instruction,[5] in order to maintain the tradition of interpretation that is proper to the Latin Liturgy.

The translations of the Scripture texts used as readings in the Lectionary are to be 'made directly from the original Hebrew, Aramaic, or Greek, as the case may be' but, since the Missal is a text 'of ecclesiastical composition', the original text is the Latin text and any translation of the implicit citations from Scripture in the Latin text are to be made 'directly from' the Latin. However, since 'the *Nova Vulgata Editio* is the point of reference as regards the delineation of the canonical text'[6] to be used in the Lectionary, one may also take into account the new and approved version of the Latin Bible, known as the *Nova Vulgata Editio*, which is to be used as 'an auxiliary tool ... to maintain the tradition of interpretation that is proper to the Latin Liturgy'.

The liturgical texts 'should be considered as the voice of the Church at prayer, rather than of only particular congregations or individuals; thus, they should be free from an overly servile adherence to prevailing modes of expression' (n. 27). Rather than avoiding 'words or expressions ... which differ somewhat from usual and everyday speech', each vernacular language should develop 'a sacred style that will come to be recognised as proper to liturgical language' (n. 27).

Liturgiam authenticam 30 outlines the general principles that should govern the translation of nouns and pronouns denoting gender:

> In many languages there exist nouns and pronouns denoting both genders, masculine and feminine, together in a single term. The insistence that such a usage should be changed is not necessarily to be regarded as the effect or the manifestation of an authentic development of the language as such. Even if it may be necessary by means of catechesis to ensure that such words continue to be understood in the 'inclusive' sense just described, it may not be possible to employ different words in the translations themselves without detriment to the precise intended meaning of the text, the correlation of its various words or expressions, or its aesthetic qualities. When the original text, for example, employs a single term in expressing the interplay between the individual and the universality and unity of the human family or community (such as the Hebrew word *Adam*, the Greek *anthropos*, or the Latin *homo*), this property of the language of the original text should be maintained in the translation. Just as has occurred at other times in history, the Church herself must freely decide upon the system of language that will serve her doctrinal mission most effectively, and should not be subject to externally imposed linguistic norms that are detrimental to that mission.

Rejecting the view that using nouns and pronouns that denote 'both genders, masculine and feminine' is 'necessarily to be regarded as the effect or the manifestation of an authentic development of the language as such', *Liturgiam authenticam* 30 insists that 'it may not be possible' to avoid gender-specific terms used in an 'inclusive' sense 'without detriment to the precise meaning of the text, the correlation of the various words or expressions, or its aesthetic qualities.' Some examples of the 'nouns and pronouns denoting both genders, masculine and feminine, together in a single term' might be the German singular and plural nouns, *Mench* and *Geschwister* and their English equivalents, individual and siblings, the Spanish singular noun, *persona*, and its English equivalent, person, and the Italian singular noun, *pilota*, and its English equivalent, pilot. Although the Spanish *persona* and the Italian *pilota* are, respectively, feminine and masculine gender from the point of view of grammar, these words are commonly used to refer to an individual of either gender. There are also words, however, that have generally been used in a way that includes both genders, even though the words in question are, as such, also used specifically for one gender rather than another. Examples might be the grammatically masculine nouns, *Vorfahr* (German), *antepassado* (Spanish) and *antenato* (Italian), that designate an individual masculine ancestor but that are also commonly and correctly used in the plural (*die Vorfahren, los antepassados*, and *gli antenati*) to designate groups of ancestors of either gender or of mixed gender. A contemporary equivalent in English slang might be the word 'guys'. *Liturgiam authenticam* does not accept that translations of the liturgical text into vernacular languages should necessarily abandon such common usage of words that can be, but are not necessarily, gender-specific. *Liturgiam authenticam* 30 says that, when the Hebrew word *Adam*, the Greek *anthropos*, or the Latin *homo* are used in contexts where the original text involves 'an interplay between the individual and the universality and unity of the human family or community', this interplay 'should be maintained in the translation'. In the Hebrew and Septuagint account of creation in Genesis 2:7-20, and in the *Nova Vulgata Editio* of that text, for example, *Adam*, *anthropos* and *homo* represent both the universality of the human family and the individual human being who was the first member of that family.

Particular directives relating to the translation of nouns and pronouns relating to gender are given in *Liturgiam authenticam* 31:

> In particular: to be avoided is the systematic resort to imprudent solutions such as a mechanical substitution of words, the transition from the singular to the plural, the splitting of a unitary collective term into masculine and feminine parts, or the introduction of impersonal or abstract words,[7] all of which may impede the communication of the true and integral sense of a word or an expression in the original text. Such measures introduce theological and anthropological problems into the translation.

Among the 'particular norms' listed are the following:

> Insofar as possible in a given vernacular language, the use of the feminine pronoun, rather than the neuter, is to be maintained in referring to the Church.

> Words which express consanguinity or other important types of relationship, such as 'brother', 'sister', etc., which are clearly masculine or feminine by virtue of the context, are to be maintained as such in the translation.

Liturgiam authenticam 33 outlines the norms governing capital letters as follows:

> The use of capitalisation in the liturgical texts of the Latin *editiones typicae* as well as in the liturgical translation of the Sacred Scriptures, for honorific or otherwise theologically significant reasons, is to be retained in the vernacular language at least insofar as the structure of a given language permits.

Ratio translationis for the English Language (2007)

Liturgiam authenticam n. 9 envisaged the production of a *ratio translationis* by the Congregation for Divine Worship and the Discipline of the Sacraments that would apply the principles of translation 'in closer detail to a given language'. Developed over a number of years, the *Ratio translations for the English Language* (2007) was 'the fruit of extensive examination and discussion of the Instruction *Liturgiam authenticam* and of practical experience of work on the translation of the Roman Missal … under the auspices of the Vox Clara Committee, a group of senior Bishops from different parts of the English-speaking world' appointed by the Congregation for Divine Worship and the Discipline of the Sacraments in 2002.[8] A working draft text was sent to the anglophone Bishops' Conferences in 2005 and the comments and suggestions received were incorporated into the final draft of 2007.

The first part, Presuppositions for an Authentic Translation of the Roman Rite, recognises seven principal characteristics of the language of the Roman Rite. It is by nature Trinitarian, eschatological in purpose, a primary source for liturgical prayer, reliant upon patristic teaching, direct and compact in its expression, pedagogical in its ability to inculcate truth and intended to engage the whole person (nn. 4–12). It insists that 'translators must first take care to locate the biblical and patristic sources of the prayers they translate' (n. 19) and that, 'rather than substituting other words that are alien to it', translators should retain the 'coherent system of words and patterns of speech consecrated by the books of Sacred Scripture and by ecclesiastical tradition, especially by the Fathers of the Church' (n. 20). It says that translators must 'really translate the Latin of the Roman Rite, and not merely allow themselves to fashion what is essentially a new composition inspired in some manner by the Latin text' (n. 25).

Part 2, Principles of Translation for the Liturgy of the Roman Rite, begins with a number of principles regarding the identity and unitary expression of the Rite. These include maintaining the identity and unitary expression of the Roman Rite down the centuries (nn. 29–35), giving first place to biblical language and expression (nn. 36–40) and translating the Latin texts of the *editiones typicae* fully and accurately rather than paraphrasing them (nn. 41–52). They also include maintaining the manner of expression of the Roman Rite, including syntax and rhetorical form (nn. 53–61) and ensuring that any anthropomorphisms, metaphors or images in the original text are fully included in any translation (nn. 62–63). Among the principles listed regarding adaptation to the qualities and exigencies of the vernacular language are accepting the guidance of the principles of inculturation developed in tandem with *Varietates legitimate*[9] and *Liturgiam authenticam* (n. 74), avoiding expressions overly dependent on colloquial language (nn. 75–77) and recognising that special rules apply to liturgical expression and that academic style manuals should not serve as standards (nn. 78–79). They also include rejecting the replacement of moral or doctrinal expressions by psychological or emotive language (n. 80), striving for consistency (n. 81) and maintaining stability when texts are translated and re-translated (n. 86). The principles related to the oral-aural-mnemonic dimensions of the translation include respect for the oral-aural dimensions and for the exigencies of the musical proclamation of a text (nn. 87–93) and the need to enhance the memorability of texts prayed by the faithful (n. 94). They also include the preservation of both the denotation (the dictionary definition) and the connotation (the finer shades of meaning evoked) of words (nn. 95–98) and the need for a text to correspond to the ritual act that accompanies it (nn. 99–101).

Part 3, Application of the Principles of Translation to the English Language, begins with a number of applications in relation to the syntax of the Roman Rite. It says that care must be taken to preserve the structure of a text expressing a theological statement (nn. 102–104), the syntax of a text that expresses a prayerful posture before God (n. 105) and any expressions of faith which contain Catholic doctrine (n. 106). Care must also be taken to preserve, as far as possible, the relationship between all elements of the Latin syntax of a given text (n. 108) and to preserve the nuances of causality, purpose and consequence (n. 109). Any biblical expressions commonly used in catechism or religious devotions should be respected (n. 107) and a 'liturgical vernacular' of sacral language should be created (n. 110). The applications in relation to genre and style include the need to preserve the genre of the original Latin text (n. 111), to preserve any Latin style that expresses content (n. 113) and to preserve the impact of Latin style even when the precise Latin style itself cannot be duplicated (n. 115). These applications also include the maintenance of the unique style of the Roman Rite (n. 112) and the cultivation of a translation style that constitutes a true liturgical vernacular (n. 114). In relation to capitalisation, the application of the principles requires the careful and consistent observance of the special rules for capitalisation that conveys theologically or otherwise liturgically significant meaning (nn. 116–120). Specifically, words used to refer to realities that 'denote a single, unrepeatable and irreducible reality, pertaining at least in part to the supernatural realm', such as the words 'Body' and 'Blood' that refer to the Eucharistic species, are to be capitalised in order 'to keep readers and celebrants mindful of the special reverence' that is needed in relation to them (nn. 117–119). Examples of capitalisations are given in n. 120 and in section VI of Appendix 1 to the *Ratio translationis*. In relation to person, number and gender, the applications require that the same person, number and gender is to be maintained in translations insofar as possible (nn. 121–124), that any systematic substitution for genderised terms should be avoided (nn. 125–129) and that it is unnecessary and inappropriate to alter biblical or liturgical texts simply because some might take offence at their apparently discriminatory wording (nn. 130–131). In relation to Greek and Hebrew terms, the application requires that the Greek and Hebrew terms that are preserved in the Latin text should be maintained in vernacular translations (n. 132).

The Appendix, which has the title 'Dignity, Design and Style in the Liturgical Books', is divided into six sections. The first, The Distinctive Character of Liturgical Books, says that these books 'serve as a deposit for the texts and rites which belong to the entire Church' and 'may not be changed or altered except by competent ecclesiastical authorities'.[10] The second section, The Publication of Liturgical Books, points out that the Congregation for Divine Worship and the Discipline of the Sacraments 'is the sole authority for the promulgation of any liturgical books for the Roman Rite'.[11] Among other things, the third section, Style in the Roman Liturgical Books, lists the five traditional elements that have remained a part of such books since the advent of the printing press: black ink for ritual texts, red ink for rubrics, using headings and divisions, including decrees of promulgation at the beginning and liturgical art.[12] Section IV, The Regulation of Style in Vernacular Editions, recommends greater coordination on the page between the musical notation and the words to be sung, as well as specifying that any notes to the text are to be in the form of footnotes rather than endnotes.[13] The fifth section, Punctuation, recognises that the punctuation used in the *Missale Romanum* derives from four principal sources: the Neo-Vulgate Bible, the oratorical tradition of late antiquity, the Latin 'texts which offer a distinctive expression of the faith' and the rules of modern punctuation. It laments the fact that the punctuation 'of recent compositions within the postconciliar *Missale Romanum* is derived from modern rules exclusively.'[14] The final section, Capitalisation, gives a number of lists of terms that should be translated in uppercase and a short list of terms that should be translated in lowercase.

The *Ratio translationis* concludes with an Annexe entitled 'Physical Elements of Style' that gives some principles concerning the layout and design of liturgical books, the use of 'sense lines' or 'colometry', the printing of prayer texts and rubrics, the use of art, graphics and colour, and the physical materials to be used in constructing liturgical books.

The 2011 Translation of the Ordinary of the Mass

Liturgiam authenticam said (n. 19) that the words spoken in liturgical celebrations 'express truths that transcend time and space' because 'by means of these words God speaks continually with the Spouse of his beloved Son … and the Church perpetuates and transmits all that she herself is and all that she believes' (n. 19). Although those words express timeless truths that contain the voice of God and the transmission of all that the Church is and believes, *Liturgiam authenticam* 20 permitted translators to arrange 'the wording, the syntax and the style in such a way as to prepare a flowing vernacular text suitable to the rhythm of popular prayer.' In other words, there should be some kind of balance between the fidelity and integrity of the translation, on the one hand, and the readability and accessibility[15] of the translation, on the other.

King is generally positive about the readability of the new translation, describing 'And with your spirit' as an 'entirely sensible' translation in view of how 'it exactly catches the Latin' and the way this translation or its equivalent 'has been adopted everywhere else in the world'.[16] Chupungco implicitly questions the readability of the text when he describes 'And with your spirit' as a 'literal translation' that 'requires a comprehensive catechesis grounded on a theological anthropology that finds resonance in the *Magnificat* ("My spirit rejoices in God my Saviour"; Luke 2:48-55).'[17] Catherine Vincie comments that, in the new translation of the Gloria, 'the words more rhythmically tumble out one upon another; it is as if we cannot say enough to acknowledge the greatness of God.'[18] Recognising that, in the Latin text of the Gloria, the location of *Deus Pater omnipotens* at the end of a series of five acclamations 'is probably where it is best', Chupungco argues that, in English, the phrase 'O

God, almighty Father' might have been at the beginning since 'it is cumbersome to recite a series of acclamations whose addressee appears only at the end.'[19] Pecklers notes that the translation of *consubstantialem* as 'consubstantial' was 'a more literal translation of the Latin' but that it had been 'one of the most hotly debated subjects among the bishops of various conferences', and he comments that it had been introduced 'despite pastoral questions to the contrary.' He speaks positively about the change from 'born of the Virgin Mary' to 'was incarnate of the Virgin Mary' in the Creed, noting that it now matches 'the text used by Anglicans, Lutherans, and other Christians'.[20] Although Chupungco holds that the English adverb 'well' corresponds to the Latin *bene* and 'does not sufficiently translate the Latin *competenter*, which means proficiently, knowledgeably, and adeptly',[21] it could also be argued that the translation of *digne et competenter* as 'worthily and well' avoids the redundancy of the overly literal translation 'worthily and competently'. Elich is balanced in his assessment of the new translation of the Communion Rite, noting both positive[22] and negative[23] aspects, and he concludes that, 'with the exception of one or two phrases, priest and assembly should be able to adopt these texts easily as a heartfelt expression of their worship at communion time.'[24] He is similarly balanced in assessing the new translation of the Concluding Rites, recognising many positive aspects[25] but noting also some negative points.[26] King is happy with the different alternatives[27] given for the phrase *Ite missa est* because, although 'the journey that the word *missa* has travelled … is probably irrecoverably lost in history', the phrase 'clearly has something to do with bringing the Eucharist to an end, and something to do with entrusting a mission ("sending") to the people of God'.[28]

The 2011 text translates almost all the words and phrases of the Latin text that the 1973 text left untranslated. In the *Confiteor*, for example, it translated *peccavi nimis* as 'I have greatly sinned',[29] apparently respecting the fact that *nimis* is found in many texts of the *Confiteor* since the fourteenth century[30] and the implicit reference to King David's 'I have greatly sinned (*peccavi nimis*)' in 1 Chronicles 21:8. *Liturgiam authenticam* n. 56 had instructed that 'the expression *mea culpa, mea culpa, mea maxima culpa*' was to be 'respected by a translation that is as literal as possible' because it belongs 'to the heritage of the whole or of a great part of the ancient Church'. Respecting this instruction, the new translation of the *Confiteor* restored 'through my fault, through my fault, through my most grievous fault'.[31] There are a number of other cases where the restoration of omitted words and phrases in the 2011 text parallels the *Nova Vulgata Editio* version of biblical texts that are implicitly cited in the Introductory Rites[32] and in the Liturgy of the Word.[33] Although he notes that the Latin genitive can be either possessive or objective, Chupungco suggests that by translating *bonae voluntatis* literally, as 'people of good will' (cf. Luke

2:14), the new version 'ignores the findings of biblical exegesis by opting for the possessive genitive.'[34] The *Ratio translationis* (2007) had specified, however, that any biblical expressions commonly used in catechism or religious devotions should be respected (n. 107). The 2011 text also translates most[35] of the adverbial and adjectival qualifiers[36] and the other words[37] and phrases[38] that the 1973 text did not translate. Vincie describes the inclusion of the omitted 'holy' before 'Church' (n. 29) as 'a more literal translation of the Latin text.'[39]

The 2011 text omitted all the words that the 1973 text added in its translation of the Introductory Rites, the Liturgy of the Word, the Liturgy of the Eucharist, and the Communion and Concluding Rites.[40] The inherent difficulties of translating *Ite, missa est* because of the likely missionary implications of *missa*,[41] and the validity of interpreting *Ite* as 'Go in peace', are clear from the three alternative translations given in the 2011 text, which had been approved by the Pope in 2008:[42] 'Go and announce the Gospel of the Lord', 'Go in peace, glorifying the Lord by your life' and 'Go in peace'.[43] The 1973 translation, 'The Mass is ended, go in peace', is nevertheless amended to the more literal 'Go forth, the Mass is ended' in the first of the four options given in the 2011 Missal.

Liturgiam authenticam n. 56 instructed that 'the people's response *Et cum spiritu tuo*' was to be 'respected by a translation that is as literal as possible' because it belongs 'to the heritage of the whole or of a great part of the ancient Church'. In line with this instruction, the 2011 text translated *Et cum spiritu tuo* as 'And with your spirit' and King comments that it 'exactly catches the Latin'.[44] The surprisingly negative response of some commentators to this more literal translation can be explained, at least in part, by the fact that it is now somewhat 'unusual' and 'remote from everyday speech'.[45] There is, however, a worrying lack of familiarity with New Testament language evident in the unease of some who think the reference to our human spirits 'sounds as if our bodies no longer matter?'[46] Although somewhat unfamiliar to many today, phrases like 'And with your spirit' seem to have been part of the everyday vocabulary of St Paul, and three of his letters conclude with a prayer asking that the grace of Christ be with the human spirits of the individuals[47] to whom the letters were addressed. In 2 Timothy 4:22, the inspired author uses a slightly different greeting, 'The Lord be with your [sing.] spirit. Grace be with you [pl.]', and the implication would seem to be that the Lord Jesus Christ would be with the spirit of Timothy and that the grace of the Lord Jesus would be with (the spirits of) the others in Ephesus whom Paul had already mentioned (Prisca, Aquila and the household of Onesiphorus; cf. 2 Tim 4:19).[48] From this perspective, 'The Lord be with you' should probably be read as a prayer that, although now invisible, the Lord Jesus Christ would be spiritually present among those present throughout the celebration of the Mass,[49] and the response 'And with your spirit' should probably be read as a prayer by those present that the Lord Jesus Christ would be spiritually with the celebrant in what he was about to do in Christ's name during that Mass.[50] The exchange *Dominus vobiscum* and *et cum spiritu tuo*, which dates from the third century at the latest,[51] is always found in a context where 'The Lord be with you' is said by a bishop, priest or deacon[52] and this tradition is continued in the rites of the Catholic Church after Vatican II.[53] St John Chrysostom (347– 407 AD) interpreted it as an acknowledgment that the sacrifice 'is brought about by the grace of the Holy Spirit and his hovering over all'.[54] Reflecting the usage in the Pauline letters, and the emphasis on the spiritual presence of the Lord in the liturgical tradition,[55] the 2011 text replaced the paraphrase in the 1973 text with a literal translation: 'And with your spirit.'[56]

There is a general tendency to adopt a more grammatically accurate style of translation in the 2011 text, such as the translation of the vocative *Domine* as 'O Lord'[57] except in the 'Lord, have mercy' and in the phrase *Domine Deus*, which is translated as 'Lord God'.[58] Compared to the 1973 translation of the texts other than the Eucharistic Prayers, which had some fifty-nine paraphrases, there are only ten paraphrases in the 2011 translation[59] and many of these are more literal than the 1973 text paraphrases. The 2011 text restored the allocation of the texts in the Penitential Rites to what is found in the Latin text[60] and, in keeping with the implied citation of John 1:29,[61] it replaced the paraphrase 'This is the Lamb of God who' with the more literal 'Behold the Lamb of God, behold him who'.[62] With three exceptions and a small number of more literal paraphrases,[63] it substituted literal translations for all of the other paraphrases we have noted in the Introductory Rites,[64] the Liturgy of the Word,[65] the Liturgy of the Eucharist[66] and the Communion and Concluding Rites.[67] The first of the three exceptions was the translation of *iube ... benedicere* as 'Your blessing, Father' rather than 'Father, give me your blessing' as in the 1973 text or the more literal 'Father, command the blessing'.[68] The second was that, rather than translating literally, the 2011 text accepted the slight paraphrase by which the 1973 text rendered *et operis manuum hominum* as 'and work of human hands' rather than as 'and of the work of human hands'.[69] The third was the translation of *meum ac vestrum sacrificium* as 'my sacrifice and yours',[70] which Chupungco describes as 'an ambiguous construction' because 'it can mean "my sacrifice and your sacrifice," which is prone to misinterpretation'.[71] He suggests 'our sacrifice', as in the 1973 text, or 'my sacrifice, which is also your sacrifice' as a more faithful rendering of the Latin.[72]

Liturgiam authenticam 65 insists on translating the Creed 'according to the precise wording that the tradition of the Latin Church has bestowed on it, including the use of the first person singular' and, accordingly, the 2011 Missal changed 'We believe' to 'I believe (*Credo*)'. Noting that the 2008 draft ICEL text did not have 'I believe' before the second and third sections of the Nicene Creed, Chupungco comments that 'Happily' the 2010 text 'reinserted "I believe" before the sections on Jesus Christ and the Holy Spirit'. Noting that the formulation 'I believe in (*credo* in)' is reserved for the profession of faith in the Holy Trinity, he bemoans the fact that the new translation follows the 1973 text in putting the preposition 'in' before 'one, holy, Catholic and apostolic Church'.[73] Citing Peter Jeffery,[74] Pecklers holds that adopting the 'I believe (*Credo*)' form is not 'consistent with the tradition of the Latin Church' because the 'We believe (*Credimus*)' form is found in the original texts of that Creed published in Greek and Latin and in the usages of Pope Leo the Great, of early Roman collections of Canon Law and of the Spanish or Mozarabic Rite.[75] It could be argued, however, that the predominance of the 'I believe (Πιστεύω)' form in the Greek and Byzantine liturgical texts and of the 'I believe (*Credo*)' form in Gregorian chant, in the later Latin tradition and in the many musical settings of the Creed in recent centuries, should probably be taken into account in deciding this question. Noting that 'the *lex orandi* must always be in harmony with the *lex credendi*', *Liturgiam authenticam* 80 said that 'liturgical translations will not be capable of being worthy of God without faithfully transmitting the wealth of Catholic doctrine from the original text into the vernacular version, in such a way that the sacred language is adapted to the dogmatic reality that it contains.' The literal translation of *consubstantialem* as 'consubstantial' in the Nicene Creed, rather than as the paraphrase 'one in Being', may have been motivated by a sense that, since all that God has created shares in Being to some extent, the term 'one in Being' was too vague to grasp the dogmatic intention of the Council of Nicea. Although it may sound strange to the ears of many, 'consubstantial' was probably considered a better translation because *consubstantialis* is the translation into Latin of the Greek term *homoousios* that was coined specifically to describe and define the disputed relationship between the Father and the Son.[76] Chupungco hopes that 'with catechesis and frequent recitation the word "consubstantial" will cease to be an unfamiliar entry in the liturgical lexicon and a tongue twister for the assembly.'[77]

Although the Apostles' Creed[78] distinguishes between 'suffered (*passus*)' and 'died (*mortuus*)', the translation of *passus* as 'suffered death' rather than as 'suffered, died' in the Nicene-Constantinopolitan Creed may have been intended to clarify that, in this case, the word refers to the death that Christ underwent on the cross. Rather than following the 1973 text, 'He descended to the dead', or its own translation of *inferos* as 'the realm of the dead' in another place,[79] the 2011 text translated *descendit ad inferos* in the Apostles'

Creed as 'he descended into hell' and, noting that it 'does not correspond to the current understanding of hell', Chupungco comments that this new translation 'will require much catechesis.'[80] Rather than choosing a more modern or literal translation of the *Pater noster*, the translators of the 2011 text followed the 1973 text in opting for the sixteenth-century version that is commonly used by most of the mainline Christian Churches and ecclesial communions: 'Our Father, who art in heaven … .'[81]

There are a number of cases where the 2011 text seems to have changed the way in which the 1973 text translated certain words or phrases to bring them into line with other translations of the same text. Instead of 'the fellowship of the Holy Spirit', which might be regarded as insufficiently inclusive from the perspective of gender,[82] it follows the majority of English Bibles in translating the phrase *communicatio Sancti Spiritus* (see the *Nova Vulgata Editio* of 2 Corinthians 3:14) as 'the communion of the Holy Spirit'. The translation 'communion' is consistent with the translation of *Communicantes* as 'In communion with'[83] and with the association of *communicatio* with communion in other ecclesiastical contexts.[84] The 2011 text did not accept the 1973 text's paraphrase of *Gratia vobis et pax a Deo Patre nostro et Domino Iesu Christo* and it translated the phrase as 'Grace to you and peace from God our Father and the Lord Jesus Christ'. The new translation is in keeping with both the original Greek greeting found in a number of the letters written by, or associated with, St Paul[85] and the Latin translations of those greetings in the *Nova Vulgata Editio*. With the exception of the conclusion to the Apostles' Creed, where many traditions[86] and the 1973 text[87] use the translation 'everlasting life',[88] the 2011 text follows the lead of n. 458 of the Catechism (1992)[89] when it translates *aeternus* in John 3:16 as 'eternal'.[90] *Liturgiam authenticam* had instructed that 'an appropriate degree of coordination should be sought between the liturgical text and the authoritative vernacular translation of the Catechism of the Catholic Church (n. 50a). There are a number of similar examples of the influence of implicit biblical citations in the Introductory Rites,[91] the Liturgy of the Word,[92] the Liturgy of the Eucharist[93] and the Communion and Concluding Rites.[94]

Liturgiam authenticam 30 rejects the view that using nouns and pronouns that denote 'both genders, masculine and feminine' is 'necessarily to be regarded as the effect or the manifestation of an authentic development of the language as such.' It insists that 'it may not be possible' to avoid gender-specific terms used in an 'inclusive' sense 'without detriment to the precise meaning of the text, the correlation of the various words or expressions, or its aesthetic qualities.' It specifically mentioned the Latin word *homo* as among those terms that express 'the interplay between the individual and the universality and unity of the human family or community' and, accordingly, the

2011 text follows the 1973 text in translating *homo* as 'man' and *homines* as 'men'.[95] Like the 1973 text, the 2011 text also translates *fratres* as 'Brethren' or as 'brothers and sisters'.[96]

Noting that the editing of liturgical texts during the period after Vatican II 'sometimes incorporated punctuation … from several past eras into a single redacted text' or 'selectively eliminated certain medieval punctuation practices', the *Ratio translationis* says that 'translators must remain open to the possibility that, in certain instances, the punctuation found in a given phrase or sentence … reflects a legitimate autonomy of expression of the faith.'[97] It was, perhaps, with this in mind that the 2011 text tends to match the punctuation of the Latin more than the 1973 text as, for example, when it translates as a single English sentence a Latin sentence that the 1973 text translates as two,[98] three[99] or more[100] sentences. In addition to the two occasions where it follows the 1973 text in combining two Latin sentences into a single English sentence,[101] there are four other occasions where it again combines two Latin sentences into a single English sentence.[102] One of the problems identified by the *Ratio translationis* was the need to recognise that, rather than indicating 'an equivalence between two phrases, or the start of a list of grammatically equal items', the full colon between significant clauses in mid-sentence could also signal 'a pause at the end of the phrase or line which leads up to it'.[103] As examples of such a pause, it pointed to the use of a semi-colon or comma and the colometric arrangement of the text in the proposed English translations of the *Communicantes* and of the *Supra quae* in Eucharistic Prayer 1.[104] Of the sixteen full colons found in the Latin text of the sections of the Missal that are not Eucharistic Prayers, only eight are translated in the same way as the 1973 text.[105] Those full colons translated by semi-colons[106] or commas[107] in these texts should, presumably, be understood as other examples of such pauses. Of the remaining four full colons, one is omitted in translation and three are translated by a full colon.[108] Because the triple *mea culpa* 'is separated from the preceding sentence by a colon' and because the phrase after a colon 'expands or explains the preceding sentence', Chupungco argues that, 'unlike the preceding *cogitatione, verbo, opere et omissione*', *mea culpa* 'is in the nominative case with unexpressed or implicit verb' rather than in the ablative case and should have been translated as 'I am at fault; I am guilty; I have grievously sinned.'[109] Since the colon in question could also signal 'a pause at the end of the phrase or line which leads up to it', it seems more probable that *mea culpa* should be understood as being in the ablative rather than in the nominative case.

In line with n. 33 of *Liturgiam authenticam* and n. 120.i of the *Ratio translationis*, which laid down that translations capitalise all words capitalised in the Latin text, the 2011 text consistently corrects the lowercase translations used by the 1973 text in the Introductory Rites,[110] the Liturgy of the Word,[111] the Liturgy of the Eucharist[112] and the Communion and Concluding Rites.[113] In accordance with the lowercase *omnipotentem* in the Latin text, it corrects the 1973 text's 'Almighty' to 'almighty'.[114] In keeping with the specific norms for capitalisation in the *Ratio translationis*, which insist on the use of the uppercase form of the terms Father (as title), Gospel and Mass,[115] the 2011 text accepts the 1973 text's translations of *domne* as Father and of *missa* as Mass[116] and it also used the uppercase Gospel.[117]

The 2011 Translation of the Eucharistic Prayers

The difficulty of reading some parts of the new translation of the Eucharistic Prayers out loud has been noted by many. Although he notes some significant reservations,[118] King is, in general, more appreciative than negative concerning Eucharistic Prayer 1.[119] Comparing it with the 'pastoral approach' of the 1973 translation, Ostdiek described the new translation of Eucharistic Prayer 1 as the product of 'a literal, word-for-word approach'.[120] While recognising many positive aspects[121] and noting that the translators have 'at times, and wisely so, departed from the principle of strict formal equivalence', he is, in general, more negative in his appraisal of the new translation,[122] noting that its language 'often does not flow naturally for an English speaker'.[123] Mark Wedig seems to want to strike a balance between the strengths and weaknesses of Eucharistic Prayer 1 when he acknowledges that the *Te igitur* (n. 84) 'evokes awe with a mystifying and formal tone' but comments also that the phrase 'serene and kindly countenance' (n. 93) 'does not resonate with the speech of twenty-first-century people'.[124] In addition to the points noted by King, Ostdiek and Wedig, the 2011 Missal seems to have translated *Nobis quoque* as 'To us, also' rather than 'For ourselves, too', because 'To us' is subject to the verb 'grant (*donare*)' and because this translation avoids the possibly confusing verbal inelegance of 'To us, too'.[125]

King refers to the serious shortcomings of certain parts[126] but he also notes the more attractive features[127] of the new English translation of Eucharistic Prayer 2. Elich says that, in general, the new translation 'handles the theology well without becoming obscure', describing as 'delightful surprises' the 'strong and concrete images that it uncovers from the Latin text (e.g., "break the bonds", "fount", "dewfall", "face"', and he adds that it 'should quickly be possible for the Body of Christ to make this text its own and to pray it worthily'.[128] In his detailed analysis of the text, his positive[129] and negative[130] assessments seem to be fairly evenly matched. Joyce Ann Zimmerman appreciates what she describes as the 'beautiful parallelism' in 'It is truly right and just, our duty and salvation' and she comments favourably on the active nature of the word 'dew*fall*' in comparison to the word 'dew.'[131] Although King[132] and Elich liked the phrase, some have found the prayer asking God to welcome those who have died 'into the light of your face'[133] somewhat strange, presumably because they were unfamiliar with the Old Testament blessing asking that God 'make his face to shine on you and be gracious to you' (Num 6:24).[134]

King is essentially positive concerning some parts of the new translation of Eucharistic Prayer 3[135] but, in addition to having some difficulties with the theology implicit in the Latin text,[136] he also notes some issues concerning the readability of the new translation.[137] Elich describes the new translation as 'a serious attempt to express' the 'complex and rich theological ideas' of Eucharistic Prayer 3 'in a full and nuanced way.' In terms of readability, it 'is unlikely to be transparent in its meaning at the first hearing but is not impenetrable.'[138] Recognising the many positive aspects of the new translation,[139] he also notes some defects.[140] Elich, King and Pecklers all prefer 'from the rising of the sun to its setting' in the new translation to 'from east to west' in the old.[141]

King is also essentially positive about the new translation of Eucharistic Prayer 4,[142] the *Confitemur tibi* in particular,[143] but he identifies some parts that present particular problems from the perspective of readers.[144] Ostdiek describes it as 'one of the most beautiful and powerful' of the Eucharistic Prayers but, echoing King, he questions its readability, noting that its long, unbroken sentences and its 'fidelity to the principles of literal equivalence' could 'inhibit the smooth flow of the prayer for priests who have not carefully prepared the proclamation in advance.'[145] In his detailed analysis of the text, Ostdiek lists a significant number of deficiencies[146] but he also recognises a number of positive points.[147]

Almost all the words that the 1973 text left untranslated in the Eucharistic Prayers (which are listed in the previous chapter of this book) were translated in the 2011 translation. In Eucharistic Prayer 1, the exceptions were the phrase describing Joseph as *eiusdem Virginis Sponsi*, which was translated as 'her Spouse' rather than 'her husband',[148] and the translation of *placatus* as 'graciously'[149] rather than as 'having consented to being reconciled'. Apart from these, all the omitted phrases,[150] all the adjectival terms, which were divided more or less evenly between the section up to and including the Consecration,[151] and the section after the Consecration,[152] all the adverbs,[153] and the other omitted terms[154] were translated literally. Recognising the implicit citation of Hebrews 11:4 (*Abel ... justus*), the 2011 text translates *munera pueri tui iusti Abel* as 'the gifts of your servant Abel the just'.[155] With one exception,[156] the 2011 text translates all the untranslated adjectives,[157] adverbs[158] and other terms[159] left untranslated in the 1973 text of Eucharistic Prayer 2. In Eucharistic Prayer 3, the 2011 text also translated all the adjectives,[160] adverbs[161] and other terms[162] that had not been translated previously. There are two cases in Eucharistic Prayer

3, however, where the 2011 text introduced adjectives that are not found in the Latin text.[163] With three exceptions,[164] the 2011 text also translated all the adjectives[165] adverbs,[166] and other terms[167] left untranslated in Eucharistic Prayer 4. The 2011 translation omitted all the insertions that the 1973 text had added in its translation of Eucharistic Prayers 1, 2, 3 and 4 but, in one case, it added the adjective 'unfailing' to the literal translation given in the 1973 text.[168]

Although *Comme le prévoit* n. 33 foresaw the possibility of using paraphrases, particularly in the more ancient texts, it did not envisage any variations in the translations of the Eucharistic Prayers. The 2011 text does not seem to have considered the majority of the reformulations used in the 1973 translation of the Eucharistic Prayers as necessary, eliminating all the variations that fundamentally altered the original meaning and significantly reducing the number of paraphrases from 133 to fifteen.[169] In an apparently systematic manner, it addressed all the variations from the original meaning that we have noted in the 1973 translation of Eucharistic Prayers 1,[170] 2,[171] 3[172] and 4.[173] A number of the corrected variations are found in all four Eucharistic Prayers because the Preface Dialogue, the *Sanctus*, the words of consecration over the chalice and the Memorial Acclamation are common. Pecklers notes that the translation 'It is right and just' in the Preface Dialogue brings the new English translation into line with what 'has been the case for years in the other major language groups: *Cela est juste et bon* in the French, etc.'[174] As well as respecting the literal meaning of the Latin text, some of these corrected variations also recognise implicit citations of the *Nova Vulgata Editio* and Isaiah 6:3 (*Sanctus, Sanctus, Sanctus Dominus exercituum*), for example,[175] seems to have been taken into account when the 2011 text translated *Sabaoth*[176] as 'of Hosts'.[177] Some of the other corrected variations seem to have taken account of the tradition enshrined in the Latin text of the ancient Eucharistic Prayers and, rather than following the New Testament texts that refer to it as a 'cup (*potérion*)', the 2011 text reflects the tradition in the Roman Canon that the cup used during the Last Supper was a chalice (*calix*), a cup with a foot rather than some other kind of cup, when it translates *calix* as 'chalice/ Chalice'.[178] The word *calix* is probably translated as 'Cup' in the mystery of faith[179] because, in that context, 'When we ... drink this Cup' refers not to the historical text of the Roman Canon, but to the vessel being used at a particular Mass, which might not take the form of a chalice.

In Mark 10:45, Jesus says that he came to give his life as a ransom 'for many', echoing the Suffering Servant who 'bore the sin of many' (Is 53:12), but, in 1 Timothy 2:6, he is described as having given himself as a ransom 'for all'. The problem of the apparent contradiction between 'for many' and 'for all' was addressed in the Roman Catechism (1566) of the Council of Trent, which recognised that the fruits of Christ's saving death were intended by him 'for all' but that, in the concrete circumstances determined by providence, by history and by our free will, his death is only an effective means of salvation for the 'many' who are able and willing to receive them.[180] In 1653, the 'for all' of 1 Timothy 2:6 was underlined when Pope Innocent X condemned the view that Christ did not die for all human beings without exception in his Apostolic Constitution *Cum occasione*.[181] In 1935,[182] Joachim Jeremias argued that, in the light of Old Testament parallels, 'for many' meant, in effect, 'for all' and for some decades this view was widely accepted. In Mark 14:24 and Matthew 26:28, Jesus says that what still looks like wine is his blood and that it is 'poured out for many' and, in 1947, Joseph Pascher argued that, in this context, being 'poured out' referred to the cup rather than to its contents.[183] In 2008, Norbert Baumert and Maria-Irma Seewann argued that being 'poured out for many' referred, not to the outpouring of Christ's blood 'for all' on the Cross, but to 'an active outpouring of the blood from the chalice' that, as a sacramental action, was intended for the 'many' who might drink it, rather than 'for all'.[184] Writing as a theologian, Pope Benedict XVI accepts that 'Our participation in Christ's body and blood indicates that his action is "for many", for us, and that we are drawn into the "many" through the sacrament'[185] and he recognises that the problem of the word 'many' is 'partly explained' by the interpretation proposed by Baumert and Seewann.[186] He suggests that the apparent contradiction between the 'many' in Mark 10:45 (and in Isaiah 53:12) and the 'all' in 1 Timothy 2:5 can best be understood in the light of the parallels in some of the Qumran documents. Independently, Rudolf Pesch and Ulrich Wilckens have argued that, for both Isaiah and Jesus, 'many' refers to the 'totality' of Israel.[187] For Pope Benedict, Mark 10:45 should be understood as a 'new interpretation' and 'universalization' of Isaiah 53:12 by Jesus who 'knew that the mission of the Suffering Servant and the mission of the Son of Man were being fulfilled in himself'. Under the guidance of God's Spirit (cf. Jn 14:26), 'the infant Church was slowly arriving at a deeper understanding of Jesus' mission' and this deeper understanding of the universal salvific meaning of Christ's death was 'made crystal clear' in 1 Timothy 2:6, where Jesus is described as giving himself 'as a ransom for all'.[188] In 2005, the presidents of all the episcopal conferences were consulted on whether *pro multis* should be translated as 'for many' or 'for all' in vernacular translations of the Missal and, the following year, Cardinal Francis Arinze, Prefect of the Congregation for Divine Worship and the Discipline of the Sacraments, wrote again to the presidents noting that the Anglicans and Lutherans, and many Eastern Rites, used the equivalent of 'for many' and informing them that 'for many' was considered the more faithful translation.[189] The 2011 Missal translated *qui pro vobis et pro multis effundetur in remissionem peccatorum* as 'which will be poured out for you and for many for the forgiveness of sins'.[190]

There are also a number of variations that are found in some Eucharistic Prayers but not in others. Since the literal translation of *Pater sancte* or *sancte Pater* as 'holy Father' is found in most of the prefaces and prayers,[191] the translation of *Pater sancte* or *sancte Pater* as '*most* holy Father' that is found in Eucharistic Prayers 2 and 4[192] and in some prefaces and prayers[193] should probably be regarded as a variation on the original literal meaning. Although the *Ratio translationis* notes that it is necessary 'to avoid expressions that are confusing or ambiguous when proclaimed orally and heard' (n. 93) and although the translation 'most holy Father' might prevent anyone listening to the prayer being read aloud from thinking that it referred to the Pope,[194] the small number of occasions where this variation is used suggests that it may be an oversight. In Eucharistic Prayer 4, the translation of *pluries* as 'time and again' rather than 'again and again'[195] seems to have been motivated by the desire to indicate a simple plurality of covenants rather than something more frequent. Instead of following the translation of *ad inferos* as 'among the dead' in the 1973 text, the 2011 text prefers 'to the realm of the dead',[196] in keeping with the biblical emphasis on the phrase referring to a place rather than to a group of individuals.[197] King accepts that 'Made incarnate by' in the 2011 text 'is closer to the Latin' *incarnatus de* than the 1973 text's 'He was conceived through the power of'[198] but his comment that the Latin *de* is neither 'by' nor 'through the power of' implies that both translations are variations.[199] Although King is correct that *de* with the ablative is not normally translated by the English preposition 'by', the context of the translation of *de Spiritu Sancto* as 'by the Holy Spirit' here and in both Creeds suggests that it should probably be understood as instrumental and equivalent to 'by (means of) the Holy Spirit'.

The paraphrase found in the 2011 text of Eucharistic Prayer 1, 'Be pleased, O God, we pray, to bless, acknowledge, and approve this offering in every respect; make it spiritual and acceptable', appears to recognise that a literal translation of the five Latin adjectives would not work in English, since it turns the first three into verbs.[200] The new translation of this text also appears to acknowledge the implicit citation of *rationabile* in Romans 12:2, where it is used in the sense of 'spiritual'.[201] There are a number of other, generally more literal paraphrases.[202] With these exceptions, the 2011 text replaced all the paraphrases in the 1973 text with a literal translation in Eucharistic Prayers 1,[203] 2,[204] 3[205] and 4.[206] In keeping with *Liturgiam authenticam* 20, Elich has noted that, in the preface dialogue and *Sanctus*, which are common to all the Eucharistic Prayers, the 'key changes ("It is right and just" and "Lord God of hosts") translate the actual words without making the translation into an explanation.'[207] As *Comme le prévoit* 33 might have led us to expect, the number of paraphrases per 100 Latin words in the recently composed

Eucharistic Prayer 3 (0.51)[208] was less than in the more ancient texts of Eucharistic Prayers 1 (0.57)[209] and 4 (0.89)[210] but, surprisingly, it is greater than the number in the more ancient text of Eucharistic Prayer 2 (0.46).[211] The small number of paraphrases involved, however, may well render any such comparisons of little account. The new literal translations restored the passive voice of verbs when it had been paraphrased as active voice.[212] Taking account of the implicit citations from John 6:35 and 6:48, the 2011 text of Eucharistic Prayer 2 translates *panis vitae* as 'Bread of life'[213] and there are a number of other examples of implicit biblical citations reinforcing the literal translations in the 2011 text of Eucharistic Prayer 2,[214] 3[215] and 4.[216]

Pecklers holds that 'While the problem of inclusive language does remain in Eucharistic Prayer IV, it needs to be said that a good deal of the exclusive language found in the current Sacramentary has been eliminated'.[217] In terms of the Eucharistic Prayers as a whole, Pecklers may have had in mind the way in which the new translation does not try to interpret which Person of the Blessed Trinity is referred to by the noun *Domine*, as the 1973 text had done in some cases, but always translates the word literally as 'O Lord'[218] or as 'Lord'.[219] In relation to Eucharistic Prayer 4, he seems to have been thinking of the way in which the translation of *homo* as 'man' in the 1973 translation is continued in the new translation rather than being replaced 'with the more inclusive "we" or "man and woman"':[220] 'You formed man (*Hominem*) in your own image and entrusted the whole world to his (*eique*) care, so that ... he might have dominion ... you did not abandon him (*eum*).'[221] While the word 'man' is considered 'exclusive' by many today, it was not so until relatively recently and, in certain contexts,[222] it may not be possible to communicate the sense of the original text without using this word in an inclusive or generic sense. According to *Liturgiam authenticam* 30, when the Latin *homo* is used in contexts where the original text involves 'an interplay between the individual and the universality and unity of the human family or community', this interplay 'should be maintained in the translation'. Article 31 describes 'the transition from the singular to the plural' (such as the replacement of 'man' by 'we'), 'the splitting of a unitary collective term into masculine and feminine parts' (such as the replacement of 'man' by 'man and woman') or 'the introduction of impersonal or abstract words' (such as 'humankind')[223] as 'imprudent solutions'. Pecklers comments that, within common English usage, the use of 'what is now considered the exclusive term "man"' in the new translation

> ... means that the newly published text will be problematic or outdated even before the ink has dried! Sadly, I fear that this will place us in the situation in which we were before the textual revisions: either priests

will avoid Eucharistic Prayer IV altogether because of the masculine references it contains, or they will begin altering the text *ad libitum* despite the fact that they are not permitted to do so. There is little that we can do about that now, however, and we must learn to live with the texts we have been given.[224]

In the Eucharistic Prayers, there are two cases where both the 1973 and 2011 texts translate a particular Latin sentence as two English sentences[225] and one case where a single Latin sentence became three English sentences in both the 1973 and 2011 texts.[226] In general, however, the 2011 text tends to reduce the number of English sentences to conform to the Latin punctuation. With some frequency, it translates as a single English sentence a Latin sentence that the 1973 text translates as two[227] or three[228] sentences and there are cases where a sentence that became four English sentences in the 1973 text was translated by only two English sentences in the 2011 text.[229] There are also cases where the 2011 text combines two Latin sentences into a single English sentence.[230] In the 2011 text, only eighteen[231] of the thirty-five full colons in the Eucharistic Prayers are translated by the same punctuation as the 1973 text. We have already noted that the *Ratio translationis* recognised that a full colon could sometimes be used in the Latin to signal 'a pause at the end of the phrase or line which leads up to it' and that it pointed to the semi-colon or comma and the colometric arrangement of the text in the proposed English translations of the *Communicantes* and of the *Supra quae* in Eucharistic Prayer 1 as examples of this practice.[232] The nine cases where full colons in the Eucharistic Prayers are translated by commas[233] and the three cases where full colons are translated by semi-colons[234] are, presumably, also examples of such pauses. Of the remaining twenty-three full colons, twenty-one are translated by full colons,[235] one by a full-stop and one by no punctuation.[236] The full colons before 'for' in the words of consecration[237] in Eucharistic Prayers 1, 2 and 3 are replaced by a comma in the words of consecration in Eucharistic Prayer 4,[238] suggesting that these full colons should not be understood as the equivalent of full stops and that the 'for' serves as a connection between what went before and what comes after. If so, the placing of 'for' after a full colon is not in violation of the enclitic nature of *enim* in Latin, the grammatical rule that it never begins a sentence, and, rather than distracting the hearer from 'this is my body' or from 'this is the chalice of my blood', it draws attention to these statements when read properly.[239] On occasion, the 2011 text also inserts a full colon, apparently as a pause, where there is a full stop, a comma or no punctuation in the Latin.[240] The *Ratio translationis* suggests that, on certain rare occasions, the punctuation used in the Latin text can reflect 'a legitimate autonomy of expression of the Faith', and it gives as an example the stark simplicity and the lack of a predicate of *Mysterium fidei*.[241] We have already noted that the 1973 text gave 'Let us proclaim the mystery of faith' as a translation but, in line with the intention of Pope Paul VI who had originally moved it from the words of consecration to becoming an independent and unadorned acclamation, the 2011 text translated it as 'The Mystery of faith'.[242]

In line with *Liturgiam authenticam* n. 33 and with the specific requirement in n. 120.i of the *Ratio translationis* (2007) that all words capitalised in the Latin text be capitalised in any translation, the 2011 text consistently corrects the lowercase translations in the 1973 text of the Eucharistic Prayers. In Eucharistic Prayer 1, for example, we find 'N. our Pope and N. our Bishop', 'Virgin Mary, Mother', 'Apostles ... Martyrs ... Saints', 'Body ... Blood', 'Bread ... Chalice', 'Angel ... Body and Blood' and 'Apostles ... Martyrs ... Saints'.[243] There are similar examples in Eucharistic Prayers 2,[244] 3[245] and 4.[246] For some reason, perhaps an oversight or a typographical error, the 2011 text did not capitalise 'hosts (*Sabaoth*)'[247] or 'father (*Patriarchae*)'.[248] In keeping with the specific norms of the *Ratio translationis* concerning the capitalisation of Angel(s), Ascension, Cross (of Christ), Only Begotten (Son), Passion (of Christ), Resurrection (of Christ) and Saviour,[249] the 2011 text capitalises these words even though they are not capitalised in the Latin text.[250] The term Order of Bishops,[251] like the terms Bishop and Pope, is, presumably, capitalised for honorific reasons.[252] The term Death (of Christ),[253] like the term Passion (of Christ), and the terms Bread and Chalice denoting the Eucharist,[254] like the terms Body and Blood of Christ,[255] would seem to be capitalised by extension.

The 2011 Translation of the Prefaces and Other Presidential Prayers
In this section, the 2011 translation of some sections from the Prefaces and of some of the other Presidential Prayers will be analysed in terms of their readability, their omissions or additions, their use of paraphrase, their approach to the translation of gendered words and their use of punctuation and capitalisation.

The 1973 translation was notable for the simplicity and readability of its prayers, but less so for its fidelity to the Latin text. The 2011 translation, while it is aware of the need for both readability and fidelity, seems to be less concerned about providing a text that is easy to read and understand than with giving a faithful translation of the Latin. Pecklers describes the new Prefaces as concluding 'more strongly in a way that leads better into the Holy Holy', noting that these concluding phrases 'are deliberately signed to produce a good sound when sung'.[256] Commenting on the proposed new Collects as a whole, he notes that 'their overall quality ... remains somewhat uneven despite the fact that some of the prayer texts are well crafted'. He suggests that the reason for this is that some translators 'were more gifted or competent' than their colleagues who 'felt more constrained by the need to translate literally from the Latin original, resulting in texts that flow less naturally in English.' Acknowledging the 'gradual improvement ... both in terms of their language as well as their proclamability' that had taken place during the process of drafting the new Collects, Pecklers points out that their 'elevated style' may require that they 'be proclaimed aloud beforehand and rehearsed by the presider' and that there be some 'adjustment in the way the presider speaks or chants them, and also in the way the assembly hears them'.[257] Citing Paul Turner,[258] he comments that, even where 'problems do remain, ICEL translators are optimistic that the length of the Collects will be a non-issue once we begin using them' because we will 'become increasingly acquainted with' their 'syntax and style as we grow comfortable with the texts.'[259]

With one exception,[260] the 2011 translation of the Prefaces reinstates any words or phrases that had been omitted in the 1973 translation.[261] The new translation also reinstates all the words and phrases omitted in the older translation of the other Presidential Prayers,[262] including the reference to 'one' heavenly Bread that would seem to be an implied citation from John 6:32 and 1 Corinthians 10:17.[263] Using the translation 'we beseech you' (rather than 'we pray') from the already well-known English translation of the prayer as part of the Angelus,[264] the 2011 text also restores the words that the 1973 translation had omitted in the Collect of the Fourth Sunday of Advent. All the additions introduced by the older translation into the Prefaces and other Presidential Prayers we are considering were omitted by the new translation[265] but 'Christ' was inserted in place of 'him' on one occasion,[266] presumably to point up the implied parallel between Christ and us.

The paraphrases introduced in the 1973 translation of the Prefaces we are considering were all rejected in favour of a more literal treatment by the 2011 Missal.[267] In the other Presidential Prayers we are considering, the words *Deus* and *Domine* are always translated as 'God'[268] or as 'Lord'[269] and Pecklers comments that if the literal translation of *Deus* as 'God' 'may render the address of the Prayer to the Father less evident, it nonetheless will make the address to God more gender-inclusive'.[270] The *Ratio translationis for the English Language* (2007) insists that 'translators must first take care to locate the biblical and patristic sources of the prayers they translate' (n. 19) and that, 'rather than substituting other words that are alien to it', translators should retain the 'coherent system of words and patterns of speech consecrated by the books of Sacred Scripture and by ecclesiastical tradition, especially by the Fathers of the Church' (n. 20). In keeping with these guidelines, the other paraphrases in the older translation of the other Presidential Prayers we are considering were, for the most part, abandoned in favour of more literal translations.[271]

Rather than using the paraphrase 'the Resurrection,' for example, the new translation restores the literal meaning (paschal festivities)[272] of the phrase *festa paschalia*, dating at least from the seventh century,[273] that had been inserted into a prayer from the *Hadrianum* (758–786).[274] Restoring the literal translation, 'illuminate our hearts ... with the splendour of your grace',[275] the 2011 translation allowed the echo of the implicit citation from St Ambrose[276] in the eighth-century prayer by Alcuin of York[277] to be heard in English.

Some of the exceptions where the 2011 Missal opts for a paraphrase rather than a more literal translation are associated with the terms 'flesh', 'heart', 'mind' and 'spirit'[278] and we begin by considering those that relate to flesh and heart/mind. Restoring the omitted reference to the flesh in the Prayer after Communion of the Third Sunday of Easter,[279] newly composed for the *Missale Romanum* of 1969,[280] the 2011 translation used the paraphrase 'attain in their flesh the incorruptible glory of the resurrection',[281] presumably to avoid translating the Gerundive. In the historical context of the late patristic period, the word 'heart' could be used to denote our capacity either to be illuminated internally with 'the splendour' of God's 'grace' so that we might ponder on what pleases God and love him in all sincerity,[282] or to have the sanctification we received in Baptism confirmed internally[283] by the light of the Pentecost Spirit.[284] The *Ratio translationis* lists being reliant on patristic teaching as one of the seven principal characteristics of the language of the Roman Rite (n. 7) and, while the 'heart' could denote both the capacity to ponder and to love during that patristic period, the mind seems to have been seen as the focus of our capacity to reason. There is a similar distinction in the sixth or seventh-century Collect for the Fourth Sunday in Ordinary Time,[285] which prays that we may 'honour' the Lord our God 'with all our mind' and love everyone 'with rational good will (*rationabili ... affectu*)'.[286] *Liturgiam authenticam* reminds us that 'a literal translation of terms which may initially sound odd in a vernacular language may for this very reason provoke inquisitiveness in the hearer and provide an occasion for catechesis' (n. 43). Although, from that perspective, the somewhat awkward paraphrase used by the 2011 Missal, 'in truth of heart (*rationabili affectu*)', might be warranted, it does not do justice to the way in which honouring God 'with all our mind' is given concrete shape in the second part of the sentence by insisting that we love everyone that God has created with good will governed by reason. The Collect of the Fourth Sunday of Advent[287] and the Prayers after Communion for the Second Sunday of Easter[288] and for the Twenty-Third Sunday in Ordinary Time[289] all date from the sixth, seventh or eighth centuries. The 2011 Missal translates *sensibus* as 'minds and hearts' in the first of these prayers, *mentibus* as 'hearts' in the second, and *mentibus* as 'minds and hearts' in the third. The word *mentibus* should probably be translated as 'minds', as it is in the contemporary Prayers after Communion for the Twenty-Fourth[290] and Twenty-Sixth[291] Sundays in Ordinary Time. The 2011 Missal also translates *mentes* in the seventh or eighth-century Prayer over the Offerings for the Second Sunday of Lent[292] as 'in ... mind' rather than 'in heart'. Using the paraphrase 'hearts' when translating *sensibus* or *mentibus* in the three texts mentioned above should probably be regarded as a departure from what the *Ratio translationis* describes as the 'coherent system of words and patterns of speech consecrated by the books of Sacred Scripture and by ecclesiastical tradition, especially by the Fathers of the Church' (n. 20). During the period in question, the human mind (*mens*) or intellect was regarded as the location of God's image in us[293] and it designated our rational or reasoning capacity,[294] rather than the hidden interior dimension of our being in general, which was usually designated by 'heart'. While *sensibus* can denote physical sensation or mental perception, moral or aesthetic sense, as well as feeling, inclination[295] and mind, the emphasis on the divine gift of sincere prayer and peace, on doing fitting homage to God's divine majesty and on our partaking of the sacred mystery, suggest that being faithfully united in our intellectual or spiritual perceptions and judgements thanks to our communion with Christ is intended.

The phrase *ut eorum et corporibus nostris subsidium non desit et mentibus* in the sixth-century Prayer over the Offerings for the Eleventh Sunday in Ordinary Time[296] should perhaps be translated as 'that we not be without their help in our bodies or in our minds' rather than as 'that the sustenance they provide may not fail us in body or in spirit'. Inspired by some of the writings of St Augustine (354–430),[297] three twelfth-century writers, Hugh of St Victor (1096–1141),[298] Gilbert of Poitiers (c. 1080–1154)[299] and Peter Lombard (1095–1160),[300] interpreted the union of the human soul and body as the union of the life of the human spirit, the rational human mind, and the life of the human body, which they regarded as inherently inferior to the life of the spirit. It was not until the Fourth Lateran Council of 1215, however, that it became commonplace to describe human nature as being 'composed of spirit and body'[301] rather than of soul and body.

Some of the situations where the 2011 Missal opts for a paraphrase rather than a more literal translation are associated with the terms 'spirit' and 'soul'.[302] The first part of the Collect of the Third Sunday of Easter[303] is a revised version of a prayer said over the people as part of the final blessing at Mass in the *Gelasian Vetus Sacramentary* (c. 628–715 AD)[304] that includes the phrase *renovata animae iuventute*.[305] The 2011 Missal's translation of this Collect as 'in renewed youthfulness of spirit (*animae*)' suggests that the renewed youthfulness in which God's people now exult is specifically spiritual rather than embracing the entire dimension of the soul's life that both includes and transcends the bodily dimension.[306] Sources contemporary with the prayer suggest, however, that the paraphrase 'spirit' for *anima* is anachronistic. In the roughly contemporary Prayer after Communion for the Solemnity of the Most Holy Trinity,[307] *salutem corporis et animae* is paraphrased by the 2011 Missal as 'health of body and soul' rather than as 'health of body and spirit'. Some developments that took place between the fifth and sixth centuries also make the paraphrase of *anima* as 'spirit' unlikely. In 450 AD, the Council of Chalcedon confessed that Jesus was 'perfect in divinity and perfect in humanity, the same truly God and truly man composed of rational soul and body'.[308] The terminology of soul and body was also used by Pope Boniface II when he approved a decree of the Second Council of Orange (529) against the Semi-Pelagians, declaring anathema anyone who says that 'through the offence of Adam's sin, the whole person, body and soul, was not changed for the worse, but believes that only the body was subjected to corruption while the freedom of the soul remained unharmed'.[309] The hypothesis of the pre-existence of the human soul had been proposed by Origen (c. 184–253), who understood the word *psyche* (soul) as referring to those created pure intelligences (*noes*) whose initial fervour had cooled.[310] When this theory was revived by some Jerusalem monks in 543, it was condemned by a provincial council held under Patriarch Menas of Constantinople[311] because, in effect, it undermined the unity of the human soul and body that the Council of Chalcedon had implicitly affirmed when it had described Christ as 'truly God and truly man composed of rational soul and body'. A later revival of the same theory by Priscillian was condemned by the Council of Braga in 561.[312] In the light of these fifth and sixth-century developments highlighting the fallen nature of the human soul and rejecting the theory that we already existed as some kind of purely spiritual soul before being conceived, the Latin phrase *renovata animae iuventute* in a slightly later prayer should probably be translated as 'in renewed youthfulness of soul' rather than as 'in renewed youthfulness of spirit'.

There are also situations where the 2011 Missal opts for a paraphrase rather than a more literal translation because of the way that the verbs *mereamur* and *satiare* are used.[313] The paraphrase 'that we may heed his lesson of patient suffering and so merit a share in his Resurrection' does not do justice to the implied parallel between the Incarnation and the Cross as examples of Christ's humility or to the prayer that we may merit to heed his lessons of patience and [become] sharers of [his] Resurrection.[314] Similarly, the translation asking God to pour the Spirit of his love on us and to make those he has 'nourished by this one heavenly bread one in mind and heart' does not do full justice to this late patristic prayer[315] asking that the outpouring of the Spirit of divine love make those 'filled by this one heavenly Bread harmoniously united through one and the same sense of dutiful conduct'.[316] In this context, Thomas Merton translated *pietas* as 'care'[317] but the richer notion of a 'sense of dutiful conduct'[318] is suggested by the citations of this prayer by Pope Pius XII, who spoke of 'the bond of that love that unites us in a fraternal covenant' in association with this prayer,[319] by a recent translation of Vatican II's *Sacrosanctum Concilium* 10, which translated *una ... pietate* as 'one in their commitment to you',[320] and by the reference to the translation of *pietas* in the *Ratio translationis* (n. 80).

The 2011 translation of the Prefaces and Presidential Prayers opted, in general, for a more literal translation of both the abstract and concrete terms that designate human nature and gender. Instead of 'by becoming man', which did not do justice either to this eighth-century text's emphasis on the concrete reality of the flesh that Christ shares with us[321] or to the parallel between being carnal and spiritual in the implied citation from Tertullian,[322] it opts for the paraphrase 'has appeared in our very flesh',[323] presumably because 'in the substance of our flesh' might not be easily understood today. Similarly, instead of 'by becoming man', which did not do justice to the text's emphasis on Christ's humility being manifested in the Incarnation, the 2011 Missal prefers the literal translation 'to take flesh'.[324] Instead of the paraphrases 'a Father's love', 'coming as man', 'faithful people' and 'sons and daughters', it also adopts the more literal translations 'care', 'Incarnation', 'faithful' and 'adoption'.[325] The 2011 text changes the paraphrases 'you bring the image of your Son to perfection within us' and 'your family' to 'they may be led to the fullness of grace that you bestow on your sons and daughters' and 'your children'.[326] Referring to the Incarnation, the phrase *homo genitus* in the Prayer over the Offerings for the Christmas Day Dawn Mass[327] is translated literally as 'was born a man'[328] and, referring to human beings in general, the word *homo* is translated by the gender-inclusive word 'everyone' in both the singular and the plural.[329]

In each of the prayers given in the Appendix, the 2011 text translates a single Latin sentence as a single English sentence except for the one case where it unites two Latin sentences into a single English sentence.[330] The two full colons are translated by commas.[331] The uppercase Latin words translated by lowercase English words in the older translation are all corrected[332] to uppercase[333] and, with one exception,[334] the lowercase Latin words for 'Cross', 'Passion', 'Resurrection' and 'Sacrament'[335] and for the Eucharistic 'Body and Blood'[336] are translated as uppercase English words, in keeping with the *Ratio translationis*. The lowercase Latin words for 'Bread', 'Death' and 'Nativity' are also translated as uppercase English words, presumably by extension of the norms for the translation of 'Body and Blood', 'Passion' and 'Christmas'.[337]

Evaluating the 2011 Translation

In this chapter, I have outlined the nature of the changes that have been made in the 2011 translation and I have tried to identify the apparent reasons for those changes.

The approach to translating liturgical texts in the 2001 instruction, *Liturgiam authenticam*, and in the *Ratio translationis for the English Language* (2007), differs in many respects from the approach in the 1969 instruction *Comme le prévoit,* but there are also significant elements of continuity. In keeping with the principles concerning fidelity of translation outlined in 2001 and in 2007, the 2011 translation seems to have corrected the great majority of the omissions and additions, and significantly reduced the number of paraphrases, that are found in the 1973 translation. Among the few omissions retained was 'her Spouse (*eiusdem Virginis Sponsi*)', which avoids the possibly confusing expression, 'Husband of the same Virgin'. The paraphrases 'And also with you' and 'Lord, I am not worthy to receive you, but only say the word, and I shall be healed' were replaced by the literal translations 'And with your spirit' and 'Lord, I am not worthy that you should enter under my roof, but only say the word and my soul shall be healed'. While almost all the variations from the original meaning found in the 1973 translation were corrected in the 2011 translation, the new translation did not eliminate all paraphrases. It significantly reduced the frequency with which paraphrases were used, however, and overall the number of paraphrases was reduced from 192 to twenty-three and the number of paraphrases per 100 Latin words was reduced from 5.88 to 0.77,[338] a reduction of 87 per cent. In keeping with the 2006 judgement by the Prefect of the Congregation for Divine Worship and the Discipline of the Sacraments that 'for many' was considered the more faithful translation, the 2011 Missal translated *qui pro vobis et pro multis effundetur in remissionem peccatorum* as 'which will be poured out for you and for many for the forgiveness of sins'. While the new translation is generally more literal than the 1973 translation, there are a number of places where the Latin word *mentes* is paraphrased as 'mind and heart' rather than translated as 'mind', or where *anima* is paraphrased as 'spirit' rather than translated as 'soul', and such paraphrases are not in accordance with the probable meaning of the original Latin sources. The 2011 translation tends to reflect the punctuation of the Latin text more faithfully than the 1973 translation but there are cases where two Latin sentences are translated as a single English sentence and vice versa. The new translation follows the more detailed norms for capitalisation that are found in the *Ratio translationis*.

The 2011 translation is generally more literal than the 1973 translation and it respects the integrity of any implicit intertextual references to the Latin texts of the Scriptures. The readability of the new translation has been questioned by many, notably in relation to some of the Collects and certain parts of Eucharistic Prayers 2 and 3. Although the need for a different approach to reading the new Presidential Prayers, paying particular attention to their colometric arrangement, has been noted, some parts of the new translation have received more favourable reviews in terms of readability and these include some of the Collects, the endings of the Prefaces and parts of Eucharistic Prayers 1 and 4. Some writers have commented unfavourably about the lack of 'inclusive language' in Eucharistic Prayer 4 but, in the light of the specific norms concerning inculturation and the use of language that concerns gender in *Liturgiam authenticam* 30–31, the translation of *homo* as 'man' in that Prayer should perhaps not be evaluated solely in terms of what has only recently become the generally accepted norm in some anglophone cultures. Some commentators have noted that the literal translation of *Deus* as 'God' rather than 'Father' makes the address to God in the new translation more gender-inclusive than in the 1973 translation.

CHAPTER III

The New Translation and the Tradition of Christian Anthropology

In the Nicene Creed, we profess that it was 'for our salvation' that Jesus Christ, 'the Only Begotten Son of God ... became man ... suffered death and was buried, and rose again on the third day'. According to Vatican II's Constitution on the Sacred Liturgy (1963), *Sacrosanctum concilium* 2, it is because the work of our redemption takes place through the liturgy, especially in the divine sacrifice of the Eucharist, that the liturgy 'is supremely effective in enabling the faithful to express in their lives and to portray to others the mystery of Christ'. Our salvation, in other words, is the fruit of Christ's redemptive work that takes place especially in the Mass. It is primarily in the Eucharistic liturgy of the new Roman Missal that English-speaking Catholics of the Roman rite will now both express the mystery of Christ in their lives and portray that mystery to others. In his apostolic exhortation on Evangelisation, *Evangelii nuntiandi* (1974), Pope Paul VI said that 'the immense sections of humankind that practice non-Christian religions ... have the right to know the riches of the mystery of Christ (see Eph 3:8)' and that, in the riches of that mystery, 'the whole human family can find, to the fullest degree and with no disappointed expectations, all those things that it is gropingly searching for concerning God, man and his destiny, life and death, and truth.'[1] Describing them as 'decisive for the meaning and orientation of our life and actions', the *Catechism of the Catholic Church* (1992) formulated these basic questions as 'Where do we come from? Where are we going? What is our origin? What is our end? Where does everything that exists come from and where is it going?' (n. 282). There are many different criteria that might be used to evaluate the new translation but, in this chapter, I want to investigate how it enables us to express in our lives and to portray to others those aspects of the rich mystery of Christ that provide the answers that the whole human family is searching for concerning our common origin, nature and destiny. Citing Vatican II's Constitution on the Sacred Liturgy, *Sacrosanctum concilium*, *Liturgiam authenticam* (2001) highlighted the need 'to preserve with care the authentic Liturgy, which flows forth from the Church's living and most ancient spiritual tradition, and to adapt it with pastoral wisdom to the genius of the various peoples' (n. 1). To what extent do the 1973 and 2011 translations of the Roman Missal reflect the living and most ancient spiritual tradition of anthropology from which they flow forth and how successful have they been in adapting that tradition to the genius of the anglophone peoples for whom they were intended?

Despite the different circumstances of their various human authors, there is a remarkable consistency in the way that the various books of the Old[2] and New Testament understand the human person as a living soul that necessarily includes the dimensions of flesh/body and spirit/breath. The *Ratio translationis for the English Language* (2007) lists being intended to engage the whole person as one of the seven principal characteristics of the language of the Roman Rite (n. 11) and, in this chapter, we will approach the whole human person using the categories of soul, body and spirit. We begin with the global description of the human person or 'soul' and we then look at the external manifestation of the person as body or flesh (*caro*) before concluding with an examination of the dimension of our being that is not necessarily manifested externally, which includes the heart (*cor*), the mind (*mens*) and the spirit (*spiritus*).

The following subsections will outline the way in which these three kinds of terms are used in Scripture, in Tradition and in the 1973 and 2011 translations of the Missal. *Liturgiam authenticam* recommended that a translation may be weakened and made trite 'by the use of a single vernacular term for rendering differing Latin terms such as ... the words *anima, animus, cor, mens,* and *spiritus*' (n. 51). Before we can proceed with an evaluation of the Latin terms used in the new translation, however, we need to have some familiarity with the way the Greek terms they represent were used in the New Testament from which they were generally adopted and with the way those Greek terms are related to the equivalent Hebrew terms used in the Old Testament.

The Human Soul in Scripture and Tradition

This section will outline the way in which the term 'soul' is used in the Old and New Testament and in the Tradition of the Church, focusing on those aspects that are most significant in terms of the use of the word 'soul (*anima*)' in the 1973 and 2011 Missals.

The soul (*nephesh*) has been described as the central notion of Israelite anthropology[3] and it implies the true, and not merely composite, unity of flesh and spirit in which the person or soul both is flesh and spirit and experiences the tension between his or her flesh and spirit. According to Pedersen, the body/flesh was seen as 'the soul in its outward form'.[4] For the ninth-century BC Jahwist writer, the bodily shape of 'man (*Adam*)' was formed by God of dust from the ground and he became a living soul (*nephesh*),[5] like the beasts and the birds whom God had also formed (cf.Gn 2:19), when God breathed the breath of life into his nostrils (cf. Gn 2:7). Genesis 2:7 is generally recognised as the key text for understanding the anthropology of the Old

Testament[6] and the following verses (cf. Gn 2:7-25) describe how God built (*banah*) the woman, who is described as sharing his essential nature ('bone of my bones and flesh of my flesh'),[7] from the man's rib. She was to be his equal and helper[8] and, as his bodily counterpart,[9] she was to become one flesh with him. Like the Jahwist, the fifth-century BC Priestly writer recognised (cf. Gn 1:20) that each of the other animals is also a living 'soul (*nephesh*)' but this writer does not describe our creation in terms of forming the bodily shape and then breathing the breath of life into it. Instead, 'man (*Adam*)', used in the collective sense that includes both male and female,[10] is described as being made or created in God's image and likeness[11] and commanded to be fruitful, to multiply, and to fill the earth and subdue it (cf. Gn 1:26-28). It is now generally recognised that there is no significant difference between image and likeness in this context[12] and, since Adam is described as having begotten his son, Seth, in his own image and likeness (cf. Gn 5:3), it would seem that, for the Priestly writer, we resemble God in the same way a man's son resembles him. Rather than opting for one of these two Creation accounts rather than the other, the final editor of the book of Genesis included both, presumably because they were regarded as being essentially compatible and complementary despite their obvious differences.[13] The Priestly writer's account of our being created in God's image/likeness was probably regarded as being essentially equivalent to the Jahwist's account of the human form that God made from clay (the man) or from bone (the woman) becoming a living soul thanks to God's gift of the breath of life.

In the Jahwist account of creation, the garden included the tree of life and the tree of the knowledge of good and evil (cf. Gn 2:9) and the Lord God commanded the man, 'You may freely eat of every tree in the garden; but of the tree of the knowledge of good and evil you shall not eat, for in the day that you eat of it you shall die' (Gn 2:16-17). The implication would seem to be that, had the man and his wife eaten of the tree of life rather than of the tree of the knowledge of good and evil, they would have become immortal.[14] The consequences of disobeying God's command included mortality, the loss of the breath of life and the return of the bodily form of their living souls to the ground from which it had originally been taken.[15] While death in the sense of becoming mortal seems to have been an immediate consequence of the Fall (cf. Gn 3:19), as Genesis 2:17 had predicted, the reduction in life-expectation from immortality to what we consider normal today is presented as taking place gradually[16] from almost a thousand years (cf. Gn 5:5)[17] to seventy or eighty (cf. Ps 90:10).

As the expression 'living soul' suggests, soul (*nephesh*) is closely associated with life and, in many texts, the two are synonymous,[18] as in the one-time internationally recognised emergency message, 'Save our souls!'[19] In 2 Kings

10:24, for example, Jehu warns his soldiers that if one of them allows a prisoner to escape, the one responsible will forfeit his soul-life (*nephesh*), and there are also references to enemies seeking an individual's 'soul' or life.[20] The identification of the soul (*nephesh*) with the person is implicit in many Old Testament texts.[21] In Numbers 19:18, for example, the 'souls that were there' and that were to be sprinkled with water clearly refers to the people who were present. In 2 Kings 2:2,[22] the phrase, 'As the Lord lives, and as your soul lives', which is addressed to the prophet Elijah, means 'As the Lord lives, and as you yourself live'.[23] The expression 'every soul (*kol nephesh*)' is the equivalent of 'everyone' or 'every person'.[24]

Beginning about the third century before Christ, the books of the Pentateuch[25] were translated into Koiné Greek and, later, Greek translations of the other Hebrew books of the Old Testament were also produced. Some of the later books of the Old Testament were composed in Greek and the process of preparing the Greek text of the whole of the Hebrew Scriptures, now known as the Septuagint,[26] was probably completed during the first century of the Christian era.[27] There is a considerable difference between the purely spiritual meaning denoted by the Greek word *psyche* and the meaning of the Hebrew word *nephesh*, which often identifies the soul with the concrete life (cf. Prov 8:35-36) of the individual. Despite the different connotations of the words, the Septuagint translates the Hebrew word *nephesh* as *psyche* on 680 occasions[28] and, in effect, this led to a certain redefining of the meaning of the Greek word *psyche* that brought it much closer to the meaning of the Hebrew word *nephesh*. In the Septuagint text of Sirach 39:1, for example, giving one's *psyche* (soul), like giving one's *nephesh* (soul), seems to be used in the reflexive sense of dedicating or devoting oneself to something. Although the Wisdom writings that used *psyche* in place of *nephesh* were later recognised as part of the canon of the Old Testament, some writers have suggested that their Jewish authors were significantly influenced by a dualistic understanding of humanity as a purely spiritual soul (*psyche*) that is somehow allied to a material body (*soma*).[29] This approach has now been largely abandoned,[30] however, and the anthropology of these writings is now generally recognised as essentially consistent with the holistic approach of the Hebrew texts of the Old Testament, which recognises both flesh/body and spirit/breath as intrinsic dimensions of the human soul/person. Being first formed by God and then becoming a living soul thanks to the gift of breath/spirit (cf. Gn 2:7) is echoed, for example, in Wisdom 15:11, which criticises the one who 'failed to know the one who formed him and inspired him with an active soul and breathed into him a living spirit'.[31] Unlike the immortal, spiritual soul of Greek philosophy, the soul is capable of being destroyed/killed (cf. Wis 1:11).[32] The notion that the body will simply 'turn to ashes' and that the breath/spirit will 'dissolve like empty air' when the beating of our hearts is extinguished at the death of the soul is presented as the unsound reasoning of the ungodly (cf. Wis 2:1-3). Instead, reflecting the common Old Testament identification of the human soul with the person's life,[33] which was generally understood to continue some kind of existence after the breath/spirit departs at death,[34] the soul/life of those who are righteous[35] is described as being 'in the hand of God' (Wis 3:1)[36] who alone can raise them from Sheol/Hades where the gates of death imprison them (cf. Wis 16:13-14).[37] Rejecting the Greek view that the living soul is the fiery principle of our bodily life, it is God's gift of breath/spirit to the body he had formed from earth (cf. Gn 2:7; Wis 7:1) that is presented as the life-principle of the living human soul.[38] Rather than being in metaphysical opposition to the soul, the body (soma) in the book of Wisdom[39] denotes the physical aspect of human existence[40] and divine Wisdom can be described as both entering a human soul/person and as dwelling in a human body (cf. Wis 1:4).

There is almost complete unanimity among scholars on the essential continuity between the way the Old and New Testaments understand the human person as a living soul that is always and at once bodily/carnal and spiritual.[41] Many have noted the presumed equivalence between the Hebrew nephesh and the Greek word psyche (soul), which is used to translate it in New Testament quotations from the Old Testament.[42] Like nephesh, the word psyche in New Testament Greek can also designate the life of an individual person[43] or the individual person as such[44] and the expression 'every soul' means 'everyone'.[45] A number of texts present Jesus as using 'soul' both in the sense of physical life and in the sense of that personal life that survives death and can be raised to share in the eternal life of God.[46] It is only those willing to lose their psyche (soul) for the sake of Christ and his Gospel who will ultimately save their psyche (soul) in the sense of sharing forever in eternal life with God (cf. Mk 8:34-37). Matthew follows Mark's use of psyche (cf. Mt 10:39) but the substitution of the reflexive pronoun for psyche (soul) in the parallel text, Luke 9:25, implies that the word is understood in the sense of the person's life.[47] The clear import of the text is that only Christian discipleship can ultimately save a person's soul-life from annihilation.[48] The use of the same word, psyche, to describe both our soul-life before and after death suggests that, in some sense, there is an essential continuity between our carnal and spiritual soul-life now and our soul-life after death.[49] Although he does nuance it to some extent,[50] St Paul follows the anthropology of the Old Testament and his relatively rare[51] use of the word soul (psyche) mirrors Old Testament usage of the word both in the sense of person[52] and in the sense of life.[53] He implies that those who are not willing to lose their physical soul-life in order to save it for eternal life are 'dominated by their concern for their physical soul-life (*psychikos*), 'which is often translated as 'natural', 'animal' or 'unspiritual' (cf. 1 Cor 2:14-15)[54] in contrast with those who are 'spiritual (*pneumatikos*)'.[55] In 2 Corinthians 5:1-4, Paul presents his own death in terms of the destruction of the tent-like house in which he has lived (his body) and taking up residence in a new and eternal heavenly dwelling that God will prepare for him.

During the centuries after the death and resurrection of Jesus, the preaching of the Gospel among those who did not share the understanding of humanity that is found in the writings of the Old and New Testaments led to the gradual modification of the prevailing cultural understanding of humanity (an eternal soul imprisoned in a mortal body) and the emergence of a cultural anthropology that was largely shaped by Christianity. Following the lead established by St Paul, the Church adopted the language and some elements of the prevailing philosophical understanding derived from Platonism but rejected those elements, like the immortality and pre-existence of the soul, that were incompatible with the Gospel message. In the process, the Greco-Roman world was gradually Christianised and the Judeo-Christian understanding of humanity adapted itself somewhat to the prevailing Greco-Roman culture at the time, particularly in its insistence on the essential unity of soul and body.[56]

The first significant attempts to form a synthesis between Christianity and the prevailing philosophical opinions of the time are to be found in the writings of St Justin Martyr (c.100–c.165 AD), Tatian the Syrian (c.120–c.173 AD) and Athanagoras of Athens (d. c.180). Rather than using the word 'soul' to describe the person or the life of the person in both its spiritual and bodily dimensions, as in the Old and New Testaments, these writers tried to modify the prevailing soul/body dualism by using the words 'soul' and 'body' to describe the two fundamental dimensions of the human individual and correcting any dualistic tendency in the light of their faith.[57] They argued that our human souls did not always exist and that they were not essentially independent of our bodies. Our souls were given the breath of life by God when they were created (cf. Gn 2:7)[58] in such a way that there is an intrinsic and unbreakable bond between our soul (and spirit) and our body and between the experiences and destinies of our soul and body.[59] For Justin, for example, 'The body is the house of the soul, and the soul is the house of the spirit. These three, in those who have a genuine hope and unquestioning faith in God, will be saved.'[60]

For Tertullian (c.160–c.225), the salvation of each human being depended, not only on the rationality and free will of the soul,[61] but on the resurrection of the body/flesh that is our defining characteristic[62] and that is ultimately inseparable from our soul.[63] We are simultaneously a union of body and soul[64] in such a way that the human body necessarily has an associated soul and the human soul necessarily has a bodily dimension.[65] Our resurrection depends on

could be regarded as a person even when it was separated from the body by death. In the case of Christ, however, Peter argued that the union between his dead body and his divine person meant that his dead body retained its status as a person.[76] In keeping with the tradition inherited from St Augustine, these three writers interpreted the union of the human soul and body as the union of the life of the spirit, the rational human mind, and the life of the body, which they regarded as inherently inferior to the life of the spirit.[77] Peter held that, as a result of the Fall, the human soul now lived in the body as in a prison but that, following the resurrection, the body would become the dwelling-place, rather than the prison, of the soul: 'Now, therefore, the body is the prison of the soul: in the future it will be the house [of the soul] on account of [its] incorruptibility and liberty.'[78] Other writers, like William of Auxerre (c.1150–1231), developed a Christianised version of the philosophy of Aristotle in which the soul was understood to be the essential form of the body.[79] Although it proved controversial during his lifetime, and for a long time afterwards, it was the synthesis proposed by St Thomas Aquinas (1225–74) that came to dominate the later Middle Ages and that was adopted by authors like St John of the Cross during the sixteenth century. For Thomas, 'the human soul communicates its being to the body, in which it subsists'[80] and it is the substantial union of the body with its soul or substantial form, rather than the soul or the body as such, that should be regarded as a human person (homo).[81] In 1312, the General Council of Vienne rejected the view 'that the substance of the rational and intellectual soul is not truly and of itself (per se) the form of the human body'.[82]

Pope Leo X's Apostolici regimis (1513) explicitly associated the individuality and immortality of the human soul with this teaching of the Council of Vienne and, in 1517, Martin Luther (1483–1546) rejected the immortality of the soul[83] because, as he put it in 1520, 'when the Scriptures use the word "soul (Seele)," they refer not to the conscience or the inner life, but to a man's living body (lebendige Leib)', as in John 10:11, for example.[84] Although he believed that our souls were created immortal, Luther held that we lost our immortality because of the sin of Adam and Eve (cf. Gn 3) but, depending on how we lived our lives here on earth, it was possible for our souls to share in eternal life.[85] At least in his later writings,[86] and based, apparently, on Isaiah 26:20 and 57:2,[87] Luther held that, having been 'freed from the workhouse of the body',[88] the souls of the dead are 'asleep and do not know anything about human affairs – this in opposition to the invocation of the saints and the fiction of purgatory.'[89] The Catholic Counter-Reformation took a very different view of the way in which the sin of our first parents affected the human nature that all humanity inherited from them, and of the power of God's grace to restore humanity to its original state. The Council of Trent declared anathema those who deny that 'the guilt of original sin is remitted by the grace of our Lord Jesus Christ given in baptism' and those who assert 'that all that is sin in the true and proper sense is not taken away but only brushed over or not imputed' as a result of Baptism.[90] For St Teresa of Avila (1514–82), the soul (*alma*) is 'like a castle made entirely out of a diamond or of very clear crystal, in which there are many rooms, just as in heaven there are many dwelling places' (cf. Jn 14:2).[91] The body is the 'outer wall of the castle',[92] the visible, exterior dimension of the human soul.[93] Teresa's younger contemporary and fellow reformer, St John of the Cross (1542–91), seems to have been influenced by her in his understanding of the nature of the human soul, body and spirit. While emphasising its spiritual rather than its bodily dimension,[94] John normally uses the word 'soul (*alma*)' to describe the human person as a whole, the person or self[95] that is called to become the 'bride-soul' of God the Son.[96] Echoing St Teresa's understanding of the interior castle, John recognised that 'God dwells secretly in all souls and is hidden in their substance' but he points out that God dwells in some souls as though he were 'a stranger in a strange house, where they do not permit him to give orders or do anything', whereas, in others, he lives 'as though in his own house, commanding and ruling everything.'[97]

The Human Soul in the 1973 and 2011 Translations of the Missal

The 1973 translation used the nouns 'mankind (*homo*)' and 'soul (*anima*)' to designate the human person in a global way. Reflecting the way that the Hebrew word *Adam* was used in the Genesis accounts of Creation, and recognising the Latin word *homo* as its equivalent, it says that God 'made mankind' in his own 'likeness'[98] and that when 'he disobeyed' and lost God's friendship, God, who wills 'all men to be saved',[99] 'did not abandon him to the power of death'.[100] Asking that the people of God will share Christ's victory over death,[101] it recognises that God, who enlightens all who come into this world[102] (cf. Jn 1:9) and who is the 'source of ... salvation for all mankind',[103] willed that his Son should be 'born as a man so that men could be born again' in him.[104] The paraphrase 'salvation for all mankind' seems to deliberately avoid the adjective 'human (*humanus*)' even though elsewhere we read that the Father gave 'the human race Jesus Christ our Saviour as a model of humility' and that the Son fulfilled his Father's will 'by becoming man and giving his life on the cross'.[105] The noun *homines* is not translated in the prayer that calls us to 'become a living sign' of the Father's goodness[106] but the adjective *humanus* is translated in the prayer about securing 'justice and equality for every human being'.[107] Since *homines* is translated as 'people' in 'peace to his people on earth',[108] the paraphrase 'born as a man so that men could be born again' may have been chosen because of its similarity with the Creed, which says that 'For us men and for our salvation' the Son of God came down from heaven, 'and became man'.[109] The paraphrase 'and was born of the Virgin Mary'[110] seems to deliberately avoid an explicit reference to the Incarnation of the Word and this avoidance is also found in the paraphrase 'human race' when we pray that we may be sustained by the love of Christ,[111] the Son of God who shared 'in our human nature'[112] and who, as 'God and man',[113] 'offered himself as a perfect sacrifice'[114] to 'bring mankind the peace and love' of his Father's kingdom.[115] The 1973 translation seems to ignore the implicit citation of 2 Peter 1:4 when it asks that the Eucharist, which is 'a sign that even now we share' the Father's life,[116] may give us 'a share in' Christ's life[117] and 'bring us into'[118] the divine life of the Father.

Implicitly citing the Gospel, where Jesus says that the good shepherd 'lays down his life for his sheep' (Jn 10:11), the 1973 translation says that the martyr bishop, St Josaphat, 'laid down his life (*anima*) for his people' and prays that the Spirit will make us 'willing to offer our lives (*animam*) for our brothers and sisters'.[119] The translators seem to have decided to systematically avoid the term 'soul (*anima*)' by the use of paraphrase[120] or by replacing it with 'heart'[121] or with 'mind and heart'.[122] As a result, the association and distinction between heart and soul that is implicit in the citation of Acts 4:32 is either omitted[123] or lost in paraphrases like 'one in heart and mind'[124] and 'one heart and spirit'.[125] The association and distinction between 'body' and 'soul' in the Latin text is also lost in paraphrases such as 'health of mind and body'[126] and 'health of body, your grace in this life, and glory in heaven'.[127] When we recognise her Assumption as 'the beginning and pattern of the Church in its perfection' and when we confess our faith that the Blessed Virgin Mary was 'raised ... body and soul to the glory of heaven',[128] we also implicitly acknowledge our faith and hope in the resurrection of our own body and its reunion with our soul. We ask God that we may 'become the temple of your presence and the home of your glory'[129] so that (cf. 2 Cor 5:1), 'When the body of our earthly dwelling lies in death we gain an everlasting dwelling place in heaven'.[130] Apparently ignoring the implied reference to Matthew 8:8, the paraphrase 'Lord, I am not worthy to receive you, but only say the word, and I shall be healed' seems to have deliberately avoided using the word 'soul' and the implied designation of the body as the dwelling place of the soul.[131]

The 2011 Missal does not follow the 1973 translation in translating *homo* as 'mankind' and, in keeping with the recommendation that liturgical texts 'should be free from an overly servile adherence to prevailing modes of expression' (*Liturgiam authenticam*, n. 27), it consistently uses the noun 'man (*homo*)' in a gender inclusive sense to designate the human person. It also uses the associated terms 'humanity (*humanitas*)' and 'human (*humanus*)' and the noun 'soul (*anima*)' to designate the human person in a global way. Reflecting the use of the Hebrew word *Adam* in the Genesis accounts of Creation, and recognising the Latin word *homo* as its equivalent, the new translation says that God 'formed man' in his own image, creating them 'male and female'[132] and that when 'through disobedience' they had lost the divine friendship, God, 'whose will it is that all should be saved',[133] 'did not abandon him to the domain of death'.[134] In fulfilment of Genesis 2:16-17, the life that we receive at conception is 'mortal'[135] but God, who enlightens everyone who comes into this world[136] (cf. Jn 1:9) and who is the 'loving author of our salvation',[137] willed that his 'Only Begotten Son should be born from among humanity so that by a wonderful mystery humanity might be born again' from him.[138] In this prayer, the play between *hominibus* and *homines* in the Latin text is translated using the word 'humanity' rather than by using the words 'man' and 'men', as in the 1973 translation. When the play on words is between the plural *homines* and the singular *homo*, however, the translations 'men' and 'man' are used: 'For us men and for our salvation' the Son of God came down from heaven and 'became man',[139] taking on 'the reality of human flesh in the womb of the Virgin Mary'.[140] When no such play on words in involved, however, the 2011 Missal follows the 1973 Missal in translating *homines* as 'people'.[141] The term 'human family' is used on one occasion[142] and the terms *homo* and *homines* are translated as 'human race' on a number of occasions.[143] It was as 'an example of humility for the human race (*humano generi*) to follow' that God the Father 'caused our Saviour to take flesh' and to 'submit to the Cross'.[144] The 2011 Missal translates *oblatio* as 'offering' or 'sacrifice' when what is offered to God is other than a self-offering[145] but the word is translated as 'oblation' when a self-offering in the form of service or the self-offering of the Church in union with Christ's priestly offering of himself as a sacrificial Victim is involved.[146] Its use of the term 'oblation' might be regarded as an example of the 2012 translation's willingness to use 'words or expressions ... which differ somewhat from usual and everyday speech' in developing 'a sacred style that will come to be recognised as proper to liturgical language' (*Liturgiam authenticam*, n. 27). Recognising that, as 'God and man',[147] the Son of God 'offered himself' to the Father 'on the Cross as the unblemished oblation',[148] it also recognises that our fallen human nature has been 'given strength' by his 'humanity'[149] in such a way that we, too, 'may present our very selves as a holy sacrifice' pleasing to the Father.[150] The Eucharist foreshadows our future 'share' in divine life[151] and it is the means by which 'each human person may be brought to perfection'[152] as the Father makes us 'sharers for eternity in the divinity' of his Son,[153] 'sharers in the divine nature'[154] (cf. 2 Pt 1:4). Through our share in the divinity of Christ we become 'a new humanity' that has been reconciled to God in loving charity[155] and that reflects 'among all humanity the image' of the Father's 'divine goodness'.[156]

The *Ratio translationis* (2007) noted that many of the prayers in the Roman Missal 'reflect the ways in which the Latin Fathers resolved issues in … the nature of the soul which had been raised in the Greco Roman culture of their day' and it recommended that translators 'be alert … to the vocabulary, syntax and topoi which the Fathers embedded in the prayers of the Roman Liturgy' (n. 20). In the new translation, the term 'soul (*anima*)' can denote the human person as a whole from the perspective of the particular characteristics of the living person, as in 'the most gentle soul of Saint Frances de Sales',[157] and it can denote the possibility of salvation for humanity in general, as in 'salvation of'[158] or 'zeal for'[159] souls and prayers offered 'for the soul' or 'souls' of those who have died.[160] In one case where 'souls' is identified with the individual persons concerned, the word 'soul' is omitted in the translation: 'we may in charity win brothers and sisters for Christ.'[161] Implicitly citing the Good Shepherd who 'lays down his life for his sheep' (Jn 10:11), the martyr bishop, St Josaphat, is described as having 'laid down his life (*anima*) for the sheep' and we pray that 'strengthened by the same Spirit' we will not be afraid 'to lay down our life (*animam*) for others'.[162] The soul-life of an individual can also designate that dimension of the interior life of a person that can be distinguished from their bodily life so that it overlaps with mind and heart,[163] as in 'health of body and soul'[164] or 'freedom of soul'.[165] The *Ratio translationis* insists that 'translators must first take care to locate the biblical and patristic sources of the prayers they translate' (n. 19) and that, 'rather than substituting other words that are alien to it', translators should retain the 'coherent system of words and patterns of speech consecrated by the books of Sacred Scripture and by ecclesiastical tradition, especially by the Fathers of the Church' (n. 20). The 2011 text could not be described as reflecting the 'coherent system of words' in its patristic sources, however, when it renders the term 'soul (*anima*)' in late patristic prayers by means of a paraphrase.[166] It also appears to deviate from the meaning intended in its patristic source when it uses the paraphrase, 'God … who are peace itself and whom a spirit of discord cannot grasp, nor a violent mind receive'. The text in question should, perhaps, have been translated as 'God … who are peace and whom a quarrelling soul cannot possess, whom a violent mind cannot receive'.[167] The term 'soul' can also be used in relation to a corporate reality such as human society as a whole, as when the Church is described as 'the soul of human society'.[168] When 'soul' is used to designate the interior life of a group of individuals, it can also connote their shared, interior life in Christ that is the fruit of Christian initiation as distinct from their shared interior life as such, usually described as their heart. The implicit citation of Acts 4:32 in the phrase 'one heart and one soul (*cor unum et ánima una*)'[169] seems to imply such a distinction and it is difficult to understand why *cor unum et ánima una* is translated 'one heart and one mind' elsewhere.[170] The *Ratio translationis* had specified that any biblical expressions commonly used in catechism or religious devotions should be respected (n. 107). Acknowledging the close relationship and the difference between the body and the living soul whose earthly dwelling that body is, we pray for 'health of body and soul',[171] for 'health for our bodies, and grace and eternal glory for our souls'[172] and when we ask God to 'guard your body and save your soul'.[173] We have already noted the identification of the body as the earthly dwelling or house of the soul in Scripture and, in different ways, by writers like St Clement of Alexandria, Peter Lombard, Martin Luther, St Teresa of Avila and St John of the Cross. Reflecting that Tradition, and implicitly recognising Matthew 8:8 as the source of the response,[174] the 2011 translation replaced the paraphrase 'Lord, I am not worthy to receive you, but only say the word, and I shall be healed' with the literal translation 'Lord, I am not worthy that you should enter under my roof, but only say the word and my soul shall be healed'.[175] Our time 'in the body'[176] is temporary and, during that time, we are to 'become his temple and the dwelling place of the Holy Spirit'[177] so that, when the 'earthly dwelling' of those who have died as temples of the Holy Spirit 'turns to dust', 'an eternal dwelling is made ready for them in heaven' (cf. 2 Cor 5:1).[178] Recognising her Assumption as 'the beginning and image' of the Church's 'coming to perfection' and confessing our faith that the Blessed Virgin Mary was 'assumed ... body and soul into heavenly glory',[179] we also implicitly acknowledge our faith and hope in the resurrection of our own body and its reunion with our soul.

The Body and the Flesh in Scripture and Tradition

This section will outline the way in which the terms 'body' and 'flesh' are used in the Old and New Testament and in the Tradition of the Church, focusing on those aspects that are most significant in the context of the use of the words 'body (*corpus*)' and 'flesh (*caro*)' in the 1973 and 2011 Missals.

We have already noted that, unlike the traditional Greek understanding of the soul as the animating principle of the body, the Old Testament regards the breath or spirit as the source and principle of the life of both the soul and its body. The Hebrew word *bashar* can refer to the bodily dimension of our living souls in general[180] but it can also designate flesh, whether in the sense of highlighting the foolishness of putting our trust in what human flesh can achieve, rather than in God[181] or in the sense of the soft tissue that is one element of the body/flesh of all living souls, alongside blood, for example.[182] Adam recognised Eve as bone of his bones and flesh of his flesh (cf. Gn 2:23) and, from the beginning, man and woman were destined to become 'one flesh' (Gn 2:24) through sexual intercourse. The expression 'all flesh'[183] includes all the living creatures on earth in which is the breath of life[184] but, after the time of the exile, both 'flesh'[185] and 'all flesh'[186] are used to refer to the bond that unites all humanity and all the different nations on earth: 'the soul-life of every living thing, the breath of all human flesh' is in the hand of the Lord (cf. Job 12:10). In these texts, 'flesh' is a principle of solidarity designating the entire person viewed from the perspective of something that he or she shares with all other human individuals. The different experiences of the living soul/person as such can also be described as being experienced by the body/flesh, and vice versa (cf. Ps 16:9), and the psalmist describes his longing for God as causing his soul to thirst and his body/flesh to faint (Ps 63:2).[187] Because our body/flesh is visible and external, this dimension of the concrete totality of human existence is both paired with, and distinguished from, the soul's internal dimension that is concerned with decisions and choices, and this internal dimension of the soul seems to be what is described as the heart (*leb*). What affects one dimension can be described as also affecting the other[188] and, when our hearts become impervious to the call to conversion, God promises to remove those 'hearts of stone' from our body/flesh and to give us again a heart of flesh (cf. Ez 11:19; 36:26), underlining the essentially positive regard for the flesh that is typical of the Old Testament as a whole.[189]

Like the Old Testament, the New Testament recognises body/flesh (*sarx*) as something common to all those creatures, both humans and animals, who share the gift of the breath of life (cf. Rv 19:17-18).[190] As in the post-exilic books of the Old Testament, 'all flesh'[191] designates all humanity and ancestral lineage can be indicated by the phrase 'according to the flesh.'[192] Living 'according to the flesh' meant acting in a merely human and earthly manner,[193] and Jesus pointed out that our fallen body/flesh, that which is born only of body/flesh, remains body/flesh and is of no avail in coming to share eternal life.[194] While those who have eaten his life-giving Eucharistic body/flesh have already received eternal life,[195] they remain subject to the weakness of their fallen, mortal flesh[196] because 'The [human] spirit is willing, but the flesh is weak' (Mt 26:41). Following the desire or lust of the flesh means being subject to those worldly passions that are opposed to the spiritual desires of the person who has been reborn as a child of God the Father.[197] Like Jesus himself, Paul attributes the universal human failure to achieve uprightness to the consequences of the sin of Adam (cf. Rm 5:12-21) and, in particular, to the now normative way in which the sensual desires of our body/flesh[198] serve the law of sin[199] and oppose our intention to serve God's law (cf. Rm 7:18-25).[200] It was for this reason, apparently, that Paul believed that good did not dwell in his flesh (cf. Rm 7:18) and that the perishable body/flesh dimension of humanity could not inherit the imperishable kingdom of God (cf. 1 Cor 15:50).

Although Paul's Jewish background is evident in the way he uses the term body/flesh (*sarx*), his Greek culture is also evident in the way he uses the Greek word *soma*. This word has 'no immediate equivalent in Hebrew' and, while it can be used to describe the physical body[201] as an external manifestation of the interior heart and conscience (cf. Heb 10:22), most commentators do not accept Gundry's view that it is used dualistically by St Paul[202] since it can also carry the richer connotation of personal embodiment[203] as the means by which an individual engages with others and with his or her environment.[204] For Paul, a person's body (*soma*) normally referred to the living physical unity of bodily members[205] through which he or she was visibly and tangibly present in a particular place and time and capable of entering into relationship with others. Although absent in body (*soma*), one could be present to others 'in spirit' (1 Cor 5:3), in other words intentionally or spiritually present despite appearances. Nevertheless, Paul frequently identifed an individual with his or her body[206] and he reminded the Corinthians that, as such, they themselves were members of Christ and temples of the Spirit[207] with the result that they should hand themselves[208] over to Christ and ensure that all that was done 'through or by means of the body (*soma*)'[209] (2 Cor 5:10),[210] including their interpersonal relationships,[211] reflected their commitment to Christ and gave glory to God.[212] For Matthew and Luke,[213] the body (*soma*) usually designates the physical unity of bodily organs.[214] They use the word in parallel with *psyche* (soul-life),[215] which needs food in order to continue living, in order to highlight the embodied dimension of our soul-life (cf. Mt 6:22-23),[216] which requires of us that we concern ourselves to some extent also with what we wear.[217]

In their attempt to form a synthesis between Christianity and the prevailing Platonic philosophy of the time, St Justin Martyr, Tatian the Syrian and Athanagoras of Athens held that, because the eternal Word united himself permanently with our human flesh in the womb of the Virgin Mary (cf. Jn 1:14), our human flesh could also share in immortality. The Christian doctrine of the resurrection of the body (cf. 1 Cor 15:12-22) implied that the link between the dead body and the soul remained unbroken and that our soul and body could be reunited by God and be given a share in eternal life.[218] St Irenaeus (c.140–c.202) held that only the human body is mortal and that the human soul and spirit neither die nor decompose.[219] He insisted, however, that, since 'the substance of our flesh is increased and supported' by the nourishment of the Body and Blood of Christ, our mortal bodies can also be regenerated and saved and, in this way, become capable of immortality.[220] Our body/flesh is mortal and will decompose after death, but our soul and our spirit are immortal and, at the resurrection, their union with our body/flesh will be restored.[221]

For St Clement of Alexandria (150–215 AD), the authentic image of God is the incarnate Word (*logos*) and we are images of that image only in the upper or rational part of our soul, the mind (*nous*) where reason (*logos*) dwells.[222] The mortal body is not an image of the incarnate Word but only 'the house of the image'[223] but, precisely because the body is the temple of the human spirit, Clement opposed those forms of dualistic Gnosticism that defended the licentious and 'reckless mode of life (*adiaphoro zoe*)'[224] they had adopted on the grounds that the life of the body had nothing whatsoever to do with the life of the spirit. Origen (c.185–253), like Clement, denied that 'the signs of the divine image' were recognisible in our corruptible bodies[225] but, acknowledging that 'man consists of body, soul, and spirit',[226] he insisted, nevertheless, that the 'body which we now use in degradation and corruption and infirmity is not a different body from that which we shall use in incorruption and power and glory'. Having 'cast off the infirmities in which it now is, it will be made spiritual and will be transformed into glory, so that the very thing which was a vessel of dishonour, being cleansed, will become a vessel of honour and an abode of blessedness.'[227]

For St Augustine, the nature of the human body is different from that of the spirit but the body 'is not extraneous to the nature of humanity' because humanity 'is a composite of spirit and body'.[228] Understanding how the two were combined was, for us, 'a great wonder that was incomprehensible'[229] but humanity is generally understood as 'a rational soul that uses a mortal and earthly body'.[230] Although inferior to the soul, the body is, nevertheless, an intrinsic part of humanity and 'it would be false to say that humanity consists in the mind and that humanity is not found in the flesh'.[231] The external desires of the body tempt us to abandon God and so to turn away from our interior light and to lose ourselves in the external world, and it is only by entering into, and by rising above, ourselves that we can rediscover God as the light of Truth that created us.[232]

The Body and the Flesh in the 1973 and 2011 Translations of the Missal

In the 1973 translation of the Missal, the term 'body (*corpus*)' is used in relation to Christ, to Baptism, to the Church and to resurrection. It normally designates the 'body like our own'[233] from which Christ's glory shone at the Transfiguration and the body of the Blessed Virgin Mary, which God did 'not allow decay to touch' because she had given birth to the Son of God.[234] The Church both already is and is growing into its full stature as Christ's body for we pray that the Holy Spirit will gather all who share in the Eucharist 'into the one body of Christ',[235] 'that the Church, which is the body of Christ, would one day share his glory'[236] and that the Father will 'bring the Church to its full stature as the body of Christ throughout the world'.[237] At 'the resurrection of the body', Christ will 'raise our mortal bodies and make them like his own in glory'.[238] Even when there is an implicit Scriptural quotation, however, the words 'body (*corpus*)'[239] and 'bodily (*corporalis*)'[240] are sometimes omitted in paraphrases. Although there is an explicit recognition that the Word 'took flesh' or 'became flesh',[241] most references to 'flesh (*caro*)' in the Latin text are either not translated,[242] or paraphrased.[243] Reflecting their union in 'one flesh', there are prayers asking that husband and wife be joined 'in union of body and heart'.[244] There are prayers asking that those preparing for Baptism 'and all the family of man be reborn into the life of your kingdom'[245] and be 'made ... his children by water and the Holy Spirit'.[246]

The word 'body' is also distinguished from spirit, heart and mind, and the Eucharist is described as Christ's 'Body and Blood'. The corporate reality of the Church and its spiritual unity is acknowledged in prayers asking that, with all the Saints, 'we may become one body, one spirit in Christ'.[247] The union of husband and wife is described in terms of their being 'in union of body and heart'[248] and the distinction between the brain, which is part of the body, and the healthy human mind's capacity to reason seems to be implicit in the prayers for 'health of/in mind and body'[249] or for purity 'both in body and in mind'.[250] There are a number of paraphrases, however, where the Latin phrase 'mind and body' is not translated.[251] The phrase 'Body and Blood of Christ'[252] designates the Eucharist, with the connotation that Christ's Body has been separated in death from his life-Blood. The term 'blood (*sanguis*)' is also used in the related sense of a person witnessing 'with his blood'[253] or shedding (*fuso / effúso / effusio*)[254] their blood, but rather than translating 'blood' literally, the 1973 text sometimes translates it as 'martyrdom' or similar terms.[255] Two other terms, 'hands' and 'lips', are also used to describe the work done or words spoken by the body. In the Liturgy of the Eucharist, the bread that will become the Body of Christ is described as 'which earth has given and human hands have made' and the wine that will become the Blood of Christ as 'fruit of the earth and work of human hands'.[256] The term 'lips (*os*, literally "mouth", or *lingua*, literally "tongue")' is used in relation to the profession of the faith[257] but this term is paraphrased in relation to the confession or teaching of the faith.[258]

In the 2011 translation of the Missal, the term 'body (*corpus*)' is used in relation to our bodily existence, to Christ, to Baptism, to the Church and to resurrection. The phrase 'while in this body' designates our earthly life[259] and the word 'body' designates 'that bodily form which he [Jesus] shares with all humanity'[260] and, in particular, with Mary who 'from her own body ... marvellously brought forth' the incarnate Son of God.[261] Just as God the Father's 'Only Begotten Son was born of her according to the flesh'[262] so too 'those once born of earth may be reborn as citizens of heaven',[263] 'reborn', that is, 'from water and the Holy Spirit'.[264] Collectively, those who have been 'gathered into one body by the Holy Spirit'[265] are described as 'members' of God's Son[266] who have become corporately and spiritually 'one with' the Saints in heaven, 'one body and one spirit in Christ'.[267] In order that 'what so wonderfully shone forth first in its Head' is fulfilled 'in the Body of the whole Church',[268] however, Christ causes his Church, 'spread throughout the world, to grow ever more and more' as his own Body[269] and to 'flourish in harmony'.[270] At 'the resurrection of the body', Christ will 'transform our lowly body after the pattern of his own glorious body'.[271] The bodily experience of birth 'according to the flesh' highlights the close association between body and flesh (caro) and the term 'flesh (caro)' is used in relation to the Incarnation and to resurrection. For the 'Word made flesh'[272] who was 'incarnate by the Holy Spirit',[273] taking on the reality of human flesh[274] and coming to share the humanity[275] and bodily form of his sinful creatures[276] are essentially synonymous. Unlike 'body', however, the word 'flesh' often designates our mortality[277] or frailty[278] and, because it highlights the power of God to overcome the frailty of the flesh, the prayer 'may our heart and our body flourish anew by a keen sense of modesty and renewed chastity' should probably have translated caro as 'flesh' rather than 'body'.[279] Since God's Only Begotten Son appeared and rose from the dead 'in our very flesh',[280] we believe that he 'will raise up in the flesh'[281] those who have become members of the Body of which he is the Head so that they 'may attain in their flesh the incorruptible glory of the resurrection'.[282]

The word 'body' is also distinguished from spirit, heart and mind and the Eucharist is described as Christ's 'Body and Blood'. There is a close relationship between our body and our spirit, and the homage that people offer to God 'in the body', literally 'as bodily servitude',[283] can 'redound upon them as a spiritual gift' and the martyr's love can triumph 'over all bodily torments'.[284] Quoting 2 Corinthians 4:10, Christians who have been baptised into Christ's Death and Resurrection are described as 'bearing in our body the Death of Jesus' so that we may merit to live with him in glory.[285] Recognising the relationship between bodily chastity and purity of heart, we are to serve God 'with a chaste body ... with a pure heart' and to pray that 'our heart and our body flourish anew by a keen sense of modesty and renewed chastity'[286] if we have sinned in this respect. Implicitly citing the 'one flesh' or Genesis 1:26, a husband and wife are described as 'made one in the flesh'[287] or as being 'united in body and heart'.[288] The distinction between the brain, which is part of the body, and the healthy human mind's capacity to reason seems to be implicit in the prayer that God 'restrain our faults, raise up our minds, and bestow both virtue and its rewards' through 'bodily fasting'[289] and in the prayers for health,[290] help, protection, purification, restoration, or sanctification in mind and body.[291] Given that corpóribus ... et méntibus was literally translated by the 1973 Missal as 'mind and body',[292] it is not clear why *corpóribus nostris subsídium non desit et méntibus* is paraphrased as 'may not fail us in body or in spirit' on three occasions in the 2011 Missal.[293] The phrase 'Body and Blood of Christ'[294] designates the Eucharist with the connotation that Christ's Body has been separated in death from his life-Blood. The term 'blood (*sanguis*)' is also used in the related sense of a person sealing his faith 'in his blood'[295] or consecrating the fruits of apostolic activity 'by his blood',[296] in other words, to the shedding (*fuso / effúso / effusio*)[297] of their blood in martyrdom. Two other terms, 'hands' and 'lips', are also used to describe the work done or words spoken by the body. In the Liturgy of the Eucharist, the bread that will become the Body of Christ as described as 'fruit of the earth and work of human hands' and the wine that will become the Blood of Christ as 'fruit of the vine and work of human hands'.[298] The phrase 'adversaries join hands'[299] is presented as the symbolic end to mutual animosity. The term 'lips (*os,* literally "mouth", or *lingua,* literally "tongue")' is used in relation to the bodily consumption of the Eucharist as spiritual food[300] and to the confession, profession or teaching of the faith.[301]

The Heart, the Mind and the Spirit in Scripture and Tradition

This section will outline the way in which the terms 'heart', 'mind' and 'spirit' are used in the Old and New Testament and in the Tradition of the Church, focusing on those aspects that are most significant in relation to the use of the words 'heart (*cor*)', 'mind (*mens*)' and 'spirit (*spiritus*)' in the 1973 and 2011 Missals.

The Old Testament often indicates the physical or emotional state of individuals by describing the way that state is manifested in their breathing (*ruach*). Being patient and slow to anger is identified with having control over one's breath (cf. Prov 16:32)[302] and restrained breathing, and the capacity to keep silent, are regarded as a sign of wisdom and understanding (cf. Prov 17:27). The particular and normative manner of breathing (*ruach*) of particular individuals may have been identified with their characteristic attitude, mental disposition, or intentions (cf. Ez 20:32) and it would seem to be in this sense that Joshua was characterised by 'a spirit of wisdom' (cf. Deut 34:9) and that Caleb, who had followed the Lord fully, was described as having 'a different spirit' from those who had not (cf. Num 14:24). The actions of particular individuals are often presented as being the result of the Lord stirring up their spirits[303] and the characteristically 'puffed up' spirit of the proud[304] is contrasted with the 'humble and contrite/crushed spirit' of those who have learned to tremble at God's word (cf. Is 66:2).[305] Using the word *ruach* both in this sense and in its original sense of breathing, the repentant psalmist asks God not to punish him with death by taking his 'holy breath' from him but to renew 'a steadfast spirit' within him, and to uphold him with 'a willing spirit' (cf. Ps 50:10-12).

The breathing, identified with the emotional or physical state of the individual or with their mettle or characteristic mental disposition, was often associated with the heart, the hidden core of the person/soul from which thought, deliberation and love flowed, and God is described as determining the behaviour of individuals by influencing their heart and spirit. Those who provided the offerings to be used for the tent of meeting are described as having been stirred by their heart and moved by their spirit to do so (cf. Ex 35:21).[306] The refusal of King Sihon of Heshbon to allow the Israelites to pass is attributed to the fact that the Lord hardened his spirit and made his heart obstinate (cf. Deut 2:30).[307] In some texts, individuals are described as having come under the influence of a spirit (ruach) that was not, as such, their own, apparently in the sense that the emotion or condition brought about was so powerful that it could dominate their normal behaviour. Zechariah prophesies that the Lord will pour out 'a spirit of grace and supplication for grace' on the House of David and the inhabitants of Jerusalem (cf. Zec 12:10) and remove 'the spirit of uncleanness' from the land (cf. Zec 13:2).

The Hebrew word ruach is usually translated in the Greek of the New Testament as pneuma, which can also designate wind,[308] breath, or spirit.[309] Both words can designate the divine gift of life-breath,[310] an individual's characteristic or dominant disposition[311] such as that of a slave or of an adopted child (cf. Rm 8:15), and the way in which our breathing reflects emotional states like exasperation,[312] anger,[313] gentleness,[314] grief,[315] or betrayal.[316] The term 'spirit (pneuma)' is perhaps the most important word in the psychological vocabulary of St Paul, who used it 146 times.[317] Paul prays that God might sanctify the Christians at Thessalonika 'wholly,' keeping their common[318] 'spirit and soul and body ... sound and blameless' at the coming of Christ (1 Th 5:23). His use of soma (body) rather than sarx (flesh/body), together with his use of spirit, soul and body in the singular, suggests that he was thinking of the Thessalonians, not as individuals, but as collectively sharing a single spirit-breath, soul-life and corporate body with Christ.[319] In a similar way, Paul describes himself and Titus as walking/acting 'in the same spirit', presumably the 'one spirit' that characterises those who are united to Jesus, the Lord (cf. 1 Cor 6:17),[320] in their dealings with the Christian community at Corinth (cf. 2 Cor 12:18).

Presenting personal defilement as involving both dimensions, 'flesh and spirit' (2 Cor 7:1), Paul recognised that every individual human soul/person necessarily has both a material and visible flesh/body dimension and an immaterial and invisible breath/spirit dimension[321] and he held that only 'the spirit of the person' knows that individual's hidden thoughts (cf. 1 Cor 2:11).

In order to deal with immorality in the Christian community, Paul recommends that the individual involved be excluded from the corporate body of which he had been a member so that, cut off from the new life of the Spirit in that body, he might be brought to his senses by suffering 'the destruction of the flesh' and so have his spirit saved (cf. 1 Cor 5:5). Paul says that the Spirit (*pneuma*) of God that was in Christ, and that was poured out at Pentecost, 'joins itself to' (Rm 8:16) the human spirit (*pneuma*) in order to awaken it to filial prayer and pleading (cf. Rm 8:26) and, in this way, to become united to Jesus, the Lord, and to 'make with him one spirit' (1 Cor 6:17). Perhaps reflecting the 'contrite/crushed spirit' of those who have learned to tremble at God's word (cf. Is 66:2), the New Testament recognises the state of being 'poor in spirit' as blessed (Mt 5:3) and it may be in the light of the same Isaiah text that Mary describes her spirit as rejoicing in God her Saviour. Despite her humble state as a lowly servant of God, her spirit experiences joy because the Holy Spirit has chosen her for great things and all future generations will recognise the special blessings which God has given her (cf. Lk 1:47-48). Distinguishing the human spirit from the human mind, and implying that individuals are not always conscious of the synergy between their spirits and the Holy Spirit, Paul says that when, 'in the Spirit,' he speaks 'in a tongue' that he does not understand (cf. 1 Cor 14:2), his spirit prays but his mind is barren and does not understand and that he prefers to pray in a tongue that he does understand so that he prays with both his spirit and his mind (cf. 1 Cor 14:14-15).

Just as Paul had used the Greek notion of body (*soma*) to explain how the bodily dimension of the human soul could share in resurrection, he also used the Greek terms, mind (*noema*) and heart (*kardia*), to explain the way in which the hidden, interior dimension of the human soul, our forward planning and our hidden motivation, are transformed by the spirit's symbiosis with the Holy Spirit. For Paul, the human mind (*noema*) refers to a person's thoughts, strategy or planning (cf. Phil 4:7), the capacity to approve or disapprove of a particular proposal (cf. Rm 7:23), and he described determined opposition to a particular plan as a hardening of the mind (cf. 2 Cor 3:14-15). Opposition to the yearnings of the human spirit (cf. 1 Cor 14:15), or a mindless dismissal of the Gospel message (cf. Gal 3:1, 3), can only be overcome through 'the renewal of the mind' (Rm 12:2).[322] Such renewal takes place when the Holy Spirit conforms our minds to that of Christ (1 Cor 2:16) and, rather than opposing the spirit, the mind can then serve the law of God and oppose the flesh, which serves the law of sin (cf. Rm 7:25). For Paul, heart (*kardia*) overlaps the sphere of influence of mind (*noema*) to some extent, and it can also be described as the place of enlightenment[323] and decision-making.[324] It is the hidden, internal seat of the will,[325] of love,[326] and of the emotions,[327] the source of belief, trust and obedience.[328] Only God can search the human mind and heart,[329] distinguishing the rational from the emotional and volitional and enabling us to find the proper balance between them.[330] The distinction between the spirit, which is capable of perceptions that go deeper than what our eyes can see, and the heart, the hidden core of each individual, is implied in Mark 2:8, where Jesus is described as 'perceiving in his spirit' that the scribes were questioning in their 'hearts'.

For John, the human spirit, in its natural state, is not capable of a truly spiritual life and it is only after being born from above of the divine Spirit (cf. Jn 3:6)[331] that we become spirit in the same sense that 'God is spirit' (Jn 4:24). This, presumably, should be understood as the restoration of our pristine state of being created in the image and likeness of God. Just as God is love (cf. 1 Jn 4:8), humanity only becomes capable of genuine love, the love that is the life of the Blessed Trinity,[332] the love that Jesus showed when he gave his life for us sinners, when it has been given life through the Spirit (cf. Jn 6:63). Authentic worship is spiritual, worship 'in spirit and in truth' (cf. Jn 4:24).

In their attempt to bridge the gap between Christianity and the prevailing Platonic philosophy of the time, St Justin Martyr and Tatian the Syrian tried to integrate their recognition of the human spirit into the conceptual framework of soul and body in different ways. For Justin, the body is the temple of the spirit in the sense that the spirit lives within the human soul which, in turn, lives within the body.[333] For Tatian, the human soul had lost its bond with the divine Spirit because of the Fall but it was possible to re-establish that bond, and to become once again true likenesses of God, thanks to the spark of the Spirit's power that remains in us.[334] For St Clement of Alexandria (150–215 AD), we are like God only in the upper or rational part of our soul, the mind (*nous*) where reason (*logos*) dwells.[335] Origen held that 'man consists of body, soul, and spirit'[336] (cf. 1 Th 5:23) and that there was an ascending order of dignity in these three elements. The soul is rational and endowed with free will and, during the earthly life of each individual, the upper part of the soul, the dominant faculty of intelligence (*nous*), is under the influence of the spirit (*pneuma*), which is open to grace and to the Holy Spirit, and the lower part of the soul is under the influence of the concupiscence of the flesh (*sarx*), which draws it towards evil.[337] Against Apollinaris of Laodicea (d. 390), who seems to have came to believe that, having dispensed with a human soul, the divine Word himself took the place of Christ's human soul,[338] St Gregory of Nazianz (330–89) argued that if the Word did not unite himself with a human soul and mind, our human soul and mind would not have been saved.[339]

In the opening lines of his *Confessions*, St Augustine of Hippo recognises the restlessness of the human heart (*cor*) that has been created by God and longs for God: 'You have made us for Yourself, O Lord, and our heart is restless until it rests in You.'[340] He describes his conversion, which took place when he was 'in the most bitter contrition of my heart', as an enlightening of his heart: 'by a light as it were of serenity infused into my heart, all the darkness of doubt vanished away.'[341] Being unable to conceive of any substance but the sort he could see with his own eyes,[342] he had been a member of the Manichees for many years and had accepted their materialistic rejection of any true union between flesh and spirit. Reading the books of some Platonist writers, however, he was able with 'the eye of his soul (*anima*)' to enter into his 'inmost parts (*intima mea*)' and to discover there the immutable light of his creator who is above or superior both to 'the eye of his soul (*anima*)' and to his 'mind (*mens*)'.[343] For Augustine, the 'eye of the soul', the capacity of the soul to 'perceive' certain realities in a way that can be compared with the capacity to see of our bodily eyes, is to be identified with our spirit (*spiritus*) or rational mind (*mens*).[344] Because every mind is a spirit, although not every spirit is a mind,[345] and because St Paul refers to the spirit praying in a tongue when the mind is unproductive (cf. 1 Cor 14:14), he interpreted the text on being renewed in 'the spirit of your mind (*spiritu mentis vestrae*)' (Eph 4:23) as implying a distinction, not between spirit (*spiritus*) and mind (*mens*), but between the capacity of the mind/spirit to perceive mental images and the capacity of the mind/spirit to understand such images.[346] Those things that can be perceived by the bodily senses of sight and touch differ from those things 'that can be perceived by the comprehension of the mind (*quae conspectu mentis intellegi possunt*)'[347] and Augustine recognised the intellectual[348] or rational[349] or spiritual[350] part of the soul that is the realm of the human mind (*mens* or *ratio*) and spirit (*spiritus*) as 'that which is pre-eminent in the soul (*anima*)'.[351] The 'mind, intelligence and will (*mentem, intelligentiam, voluntatem*)' of the rational part of the soul is to be distinguished from the 'memory, sense-perception and appetite (*memoriam, sensus, adpetitum*)' of the 'irrational soul or life (*irrationalis anima vel vita*)'[352] that we share with animals.[353] The capacity of the mind/spirit to consider both true or invented images of bodily realities that have been seen and remembered is sometimes attributed also to the capacity for self-consciousness and rational deliberation that the Greeks called *nous* and the Romans *animus*.[354] The things that are invisible to our bodily eyes, for example, can be 'perceived by the conscious self (*animus*) and by the mind (*mens*)'[355] and the conscious self (*animus*) or spirit (*spiritus*) is the constant witness of our hidden thoughts:

> ... the conscious self (*animus*) of each man is his own proper spirit (*spiritus*), about which the Apostle Paul said, 'For who among men knows the things that are of a man but the spirit of a man (*spiritus hominis*) which is in him?' [1 Cor 2:11]. ... Nobody knows those things that are our own except our spirit (*spiritus*).[356]

The mortal flesh and both the rational and irrational parts of the human soul of the Incarnate Word are of the same nature as ours[357] for he also has 'a complete soul (*anima*), not the irrational part of the soul only, but the rational part too, which is called the mind (*mens*)'.[358] Augustine held that the image of God in us is not in our fleshly body but in our mind (*mens*) or spirit (*spiritus*): 'And where is God's image? In your mind (*mens*), in your intellect (*intellectus*)!'[359] The subordination of our human spirit to God should be reflected in the subordination of our body to our spirit:

> … let the will of God be done on earth as it is in heaven; i.e. in such a way that in like manner as the spirit (*spiritus*), following and doing His will, does not resist God so the body (*corpus*) may also not resist the spirit (*spiritus*) or soul (*anima*), which at present is harassed by the weakness of the body (corpus), and is prone to fleshly (*carnalem*) habit.[360]

Reflecting the superiority of the rational and spiritual part of the human soul and the division and antagonism that results from the refusal to recognise its superiority, Augustine's *City of God* distinguished between the 'natural (*animale*)' human community and the 'spiritual (*spiritale*)' human community. The natural community lives 'according to man (*secundum hominem*)' in the 'city of men (*hominum civitas*)' represented by Cain, who lived 'according to man (*secundum hominem*)' and was a citizen of the earthly city but a stranger to the 'city of God'. The spiritual community lives 'according to God (*secundum Deum*)' in the 'city of God (*civitas Dei*)' represented by Abel who was a stranger on earth but a citizen of heaven.[361]

We have already noted in the previous chapter that, due to the influence of St Augustine, the human mind (*mens*) or intellect was regarded as the location of God's image in us[362] by many Latin writers of the later patristic period and that it designated our rational or reasoning capacity,[363] rather than the hidden interior dimension of our being in general, which was usually designated by 'heart'. For this reason the translation of *mens* as 'heart' in Latin liturgical texts from the late patristic period should probably be considered anachronistic. In the previous chapter, we have also noted that some of the theological controversies during the fifth and sixth centuries led to a somewhat sharper distinction between 'soul (*anima*)' and 'spirit (*spiritus*)' than is found, for example, in the anthropology of St Augustine. The Council of Chalcedon (450 AD) recognised that Jesus was 'truly man composed of rational soul and body'[364] and Pope Boniface II approved a decree of the Second Council of Orange (529) declaring anathema those who denied that 'the freedom of the soul remained unharmed' as the result of Adam's sin.[365] The revival of Origen's hypothesis of the pre-existence of human souls as pure intelligences (*noes*) by some Jerusalem monks in 543 was condemned by a provincial council held under Patriarch Menas of Constantinople[366] and a similar revival of the same theory by Priscillian was condemned by the Council of Braga in 561.[367] In the light of these developments, the term *anima* in prayers composed in the late sixth or seventh centuries should probably be translated as 'soul' rather than 'spirit'.

The Heart, the Mind and the Spirit in the 1973 and 2011 Translations of the Missal

Our awareness that, at times, there may be little coherence between our bodily gestures, facial expressions or words and the hidden attitudes of our hearts[368] is expressed in the prayers referring to purity of heart[369] in the 1973 Missal. In the light of Lamentations 3:41, where lifting up our hearts as well as our hands to God in heaven is an expression of repentance and conversion, the invitation 'Lift up your hearts' and the response 'We lift them up to the Lord' should probably be read as a willingness to purify our hearts.[370] God 'prepared the heart of the Virgin Mary to be a fitting home' for the Holy Spirit[371] and we recognise that we also need God's grace to liberate our hearts so that we can serve him[372] with loving trust[373] and with simplicity of heart,[374] with all our heart,[375] or with a pure and undivided heart.[376] During the Eucharist we remember all who seek God 'with a sincere heart'[377] and we pray that God will make our hearts steadfast in faith.[378] The metaphor of enlightenment is also used to describe the process of learning to act with purity of heart and God is asked to 'fill the hearts of all believers with the light of faith'[379] and with the light of the Gospel,[380] to 'open our hearts' to understand his teaching[381] and to establish his teaching in our hearts.[382] Echoing St Paul, who described the Holy Spirit as [invisibly] pouring God's love into our hearts (cf. Rm 5:5), there are prayers asking that God fill our hearts with love,[383] that the good seed planted there may bear fruit[384] and that married couples 'will unite in love' and become 'one in love for each other.[385] Other prayers ask that, just as the Saviour invites all to 'his open heart',[386] so too the self-offering of people during the Mass may unite hearts in peace[387] and give them hearts that are open to truth, gently loving[388] and untroubled.[389] In the 1973 translation, it is not clear why some paraphrases do not translate the word *cor* (heart) at all[390] or why the implicit citation of Acts 4:32 in *cor unum et anima una* (literally, 'one heart and soul') does not seem to have been taken into account in the paraphrases 'one heart and spirit',[391] 'one in heart and mind'[392] and 'united in love'.[393]

The verbs *agnosco* and *memoro* are translated as 'call to mind'.[394] The distinction between the body (and brain) and the capacity of the mind to reason that we have already noted is evident in the prayers for purity 'both in body and in mind'[395] and for health of 'mind and body'.[396] This distinction is somewhat obscured, however, in the paraphrases 'influence our thoughts and actions', 'observance of Lent ... raise our minds' and 'health of mind and body'.[397] The phrase 'mind and body' or its equivalent is sometimes omitted in translation[398] and it is also paraphrased as 'body and spirit' on one occasion.[399] Rather than translating *cogitationes cordis nostri* as 'the meditations of our hearts' (see 'the meditation of my heart' in Ps 19:14), the 1973 text was perhaps seeking some kind of paraphrastic compromise between heart and mind when it asked God to 'Fill our hearts with the light of your Holy Spirit to free our thoughts from sin'.[400] St Paul's words, 'Let the same mind be in you that was in Christ Jesus' (Phil 2:5) was probably the inspiration for the prayer asking God to 'conform the minds of those who offer them [the gifts] to the likeness of your Son'.[401] Although the gap between the mind of Christ and our own minds seems to be implied in the original Latin, it is less evident in the paraphrases asking for the capacity 'to control our desires',[402] requesting that we love God 'with all our hearts'[403] and love 'all men' as God loves them[404] or acknowledging that, unlike those who are at peace with one another, violence and cruelty can have no part in the God of perfect peace.[405] The distinction between the loving heart and the reasoning mind that is implied in Paul's reference to being 'of the same mind, having the same love' (Phil 2:2) seems to be reflected in the prayer that those who dedicate themselves to God by religious profession 'may always raise their minds and hearts' to him.[406] This distinction between mind and hearts is obscured, however, when 'minds (*mentes*)' is paraphrased as 'heart' or 'mind and heart',[407] when it left untranslated[408] and when a reference to minds or hearts is introduced that is not found in the original Latin.[409] *Comme le prévoit* (1969) held that translators 'must follow the scientific methods of textual study as used by experts' to discover 'the true meaning of a text' (n. 9) and must ensure that words and expressions 'keep the correct signification' and must use those words and expressions 'in their proper historical, social, and ritual meanings' (n. 13). In the previous chapter, we have already noted that the paraphrase 'heart' does not reflect the proper historical meaning in relation to two of the prayers concerned[410] and, for the same reason, it also seems to be anachronistic in relation to the prayer *Quod ore sumpsimus* from the Concluding Rites of the Mass.[411] Preface I of Lent is a recent composition that is inspired, in part, by a text from the *Gelasian Sacramentary*[412] and its reference to *purificatis mentibus* comes from a Palm Sunday sermon by Pope St Leo the Great.[413] The phrase *ad reparandam mentium puritatem* in the newly composed Preface II of Lent was also taken from a sermon of Pope St Leo the Great.[414] St Leo's distinction between mind and body, and his emphasis on spiritual understanding and on our capacity for rational deliberation[415] suggest that, in these Prefaces, *mentibus* and *mentium* refer specifically to the 'mind' rather than to 'mind and heart' or 'spirit'.[416] The paraphrases of some of the words that are associated with the heart and mind, such as *affectus*,[417] *animus*,[418] *pectus*[419] and *unanimes*,[420] seem to shy away from identifying what dimension of our being might be involved. Some of the prayers that use the terms *concordes*[421] and *sensibus*[422] date from the Veronese Sacramentary, which was composed in the late fifth century. The paraphrases used to translate *concordes* echo St Augustine's use of this word in the sense of those who are peaceful and lovers of harmony and agreement in human relationships.[423] The paraphrase used to translate *sensibus*, however, could not be described as echoing the usage of St Augustine and of Pope St Leo the Great since it, in effect, ignores that word. We have already noted that, for Augustine, things invisible to our bodily eyes can be 'perceived (*sentire*) by the conscious self (*animus*) and by the mind (*mens*)'[424] and that such intellectual perception (*sensus*)[425] is distinguished from the sense-perception (*sensus*) of the 'irrational soul or life (*irrationalis anima vel vita*)'[426] that we share with animals.[427] For Pope St Leo, the saving mystery, by means of a remarkable miracle, always imprints itself on the senses of the intelligent (*sensibus intelligentium*) when we ceaselessly re-examine the Gospel accounts.[428] Since it is unlikely that a prayer would be composed asking that we be united in our sense-perception, it seems that the prayer was asking that we be faithfully united in our intellectual or spiritual perceptions and judgements.

We have already noted the close relationship between our body and our spirit in the 1973 translation where we pray 'for bodily (*temporaliter*) nourishment and spiritual growth'[429] or that 'we may become one body, one spirit in Christ'.[430] A number of the paraphrases used, including 'And also with you (*Et cum spiritu tuo*)',[431] do not translate the word 'spirit (*spiritus*)'[432] or its cognate terms[433] and some introduce the word 'spirit' when it is not found in the original Latin.[434] The human spirit seems to be confused, at times, with the Holy Spirit.[435] In two places, John 4:24 is implicitly invoked by a paraphrase that refers to worshipping 'in spirit and truth' even though the text in question seems to be based on an implicit citation of the 'right spirit' mentioned in Psalm 51:10.[436] The term 'spirit' is used, however, to describe those who live 'in the spirit of' a particular individual,[437] those who manifest the particular attitudes or dispositions known as joy,[438] love,[439] poverty of spirit,[440] wisdom[441] or zeal[442] or when asking that the world be filled with 'the spirit of Christ',[443] the 'spirit of the sons of God'.[444] The term 'spirit of loving reverence' is used to paraphrase a text about being eagerly intent on carrying out the observances of religious devotion[445] and the term 'spirit of grace' is paraphrased as 'spiritual gifts'.[446] The cognate term 'spiritual (*spiritalis*)' is used in reference to offering oneself as a 'spiritual sacrifice',[447] to the Eucharist as a 'spiritual drink'[448] and to spiritual freedom.[449]

The 2011 translation uses the word 'heart (cor)' to designate that hidden dimension of our being that is not necessarily manifested externally. As in the 1973 Missal, the invitation 'Lift up your hearts' and the response 'We lift them up to the Lord' should probably be read as a willingness to purify our hearts (cf. Lam 3:41).[450] The prayer that 'we may show in our hearts and by our deeds both fraternal charity and the light of truth'[451] implies that the light of truth that inspires our deeds of fraternal charity is directly manifest only in our hearts. Our awareness that, at times, there may be a lack of coherence between our bodily gestures or words and our hidden, interior attitudes[452] seems to lie behind the prayers asking God to receive our offerings and, in his kindness, to 'render us fully acceptable by giving us sincerity of heart'.[453] God 'prepared a fit dwelling place for the Holy Spirit in the Heart of the Blessed Virgin Mary'[454] and sent his Son 'to heal the contrite of heart'.[455] Because overcoming the discrepancy between our hidden attitudes and our visible behaviour requires God's help, however, we ask God to cleanse 'the thoughts[456] of our heart' by the outpouring of the Holy Spirit.[457] In this way, we become capable of acting 'in sincerity of heart',[458] which is, presumably, the same as acting with simplicity of heart,[459] with all one's heart,[460] or with a pure and humble heart.[461] In order to facilitate the renewal of our hearts[462] we pray that God may 'bring forth ... from the hardness of our heart, tears of sorrow'[463] and direct them 'into the way of salvation and peace'.[464] The metaphor of enlightenment is also used to describe the process of learning to act with sincerity of heart and God is asked to 'bring light ... to the darkness of our hearts',[465] to 'illuminate our hearts ... with the splendour' of his grace,[466] to 'confirm the hearts of those born again' by God's grace[467] and to grant that our hearts may grasp his teaching,[468] seek it out and treasure it[469] and hold firmly to what the Bishops and Doctors of the Church teach 'when moved by the divine Spirit'.[470] It is by his Spirit that God the Father moves 'human hearts that enemies may speak to each other again'[471] and, echoing St Paul, who described the Holy Spirit as [invisibly] pouring God's love into our hearts (cf. Rm 5:5),[472] there are many prayers asking that love may be kindled in our hearts,[473] that the good seed planted there may bear fruit,[474] and that others may be of one heart in the pursuit of charity and good works.[475] There are prayers asking for an open, generous and kind heart that is capable of caring for the needy and for strangers,[476] as 'the open Heart of the Saviour'[477] was. Like love,[478] the joy[479] and fortitude[480] that remain hidden in our hearts are also recognised as gifts from God. We have already noted that, for St Augustine, who recognises the etymology as a combination of con and corda (chord), the word concordes denotes those who are peaceful and lovers of harmony and agreement in human relationships. Apparently following an etymology based on con and cor (heart), the 2011 text translates it as 'of one heart in love'[481] when it is used together with a reference to married couples being united in heart. It was, presumably, on the basis of a similar etymology that a text referring to being *concordes* in relation to our duties towards God is paraphrased as being 'one in mind and heart'[482] rather than being translated more accurately as 'in peace and harmony' or something similar.

We have already noted that the distinction between the body (and the physical brain) and the mind's capacity to reason seems to be implicit in the prayers for 'health of mind and body'[483] or for help, protection, restoration or sanctification in mind and body.[484] This distinction does not imply a disjunction, however, for we pray that God use our bodily fasting to 'raise up our minds' to him[485] and that, being 'one flesh', husband and wife 'may be bound together ... in likeness of mind.'[486] Occasionally, the 2011 text translates 'minds (*mentes*)' as 'minds and hearts'[487] even though, as we have already seen, such a translation probably does not reflect the 'proper historical'[488] meaning of the word in late patristic texts. Unlike the 1973 version, the implied reference to St Paul's admonition, 'Let the same mind be in you that was in Christ Jesus' (Phil 2:5), seems to have been ignored in the prayer asking that the gifts offered during a prayer for the renewal of religious vows 'conform those who make this offering in mind and heart to the likeness of your Son'.[489] It is, presumably, because of the gap between our mind and the mind of Christ that the 2011 Missal recognises that our minds are in need of purification[490] if we are to honour God 'with all our mind'.[491] The reality of this gap is obscured, however, by anachronistic[492] paraphrases using the term 'heart'[493] and by paraphrases where the Latin word used probably does not denote 'heart'[494] or 'spirit'[495] in the same way that the words *cor* and *spiritus* do. The distinction between the loving heart and the reasoning mind that is implied in Paul's reference to being 'of the same mind, having the same love' (Phil 2:2) seems to be reflected in the prayer that those who dedicate themselves to God by religious profession 'may always raise their hearts and minds' to him[496] and in the prayer asking for sanctification of our minds and hearts.[497] The text referring to approaching the sacred rites of the Eucharist 'with a pure mind and a fervent heart'[498] suggests that the purity in question is concerned with reason's capacity to perceive and judge rather than with the will's capacity to love, and that having a fervent heart is concerned with the will's capacity to love rather than with reason's capacity to perceive and judge.

The term 'spirit' is both associated with, and distinguished from, the body (*corpus*) in the 2011 translation. Like the 'mind (*mens*)', the 'spirit (*spiritus*)' is seen as belonging to the interior dimension of the heart rather than to the body[499] and, apparently recognising that the Vulgate translation of Romans 12:2 uses *rationabile* in that sense, the adjective *rationabilem* is translated on one occasion as 'spiritual'.[500] Reflecting 2 Timothy 4:19 and 22 and following the explicit direction given in *Liturgiam authenticam* n. 56, the people's response *Et cum spiritu tuo*, apparently a prayer that the Lord Jesus Christ would be spiritually with the celebrant in what he was about to do in Christ's name, is translated literally as 'And with your spirit'.[501] The 2011 Missal prays that the homage[502] that people offer to God 'in the body' will 'redound upon them as a spiritual gift',[503] that the sustenance provided by the Eucharist, which is described as a 'spiritual drink',[504] 'not fail us in body or in spirit'[505] and that we may become 'one with' the Saints in heaven, 'one body and one spirit in Christ'.[506] The term 'spirit' can describe particular attitudes, capacities, dispositions or spiritual gifts[507] such as counsel and fortitude,[508] fortitude and peace,[509] freedom,[510] generosity,[511] humility,[512] humility and zeal,[513] joy,[514] love,[515] patience and charity,[516] penance and prayer,[517] poverty[518] or wisdom.[519] Those inspired by the same spiritual ideals as a particular individual can be described as living 'in the spirit of' that individual[520] or being 'afire with that same spirit'.[521] Learning how to 'grow in spiritual things',[522] how to offer ourselves as 'spiritual sacrifices'[523] to God and how to imbue the world with 'the spirit of Christ'[524] depends on having a 'right spirit' (cf. Ps 51:10)[525] by sharing in 'the Christian spirit',[526] the spirit of grace[527] or of adoption as a child of God.[528] We received the spirit of Christ when we were 'signed with his Cross and with a spiritual anointing'[529] in the Sacraments of Christian Initiation.

An Overview of the Way Soul, Body and Spirit are Presented in the 1973 and 2011 Translations

Generally speaking, the Latin text of the 1970 Missal reflects the classical anthropology of both the Old and New Testaments and of the Christian Tradition where the living human soul (*anima*) is recognised as including both a body (*corpus*) and a spirit (*spiritus*) dimension. In this chapter, I have examined the 1973 and 2011 translations of the Missal in order to determine how well they reflect that anthropology. In this overview of the chapter, I will try to directly compare the ways in which key terms are used in the 1973 and 2011 translation.

The 1973 text translated *homo* as 'mankind' when it described our creation in the likeness of God and, rather than referring to 'flesh' as in the Latin texts, it preferred the paraphrases 'becoming man' and 'born of the Virgin Mary' to describe the Incarnation. The play between *hominibus* and *homines* in the Latin text is translated using the words 'man' and 'men'. The 2011 text consistently uses the noun 'man (*homo*)' in a gender-inclusive sense and it also uses the noun 'soul (*anima*)' to designate the human person in a global way. The play between *hominibus* and *homines* in the Latin text is translated using the word 'humanity' but, when the play is between the plural *homines* and the singular *homo*, the translations 'men' and 'man' are used.

As in the Old and New Testaments, the 1973 text translated *anima* as 'life' but it seems to have systematically used paraphrase to avoid translating *anima* as 'soul' except in the context of the Assumption. As a result, the association and distinction between soul and body, and between soul and heart, was obscured somewhat. The implicit recognition of the body as the dwelling place of the soul was lost in the paraphrase 'Lord, I am not worthy to receive you, but only say the word, and I shall be healed' (cf. Mt 8:8). As in the 1973 text, the word *anima* is sometimes translated as 'life' in the 2011 text but the term 'soul (*anima*)' is also used to denote the human person as a whole, the possibility of salvation for humanity in general, as in the 'salvation of souls', and the possibility of salvation for those who have died, as in the prayers offered for the 'souls' of particular individuals. In addition to recognising our bodies as temples of the Holy Spirit, the implied identification of the body as the dwelling place of the soul or person is recognised in the translation 'Lord, I am not worthy that you should enter under my roof, but only say the word and my soul shall be healed.' The 2011 text recognises the relationship and the distinction between body and soul and the Church is described as the soul of human society. There are some cases, however, where the 2011 translation seems to introduce a paraphrase of the word *anima* that does not reflect the likely meaning of the original Latin.

Although the term 'body (*corpus*)' is sometimes omitted in paraphrases, the 1973 text used the term in relation to Christ, whose earthly body was like our own, to our rebirth in Baptism, to the Eucharist as Christ's 'body and blood', to the Church as the body of Christ and to the resurrection of our bodies. The Incarnation was described as the Word becoming flesh but most references to 'flesh (*caro*)' in the Latin text were either not translated or paraphrased. The phrase 'body and heart' recognised the distinction between the external and internal dimensions of the person and of the union of husband and wife. The phrase 'one body, one spirit in Christ' acknowledged the corporate reality and spiritual unity of the Church. The distinction between the bodily brain and the healthy human mind's capacity to reason seems to have been implicit in the prayers for 'health of mind and body' but there were a number of paraphrases where the Latin phrase 'mind and body' was not translated. In the 2011 translation of the Missal, the term 'body (*corpus*)' is used in relation to our bodily existence on earth, to Christ who shared our 'bodily form', to the rebirth of Baptism, to the Eucharist as Christ's Body and Blood, to the Church as the Body of Christ and to resurrection of our bodies. We are described as corporately and spiritually 'one with' the Saints in heaven, 'one body and one spirit in Christ'. The bodily experience of birth 'according to the flesh' highlights the close association between body and flesh (*caro*), and the term 'flesh (*caro*)', which designates our mortality and frailty, is used in relation to the 'Word made flesh' and to our being raised up 'in the flesh' at our resurrection. The close association between body and spirit is highlighted when we pray that the homage we offer God 'in the body' may bear fruit in 'a spiritual gift'. The relationship between the exterior body and the interior heart is reflected in the close association between bodily chastity and purity of heart and in the prayer that husbands and wives may be 'united in body and heart'. The distinction between the bodily brain and the healthy human mind's capacity to reason seems to be implicit in the prayer that God will raise up our minds through 'bodily fasting' and in the prayers for health, help, protection, purification, restoration, or sanctification in mind and body. In some cases, however, references to mind and body in the Latin text are paraphrased rather than being translated in the 2011 text.

The 1973 Missal recognised the need to purify and enlighten our hearts so that our outward behaviour might truly express what is hidden in our hearts and so that our hearts might be filled with love. It also included a prayer that God may unite our hearts in peace. Some paraphrases did not translate the word *cor* (heart) at all and the implicit citation of Acts 4:32 in *cor unum et anima una* (literally, 'one heart and soul') was ignored. The 2011 translation uses the word 'heart (*cor*)' to designate that hidden dimension of our being that is not necessarily manifested externally and, recognising the need for a contrite heart, there are many prayers that ask God to purify our hearts. The need for enlightenment so that our hearts may treasure and hold firmly to the truth is highlighted and the role of the Holy Spirit in reconciling hearts that have become divided is mentioned. There are many prayers asking that love may be kindled in our hearts, and being of one heart is presented as the ideal in the Christian community. In one case, rather than following St Augustine, who used the word in the sense of being harmoniously united, the word *concordes* is paraphrased as being 'one in mind and heart'.

In the 1973 text, the term 'mind (*mens*)' was left untranslated or was ignored in some paraphrases and the explicit distinction between mind and body was also sometimes left untranslated or ignored in paraphrases. The distinction between mind and heart was recognised in some cases but the paraphrases used when translating *mentes* sometimes obscured this distinction by failing to translate the word in the light of the original meaning of the Latin text. The paraphrases of words that are associated with the heart and mind, such as *affectus*, *animus*, *pectus* and *unanimes*, seem to have shied away from identifying what dimension of our being might be involved. While the translations of *concordes* echoed the usage of St Augustine, the term *sensibus* was left untranslated in the paraphrase given. The close association between mind (*mens*) and body is emphasised in some of the texts in the 2011 Missal but there are also cases where *mentes* is paraphrased in a way that does not reflect the probable meaning of the original Latin source. The need for purification of our minds is recognised in some texts but the paraphrases used sometimes conceal the distinction between heart (*cor*) and mind (*mens*) that is recognised in other texts.

A number of the paraphrases used in the 1973 Missal, including 'And also with you (*Et cum spiritu tuo*)', did not translate the word 'spirit (*spiritus*)' or its cognate terms and some introduced the word 'spirit' when it is not found in the original Latin. There are cases where the human spirit seems to have been confused with the Holy Spirit or where the reference to 'spirit' in one biblical text (Jn 4:24) was confused with another (Ps 51:10). The term 'spirit' was used to describe those who live 'in the spirit of' a particular individual and those who manifest particular attitudes or dispositions. There were also references to filling the world with 'the spirit of Christ', to the 'spirit of the sons of God' and to spiritual sacrifices. In the 2011 Missal, the literal translation 'And with your spirit (*Et cum spiritu tuo*)' explicitly asks that Christ may be spiritually with the celebrant in what he is about to do in Christ's name. The close relationship between body and spirit is recognised and our corporate and spiritual unity as Christ's Body, the Church, is also acknowledged. Like the 1973 Missal, there are texts that refer to the spirit of Christ and to spiritual sacrifices but the 2011 Missal corrects those paraphrases that confused the human spirit with the Holy Spirit or that confused an intertextual reference to Psalm 51 with a reference to John 4. The term 'spirit' is also used to denote a particular attitude, capacity, disposition or spiritual gift and those inspired by the same spiritual ideals as a particular individual are described as living 'in the spirit of' that individual.

In general, the 2011 Missal is considerably more faithful than the 1973 Missal in translating the anthropology of the Latin Missal of 1970. The new translation allows such key terms as soul (*anima*), body (*cor*), flesh (*caro*), heart (*cor*), mind (*mens*) and spirit (*spiritus*) to be heard in a way that is much richer than in the older translation. *Comme le prévoit* (1969) held that translators 'should give first consideration to the meaning of the communication' (n. 8), 'must follow the scientific methods of textual study as used by experts' to discover 'the true meaning of a text' (n. 9), must ensure that words and expressions 'keep the correct signification' and must use those words and expressions 'in their proper historical, social, and ritual meanings' (n. 13). In the light of the many inaccurate paraphrases of key anthropological terms, however, it would seem that, in many instances, the translators of the 1973 Missal did not take sufficient care in establishing the true meaning of many anthropological terms before they drew up their paraphrases. The 2011 translation corrects many of the inaccurate paraphrases of key anthropological terms that were used in the 1973 translation. On occasion, however, it does not seem to have taken sufficiently into account the requirements of the *Ratio translationis for the English Language* (2007), which insists that 'translators must first take care to locate the biblical and patristic sources of the prayers they translate' (n. 19) and that, 'rather than substituting other words that are alien to it', translators should retain the 'coherent system of words and patterns of speech consecrated by the books of Sacred Scripture and by ecclesiastical tradition, especially by the Fathers of the Church' (n. 20). The *Ratio translationis* specifies that any biblical expressions commonly used in catechism or religious devotions should be respected (n. 107) and it envisages the creation of a 'liturgical vernacular' of sacral language (n. 110). In some cases, the paraphrases used for key anthropological terms in the 2011 translation do not respect the biblical words and expressions relating to theological anthropology that are commonly used in catechism or religious devotions or the way in which such words or expressions are used in patristic sources. As a consequence of such paraphrases, there seems to be a certain weakening in the 'coherent system of words and patterns of speech consecrated by the books of Sacred Scripture and by ecclesiastical tradition, especially by the Fathers of the Church' that the *Ratio* sought to create.

Conclusion

This book tries to address some of these issues that the new translation of the Roman Missal has raised by evaluating the 1973 translation in the light of the principles of translation issued in 1969 and by evaluating the 2011 translation in the light of the principles of translation issued in 2001 and in 2007.

In Chapter One, we noted that, although the 1973 translation was 'much-loved', reservations about its effectiveness were expressed by many commentators. Although *Comme le prévoit* (1969) might have led one to expect a greater density of paraphrases in the more ancient texts of Eucharistic Prayers 1, 2 and 4 (see n. 33), the number of paraphrases per 100 Latin words in Eucharistic Prayers 3 was greater than in Eucharistic Prayers 2 and 4 but less than the density in Eucharistic Prayer 1. The frequent use of paraphrase in the 1973 translation might reflect the emphasis on addressing 'the audience for which it is intended', as *Comme le prévoit* n. 7 recommended. In many cases, however, the neglect of the implicit biblical citations indicates that this translation did not always follow 'the scientific methods of textual study as used by experts' to discover 'the true meaning of a text' (*Comme le prévoit* n. 9). Paraphrasing *unigenitum* as 'only Son', for example, obscured the distinction between our adoption as the children of God the Father and the unique and eternal relationship of the 'only-begotten Son' to the Father that the true meaning of the Latin word communicated.

Chapter Two outlines the nature of the changes that were made in the 2011 translation and tries to identify the reasons for those changes in the light of the approach to translating liturgical texts in the 2001 instruction, *Liturgiam authenticam*, and in the *Ratio translationis for the English Language* (2007). The 2011 translation corrected the great majority of the omissions and additions in the older translation and it significantly reduced the number of paraphrases. Among the few omissions retained was 'her Spouse (*eiusdem Virginis Sponsi*)', which avoids the strange sounding 'Husband of the same Virgin' and, among the additions introduced into the Latin text are the new alternative forms of the dismissal approved by Pope Benedict XVI in 2008. Almost all the variations from the original meaning found in the 1973 translation were corrected and the paraphrases 'And also with you' and 'Lord, I am not worthy to receive you, but only say the word, and I shall be healed' were replaced by the literal translations 'And with your spirit' and 'Lord, I am not worthy that you should enter under my roof, but only say the word and my soul shall be healed'. The frequency with which paraphrases were used was reduced and, overall, the number of paraphrases per 100 Latin words was reduced from 5.88 to 0.77. In keeping with the 2006 judgement by the Prefect of the Congregation for Divine Worship and the Discipline of the Sacraments, 'for many' was considered the more faithful translation of *pro multis*. While the new translation is generally more literal than the 1973 translation, there are a number of places where, rather than reflecting the probable meaning of the original Latin sources, the Latin words *mentes* and *anima* are paraphrased as 'mind and heart' and 'spirit'. The 2011 translation tends to reflect the punctuation of the Latin text more faithfully and it follows the more detailed norms for capitalisation that are found in the *Ratio translationis* (2007). The readability of the new translation has been questioned by many, notably in relation to some of the Collects and certain parts of Eucharistic Prayers 2 and 3, but there has also been some favourable comment about the readability of some Collects, of the endings of the Prefaces and of parts of Eucharistic Prayers 1 and 4. Given the now generally accepted norms in many anglophone countries, some writers have commented unfavourably about the lack of 'inclusive language' in Eucharistic Prayer 4 and in the translation of the word *homo,* but such judgements should, perhaps, be tempered by a consideration of the specific norms concerning inculturation and the use of language that concerns gender in *Liturgiam authenticam* 30–31.

In the third chapter, we explored the degree to which the classical anthropology of the Latin text of the 1970 Missal, where the living human soul (*anima*) is recognised as including both a body (*corpus*) and a spirit (*spiritus*) dimension, is evident in the 1973 and 2011 translations of that Missal. Both translations reflect that classical anthropology but, in the case of the 1973 translation, the systematic use of paraphrase to avoid translating *anima* as 'soul', except in the context of the Assumption, results in a distortion that is most evident, perhaps, in the paraphrase 'Lord, I am not worthy to receive you, but only say the word, and I shall be healed' and in the avoidance of any reference to praying for the 'souls' of the dead. The 2011 translation restores the term 'soul' in both contexts but, on occasion, it also introduces paraphrases of the word *anima* that do not reflect the likely meaning of the original Latin. The 1973 translation sometimes omitted the term 'body (*corpus*)' in paraphrases and, except in direct references to the Incarnation, references to 'flesh (*caro*)' in the Latin text were either not translated or paraphrased. These omissions and paraphrases were replaced by literal translations in the 2011 translation but, like the 1973 translation, the 2011 translation sometimes paraphrased references to 'body and mind'. Some of the paraphrases in the

1973 Missal do not translate the word *cor* (heart) and the implicit citation of Acts 4:32 in *cor unum et anima una* (literally, 'one heart and soul') seems to be ignored. The 2011 text addresses both these issues but, in one case, it also paraphrases the word *concordes* as being 'one in mind and heart'. In the 1973 text, the term 'mind (*mens*)' was left untranslated or was ignored in some paraphrases and the explicit distinction between mind and body was also sometimes left untranslated or was ignored in paraphrases. The distinction between mind and heart was recognised in some cases but the paraphrases used when translating *mentes* sometimes obscured this distinction by failing to translate the word in the light of the original meaning of the Latin text. The close association between mind and body is emphasised in some of the texts in the 2011 Missal but there are also cases where *mentes* is paraphrased in a way that does not reflect the probable meaning of the original Latin source. Some of the paraphrases used conceal the distinction between heart (*cor*) and mind (*mens*) that is recognised in other texts. A number of the paraphrases used in the 1973 Missal, including 'And also with you (*Et cum spiritu tuo*)', did not translate the word 'spirit (*spiritus*)' and there are cases where the human spirit seems to have been confused with the Holy Spirit or where the reference to 'spirit' in one biblical text (Jn 4:24) was confused with another (Ps 51:10). In the 2011 Missal, the literal translation 'And with your spirit (*Et cum spiritu tuo*)' explicitly asks that Christ may be spiritually with the celebrant in what he is about to do in Christ's name. The 2011 Missal corrects those paraphrases in the 1973 translation that confused the human spirit with the Holy Spirit or that confused an intertextual reference to Psalm 51 with a reference to John 4. In general, while the 2011 Missal is considerably more faithful than the 1973 Missal in translating the anthropology of the Latin Missal of 1970, it does not always follow the guidelines of the *Ratio translationis for the English Language* (2007) concerning the need to 'locate the biblical and patristic sources' (n. 19) and to retain the 'coherent system of words and patterns of speech consecrated by the books of Sacred Scripture and by ecclesiastical tradition, especially by the Fathers of the Church' (n. 20).

In 1969, *Comme le prévoit* recognised (n. 1) that 'after sufficient experiment and passage of time, all translations will need review' and, in 2008, Bishop Arthur J. Serratelli of Paterson, New Jersey, commented that the new translation

> ... will improve our liturgical prayer, but it will not be perfect. Perfection will come when the Liturgy on earth gives way to that of Heaven where all the saints praise God with one voice.'[1]

In preparing a translation of liturgical books, *Liturgiam authenticam* (2001) said (n. 5) that 'the greatest care is to be taken to maintain the identity and unitary expression of the Roman Rite ... as a manifestation of the theological realities of ecclesial communion and unity.' It noted (n. 6) that the 'omissions or errors which affect certain existing vernacular translations – especially in the case of certain languages – have impeded the progress of inculturation that actually should have taken place' and had prevented the Church 'from laying the foundation for a fuller, healthier and more authentic renewal'. In their desire to produce a translation whose language would be largely familiar, the translators of the 1973 text had, perhaps inadvertently, failed to maintain the identity and unitary expression of the Roman Rite, as can be seen from the many omissions, additions, variations and paraphrases that were used. The shortcomings that have since been recognised in the 1973 translation of the Missal should not blind us, however, to the extraordinary achievement of producing the first English translation of the 1970 Latin Missal in just three years. This first and well-loved translation was less than perfect but, even if it had been perfect, the changes that have since taken place in the anglophone cultures for which it was intended would probably now require at least some minor adjustments. I believe that the new 2011 translation is, in many respects, a significant improvement and that it will, in time, help to lay 'the foundation for a fuller, healthier and more authentic renewal'[2] of the liturgical life of the English-speaking Churches. Like its predecessor, however, the new translation is also less than perfect and, in due course, though not perhaps in the immediate future, it, too, will probably require some adjustments. It may be that some of the issues I have tried to raise concerning theological anthropology will be addressed when the time comes for drawing up a new translation but it is also likely that regular use of the new translation will lead to the identification of other issues that will be addressed at that time. I believe that, in due course, the new translation will also become well-loved and that its many merits will be widely appreciated.

The Changes in the New Translation of the Ordinary of the Mass

If we compare the changes introduced in the new English translation (2011) of the Latin text of the first typical edition of the Paul VI Roman Missal (2002)[1] with the translation with which most of us are now familiar, the English translation (1973) of the Latin text of the third typical edition of the Paul VI Roman Missal (2002/2008)[2] we notice that, while there are considerable differences between the two English translations, the two Latin texts are identical apart from the addition of the three alternative forms of dismissal at the end and a few other changes to the Presidential Prayers.

In the examples of the changes listed in sections A to D below, the Latin text, which, apart from the new forms of the dismissal, is common to both the first (1970) and third (2002/2008) edition of the Paul VI Roman Missal, is given first in italics, each with the identifying paragraph number used in the 2011 edition of the Roman Missal.[3] The Roman numerals assigned to the extracts from Prefaces in section E and to the selection of Collects, Prayers over the Offerings and Prayers after Communion in section F do not reflect any numbering system in the 2011 Roman Missal. Below the Latin text, the sections of the English translations in which significant changes are found are given side by side, with the 1973 text on the left and the 2011 text on the right. Ignoring any changes in word order, the words in English that have been changed are in italics. Each of the four basic parts of the Mass (Preparatory Rites, the Liturgy of the Word, the Liturgy of the Eucharist, and the Communion and Concluding Rite) are taken separately and the four Eucharistic Prayers are treated as subsections under the heading, 'The Liturgy of the Eucharist'.

A. The Introductory Rites

2. Gratia Domini nostri Iesu Christi, et caritas Dei, et communicatio Sancti Spiritus sit cum omnibus vobis.
Gratia vobis et pax a Deo Patre nostro et Domino Iesu Christo.
Et cum spiritu tuo.

Priest: The grace of our Lord Jesus Christ, and the love of God, and the *fellowship* of the Holy Spirit be with you all.
Or: *The* grace and peace *of* God our Father and the Lord Jesus Christ be with you.
People: And *also* with *you.*

Priest: The grace of our Lord Jesus Christ, and the love of God, and the *communion* of the Holy Spirit be with you all.
Or: Grace *to you* and peace *from* God our Father and the Lord Jesus Christ.
People: And with *your spirit.*

---

4. Fratres, agnoscamus peccata nostra, ut apti simus ad sacra mysteria celebranda.
Confiteor Deo omnipotenti et vobis, fratres, quia peccavi nimis cogitatione, verbo, opere et omissione: mea culpa, mea culpa, mea maxima culpa. Ideo precor beatam Mariam semper Virginem, omnes Angelos et Sanctos, et vos, fratres, orare pro me ad Dominum Deum nostrum.

My brothers and sisters, to *prepare* ourselves to celebrate the sacred mysteries, let us *call to mind* our sins.

I confess to almighty God, and to you, my brothers and sisters, that I have sinned *through my own fault*, in my thoughts and in my words, in what I have done, and in what I have failed to do; *and* I ask blessed Mary, ever *virgin*, all the *angels* and *saints*, and you, my brothers and sisters, to pray for me to the Lord, our God.

Brethren (brothers and sisters), let us *acknowledge* our sins, *and so prepare* ourselves to celebrate the sacred mysteries.

I confess to almighty God and to you, my brothers and sisters, that I have *greatly* sinned, in my thoughts and in my words, in what I have done and in what I have failed to do, *through my fault, through my fault, through my most grievous fault; therefore* I ask blessed Mary ever-*Virgin*, all the *Angels* and *Saints*, and you, my brothers and sisters, to pray for me to the Lord our God.

---

5. Sac. Miserere nostri, Domine.
Pop. Quia[4] peccavimus tibi.
Sac. Ostende nobis, Domine, misericordiam tuam.

Priest: Lord, we have sinned against you: Lord, have mercy.
People: Lord, have mercy.
Priest: Lord, show us your mercy and love.

Priest: Have mercy on us, O Lord.
People: For we have sinned against you.
Priest: Show us, O Lord, your mercy.

---

6. Qui missus es sanare contritos corde: Kyrie, eleison. Qui ad dexteram Patris sedes, ad interpellandum pro nobis: Kyrie, eleison.

You were sent to heal the contrite: Lord, have mercy.
You *plead* for us at the right hand of the Father: Lord, have mercy.

You were sent to heal the contrite *of heart*: Lord, have mercy.
You *are seated* at the right hand of the Father to *intercede* for us: Lord, have mercy.

---

8. Gloria in excelsis Deo et in terra pax hominibus bonae voluntatis. Laudamus te, benedicimus te, adoramus te, glorificamus te, gratias agimus tibi propter magnam gloriam tuam, Domine Deus, Rex caelestis, Deus Pater omnipotens. Domine Fili Unigenite, Iesu Christe, Domine Deus, Agnus Dei, Filius Patris, qui tollis peccata mundi, miserere nobis; qui tollis peccata mundi, suscipe deprecationem nostram. Qui sedes ad dexteram Patris, miserere nobis. Quoniam tu solus Sanctus, tu solus Dominus, tu solus Altissimus, Iesu Christe, cum Sancto Spiritu: in gloria Dei Patris. Amen.

Glory to God in the highest, and peace to *his* people on earth. Lord God, heavenly King, almighty God *and* Father, *we worship you, we give you thanks, we praise you for your glory.* Lord Jesus Christ, only Son of the Father, Lord God, Lamb of God, you take away the *sins* of the world: have mercy on us; you are seated at the right hand of the Father, receive our prayer. For you alone are the Holy One, you alone are the Lord, you alone are the Most High, Jesus Christ, with the Holy Spirit, in the glory of God the Father. Amen.

Glory to God in the highest, and on earth peace to people *of good will. We praise you, we bless you, we adore you, we glorify you, we give you thanks for your great glory*, Lord God, heavenly King, O God, almighty Father. Lord Jesus Christ, *Only Begotten Son*, Lord God, Lamb of God, Son of the Father, you take away the *sins* of the world, have mercy on us; *you take away the sins of the world*, receive our prayer; you are seated at the right hand of the Father, have mercy on us. For you alone are the Holy One, you alone are the Lord, you alone are the Most High, Jesus Christ, with the Holy Spirit, in the glory of God the Father. Amen.

B. The Liturgy of the Word

14. Iube, domne, benedicere.
Dominus sit in corde tuo et in labiis tuis: ut digne et competenter annunties Evangelium suum: in nomine Patris, et Filii, et Spiritus Sancti.
Munda cor meum ac labia mea, omnipotens Deus, ut sanctum Evangelium tuum digne valeam nuntiare.

Deacon: Father, *give me* your blessing. *Priest:* The Lord be in your heart and on your lips that you may worthily proclaim his gospel. In the name of the Father, and of the Son, and of the Holy Spirit. Almighty God, cleanse my heart and my lips that I may worthily proclaim your holy Gospel.	*Deacon:* Your blessing, Father. *Priest: May* the Lord be in your heart and on your lips, that you may proclaim his Gospel worthily *and well*, in the name of the Father, and of the Son, and of the Holy Spirit. Cleanse my heart and my lips, almighty God, that I may worthily proclaim your holy Gospel.

15. Dominus vobiscum.
Et cum spiritu tuo.
Lectio sancti Evangelii secundum N.
Gloria tibi, Domine.

Priest: The Lord be with you. *People:* And *also* with *you*. *Priest:* A reading from the Holy Gospel according to N. *People:* Glory to you, O Lord.	*Priest:* The Lord be with you. *People:* And with *your spirit*. *Priest:* A reading from the Holy Gospel according to N. *People:* Glory to you, O Lord.

16. Per evangelica dicta deleantur nostra delicta.

May the words of the *gospel wipe* away our sins.	*Through* the words of the *Gospel* may our sins *be wiped away*.

18. The Nicene-Constantinopolitan Creed
Credo in unum Deum, Patrem omnipotentem, factorem caeli et terrae, visibilium omnium et invisibilium. Et in unum Dominum Iesum Christum, Filium Dei Unigenitum, et ex Patre natum ante omnia saecula. Deum de Deo, lumen de lumine, Deum verum de Deo vero, genitum, non factum, consubstantialem Patri: per quem omnia facta sunt. Qui propter nos homines et propter nostram salutem descendit de caelis. Et incarnatus est de Spiritu Sancto ex Maria

Virgine, et homo factus est. Crucifixus etiam pro nobis sub Pontio Pilato; passus et sepultus est, et resurrexit tertia die, secundum Scripturas, et ascendit in caelum, sedet ad dexteram Patris. Et iterum venturus est cum gloria, iudicare vivos et mortuos, cuius regni non erit finis. Et in Spiritum Sanctum, Dominum et vivificantem: qui ex Patre Filioque procedit. Qui cum Patre et Filio simul adoratur et conglorificatur: qui locutus est per prophetas. Et unam, sanctam, catholicam et apostolicam Ecclesiam. Confiteor unum baptisma in remissionem peccatorum. Et exspecto resurrectionem mortuorum, et vitam venturi saeculi. Amen.

We believe in one God, the Father, the *Almighty*, maker of heaven and earth, of all *that is seen and unseen. We believe* in one Lord, Jesus Christ, the *only* Son of God, *eternally begotten* of the Father, God from God, Light from Light, true God from true God, begotten, not made, *one in Being* with the Father. Through him all things were made. For us men and for our salvation he came down from heaven: by *the power of* the Holy Spirit *he* was *born* of the Virgin Mary, and became man. For our sake he was crucified under Pontius Pilate; he suffered, *died*, and was buried. On the third day *he* rose again *in fulfilment* of the Scriptures; he ascended into heaven and is seated at the right hand of the Father. He will come again in glory to judge the living and the dead, and his kingdom will have no end. *We believe* in the Holy Spirit, the Lord, the giver of life, who proceeds from the Father and the Son. With the Father and the Son *he* is *worshipped* and glorified. *He* has spoken through the Prophets. *We believe* in one holy catholic and apostolic Church. *We acknowledge* one baptism for the forgiveness of sins. *We* look for the resurrection of the dead, and the life of the world to come. Amen.

I believe in one God, the Father *almighty*, maker of heaven and earth, of all *things visible and invisible. I* believe in one Lord Jesus Christ, the *Only Begotten* Son of God, *born* of the Father *before all* ages. God from God, Light from Light, true God from true God, begotten, not made, *consubstantial* with the Father; through him all things were made. For us men and for our salvation he came down from heaven, *and* by the Holy Spirit was *incarnate* of the Virgin Mary, and became man. For our sake he was crucified under Pontius Pilate, he suffered *death* and was buried, *and* rose again on the third day in *accordance with* the Scriptures. He ascended into heaven and is seated at the right hand of the Father. He will come again in glory to judge the living and the dead and his kingdom will have no end. *I believe* in the Holy Spirit, the Lord, the giver of life, who proceeds from the Father and the Son, *who* with the Father and the Son is *adored* and glorified, *who* has spoken through the prophets. *I believe* in one, holy, catholic and apostolic Church. *I confess* one Baptism for the forgiveness of sins *and* I look *forward* to the resurrection of the dead and the life of the world to come. Amen.

19. The Apostles' Creed

Credo in unum Deum Patrem omnipotentem, Creatorem caeli et terrae, et in Iesum Christum, Filium eius unicum, Dominum nostrum, qui conceptus est de Spiritu Sancto, natus ex Maria Virgine, passus sub Pontio Pilato, crucifixus, mortuus, et sepultus, descendit ad inferos, tertia die resurrexit a mortuis, ascendit ad caelos, sedet ad dexteram Dei Patris omnipotentis, inde venturus est iudicare vivos et mortuos. Credo in Spiritum Sanctum, sanctam Ecclesiam catholicam, sanctorum communionem, remissionem peccatorum, carnis resurrectionem, vitam aeternam. Amen.

I believe in God, the Father almighty, *creator* of heaven and earth. *I believe* in Jesus Christ, his only Son, our Lord. *He* was conceived by *the power of* the Holy Spirit *and* born of the Virgin Mary. *He* suffered under Pontius Pilate, was crucified, died, and was buried. He descended *to the dead*. On the third day he rose again. He ascended into heaven, and is seated at the right hand of the Father. He will come *again* to judge the living and the dead. I believe in the Holy Spirit, the holy catholic Church, the communion of saints, the forgiveness of sins, the resurrection of the body, and *the* life everlasting. Amen.

I believe in God, the Father almighty, *Creator* of heaven and earth, *and* in Jesus Christ, his only Son, our Lord, *who* was conceived by the Holy Spirit, born of the Virgin Mary, suffered under Pontius Pilate, was crucified, died and was buried; he descended *into hell;* on the third day he rose again *from the dead;* he ascended into heaven, and is seated at the right hand of *God* the Father *almighty; from there* he will come to judge the living and the dead. I believe in the Holy Spirit, the holy catholic Church, the communion of saints, the forgiveness of sins, the resurrection of the body, and life everlasting. Amen.

C. The Liturgy of the Eucharist

23. *Benedictus es, Domine, Deus universi, quia de tua largitate accepimus panem, quem tibi offerimus, fructum terrae et operis manuum hominum, ex quo nobis fiet panis vitae.*

Blessed are you, Lord, God of all creation. Through your goodness we have *this* bread to offer, *which* earth *has given* and human hands *have made*. It will become for us the bread of life.

Blessed are you, Lord God of all creation, *for* through your goodness we have *received the* bread we offer you: *fruit of the* earth and *work of* human hands, it will become for us the bread of life.

25. Benedictus es, Domine, Deus universi, quia de tua largitate accepimus vinum, quod tibi offerimus, fructum vitis et operis manuum hominum, ex quo nobis fiet potus spiritalis.

Blessed are you, Lord, God of all creation. Through your goodness we have *this* wine to offer, fruit of the vine and work of human hands. It will become our spiritual drink.

Blessed are you, Lord God of all creation, *for* through your goodness we have *received the* wine we offer *you*: fruit of the vine and work of human hands, it will become our spiritual drink.

---

26. In spiritu humilitatis et in animo contrito suscipiamur a te, Domine; et sic fiat sacrificium nostrum in conspectu tuo hodie, ut placeat tibi, Domine Deus.

Lord God, *we ask* you to *receive us* and *be pleased with the* sacrifice we *offer you* with humble and contrite hearts.

With humble *spirit* and contrite *heart may we be accepted by you, O Lord*, and *may our sacrifice in your sight this day be pleasing to you*, Lord God.

---

28. Lava me, Domine, ab iniquitate mea, et a peccato meo munda me.

Lord, *wash away* my iniquity; cleanse me from my sin.

Wash *me*, O Lord, *from* my iniquity *and* cleanse me from my sin.

---

29. Orate, fratres, ut meum ac vestrum sacrificium acceptabile fiat apud Deum Patrem omnipotentem.
Suscipiat Dominus sacrificium de manibus tuis ad laudem et gloriam nominis sui, ad utilitatem quoque nostram totiusque Ecclesiae suae sanctae.

Pray, brethren, that *our* sacrifice may be acceptable to God, the almighty Father.

May the Lord accept the sacrifice at your hands for the praise and glory of his name, for our good, and the good of all his Church.

Pray, brethren (*brothers and sisters*), that *my* sacrifice *and yours* may be acceptable to God, the almighty Father.

May the Lord accept the sacrifice at your hands for the praise and glory of his name, for our good and the good of all his *holy* Church.

C.1 Eucharistic Prayer 1

83. V. Dominus vobiscum.
R. Et cum spiritu tuo.
V. Sursum corda.
R. Habemus ad Dominum.
V. Gratias agamus Domino Deo nostro.
R. Dignum et iustum est.
Sanctus, Sanctus, Sanctus Dominus Deus Sabaoth. Pleni sunt caeli et terra gloria tua. Hosanna in excelsis. Benedictus qui venit in nomine Domini. Hosanna in excelsis.

Priest: The Lord be with you.
People: And *also* with *you.*
Priest: Lift up your hearts.
People: We lift them up to the Lord.
Priest: Let us give thanks to the Lord our God.
People: It is right *to give him thanks and praise.*

Holy, *holy, holy* Lord, God of *power and might*. Heaven and earth are full of your glory. Hosanna in the highest. Blessed is he who comes in the name of the Lord. Hosanna in the highest.

Priest: The Lord be with you.
People: And with *your spirit.*
Priest: Lift up your hearts.
People: We lift them up to the Lord.
Priest: Let us give thanks to the Lord our God.
People: It is right *and just.*

Holy, *Holy, Holy* Lord God of *hosts*. Heaven and earth are full of your glory. Hosanna in the highest. Blessed is he who comes in the name of the Lord. Hosanna in the highest.

84. Te igitur, clementissime Pater, per Iesum Christum, Filium tuum, Dominum nostrum, supplices rogamus ac petimus uti accepta habeas et benedicas haec dona, haec munera, haec sancta sacrificia illibata in primis, quae tibi offerimus pro Ecclesia tua sancta catholica: quam pacificare, custodire, adunare et regere digneris toto orbe terrarum: una cum famulo tuo Papa nostro N. et Antistite nostro N. et omnibus orthodoxis atque catholicae et apostolicae fidei cultoribus.

We come to you, Father, *with praise and thanksgiving*, through Jesus Christ your Son. *Through him we ask* you *to* accept and bless these gifts we offer you *in sacrifice. We offer them* for your holy catholic Church, *watch over it, Lord, and guide it*; grant *it* peace *and unity* throughout the world. *We offer them* for N. our Pope, *for* N. our *bishop*, and for all *who hold and teach* the catholic faith *that comes from the apostles.*

To you, *therefore, most merciful* Father, we *make humble prayer and petition* through Jesus Christ, your Son, *our Lord:* that you accept and bless these gifts, *these offerings, these holy and unblemished sacrifices, which we* offer you *firstly* for your holy catholic Church. *Be pleased to* grant *her* peace, *to guard, unite and govern her* throughout the whole world, *together with your servant* N. our Pope *and* N. our *Bishop*, and all *those who, holding to the truth, hand on* the catholic *and apostolic faith.*

85. Memento, Domine, famulorum famularumque tuarum N. et N. et omnium circumstantium, quorum tibi fides cognita est et nota devotio, pro quibus tibi offerimus: [vel qui tibi offerunt hoc sacrificium laudis, pro se suisque omnibus:] pro redemptione animarum suarum, pro spe salutis et incolumitatis suae: tibique reddunt vota sua aeterno Deo, vivo et vero.

Remember, Lord, your *people, especially those for whom we now pray*, N. and N. Remember all *of us* gathered here before *you. You know how firmly we believe in you and dedicate ourselves* to you. We offer you this sacrifice of praise for *ourselves* and *those* who are dear to *us. We pray to you, our* living and true God, *for our* well being *and* redemption.

Remember, Lord, your *servants N. and N. and* all gathered here, *whose faith and devotion* are known to you. *For them,* we offer you this sacrifice of praise *or they offer it* for *themselves* and *all* who are dear to *them: for the* redemption *of their souls, in hope of health and* well-being, *and paying their homage to you, the eternal* God, living and true.

86. Communicantes, et memoriam venerantes, in primis gloriosae semper Virginis Mariae, Genetricis Dei et Domini nostri Iesu Christi: sed et beati Ioseph, eiusdem Virginis Sponsi, et beatorum Apostolorum ac Martyrum tuorum, Petri et Pauli ... et Thaddaei: Lini, Cleti ... et Damiani) et omnium Sanctorum tuorum; quorum meritis precibusque concedas, ut in omnibus protectionis tuae muniamur auxilio.

In union *with the whole Church, we honour* Mary, *the ever-virgin mother* of Jesus Christ our Lord and God. *We honour* Joseph, her *husband, the apostles* and *martyrs*, Peter and Paul ... and Jude; *we honour* Linus, Cletus ... and Damian] and all *the saints*. May their merits and prayers grant us your *constant* help and *protection*.

In *communion with those whose memory we venerate, especially the glorious* ever-*Virgin* Mary, *Mother* of our God and Lord, Jesus Christ, *and blessed* Joseph, her *Spouse, your blessed Apostles* and *Martyrs*, Peter and Paul ... and Jude; Linus, Cletus ... and Damian] and all *your Saints; we ask that through* their merits and prayers, *in all things we may be defended by* your *protecting* help.

---

87. Hanc igitur oblationem servitutis nostrae, sed et cunctae familiae tuae, quaesumus, Domine, ut placatus accipias: diesque nostros in tua pace disponas, atque ab aeterna damnatione nos eripi et in electorum tuorum iubeas grege numerari.

Father, accept this *offering from* your whole family. *Grant us* your peace *in this* life, *save us* from *final* damnation, and *count us* among those you have chosen.

Therefore, Lord, we pray: graciously accept this *oblation of our service, that* of *your whole family; order our days in* your peace, *and command that we be delivered* from *eternal* damnation and *counted* among *the flock of* those you have chosen.

---

88. Quam oblationem tu, Deus, in omnibus, quaesumus, benedictam, adscriptam, ratam, rationabilem, acceptabilemque facere digneris: ut nobis Corpus et Sanguis fiat dilectissimi Filii tui, Domini nostri Iesu Christi.

Bless and approve *our* offering: make it acceptable *to you, an offering in spirit and in truth. Let it* become for us the *body* and *blood* of Jesus Christ, your *only* Son our Lord.

Be pleased, O God, we pray, to bless, *acknowledge*, and approve *this* offering *in every respect*; make *it spiritual and* acceptable, so *that it may* become for us the *Body* and *Blood* of your *most beloved* Son, our Lord Jesus Christ.

---

89. Qui, pridie quam pateretur, accepit panem in sanctas ac venerabiles manus suas, elevat oculos, et elevatis oculis in caelum ad te Deum Patrem suum omnipotentem, tibi gratias agens benedixit, fregit, deditque discipulis suis, dicens: ACCIPITE ET MANDUCATE EX HOC OMNES: HOC EST ENIM CORPUS MEUM, QUOD PRO VOBIS TRADETUR.

The day before he *suffered* he took bread in his *sacred* hands and *looking up* to heaven, to you, his almighty Father, *he gave you* thanks *and praise*. He broke the bread, gave it to his disciples, *and said*: TAKE THIS, ALL OF YOU, AND EAT IT: THIS IS MY BODY WHICH WILL BE GIVEN UP FOR YOU.

On the day before he *was to suffer,* he took bread in his *holy and venerable* hands, and *with eyes raised* to heaven to you, *O God*, his almighty Father, *giving you* thanks he *said the blessing*, broke the bread *and* gave it to his disciples, *saying*: TAKE THIS, ALL OF YOU, AND EAT *OF* IT: *FOR* THIS IS MY BODY WHICH WILL BE GIVEN UP FOR YOU.

90. Simili modo, postquam cenatum est, accipiens et hunc praeclarum calicem in sanctas ac venerabiles manus suas, item tibi gratias agens benedixit, deditque discipulis suis, dicens: ACCIPITE ET BIBITE EX EO OMNES: HIC EST ENIM CALIX SANGUINIS MEI NOVI ET AETERNI TESTAMENTI, QUI PRO VOBIS ET PRO MULTIS EFFUNDETUR IN REMISSIONEM PECCATORUM. HOC FACITE IN MEAM COMMEMORATIONEM.

When supper was ended, he took *the cup. Again he gave* you thanks *and praise*, gave the *cup* to his disciples, *and said:* TAKE THIS, ALL OF YOU, AND DRINK FROM IT: THIS IS THE *CUP* OF MY BLOOD, THE BLOOD OF THE NEW AND *EVERLASTING* COVENANT. *IT* WILL BE *SHED* FOR YOU AND FOR *ALL SO THAT SINS* MAY BE FORGIVEN. DO THIS IN MEMORY OF ME.

In a similar way, when supper was ended, he took *this precious chalice in his holy and venerable hands, and once more giving* you thanks, *he said the blessing and gave* the *chalice* to his disciples, *saying*: TAKE THIS, ALL OF YOU, AND DRINK FROM IT: *FOR* THIS IS THE *CHALICE* OF MY BLOOD, THE BLOOD OF THE NEW AND *ETERNAL* COVENANT, *WHICH* WILL BE *POURED* OUT FOR YOU AND FOR *MANY FOR THE FORGIVENESS OF* SINS. DO THIS IN MEMORY OF ME.

91. Mysterium fidei
Mortem tuam annuntiamus, Domine, et tuam resurrectionem confitemur, donec venias.
Vel: Quotiescumque manducamus panem hunc et calicem bibimus, mortem tuam annuntiamus, Domine, donec venias.
Vel: Salvator mundi, salva nos, quia per crucem et resurrectionem tuam liberasti nos.

Priest: *Let us proclaim* the mystery of faith:
People: A – *Christ has died, Christ is risen, Christ will* come again.

or **C** – When we eat this *bread* and drink this *cup*, we proclaim your death, Lord *Jesus*, until you come *in glory*.
or **D** – *Lord*, by your *cross* and resurrection, you have set us free. *You are the* Saviour of the World.

Priest: The mystery of faith.
People: A – *We proclaim your Death, O Lord, and profess your Resurrection until you* come again.

or **B** – When we eat this *Bread* and drink this *Cup, we* proclaim your *Death*, O Lord, until you come *again*.
or **C** – *Save us*, Saviour of the world, *for* by your *Cross* and *Resurrection*, you have set us free.

---

92. Unde et memores, Domine, nos servi tui, sed et plebs tua sancta, eiusdem Christi, Filii tui, Domini nostri, tam beatae passionis, necnon et ab inferis resurrectionis, sed et in caelos gloriosae ascensionis: offerimus praeclarae maiestati tuae de tuis donis ac datis hostiam puram, hostiam sanctam, hostiam immaculatam, Panem sanctum vitae aeternae et Calicem salutis perpetuae.

Father, we celebrate the *memory of* Christ, your Son. We, your people and your *ministers, recall his passion, his resurrection* from the dead, and *his ascension* into *glory; and* from the *many* gifts you have given us *we* offer to *you*, God *of glory and* majesty, this *holy and perfect sacrifice*: the *bread* of life and the *cup of eternal* salvation.

Therefore, O Lord, as we celebrate the *memorial of the blessed Passion, the Resurrection* from the dead, and *the glorious Ascension* into *heaven* of Christ, your Son, *our Lord*, we, your *servants* and your *holy* people, offer to *your glorious* majesty from the gifts *that* you have given us, this *pure victim, this* holy *victim, this spotless victim*, the *holy Bread* of *eternal* life and the *Chalice* of *everlasting* salvation.

---

93. Supra quae propitio ac sereno vultu respicere digneris: et accepta habere, sicuti accepta habere dignatus es munera pueri tui iusti Abel, et sacrificium Patriarchae nostri Abrahae, et quod tibi obtulit summus sacerdos tuus Melchisedech, sanctum sacrificium, immaculatam hostiam.

Look *with favour on these offerings* and accept them as once you *accepted* the gifts of your servant Abel, the sacrifice of Abraham, our father in faith, and the *bread and wine offered* by your priest Melchizedech.

Be pleased to look *upon these offerings with a serene and kindly countenance*, and *to* accept them, as once you *were pleased to accept* the gifts of your servant Abel *the just*, the sacrifice of Abraham, our father in faith, and the *offering of* your *high* priest Melchizedek, *a holy sacrifice, a spotless victim.*

---

94. *Supplices te rogamus, omnipotens Deus: iube haec perferri per manus sancti Angeli tui in sublime altare tuum, in conspectu divinae maiestatis tuae; ut, quotquot ex hac altaris participatione sacrosanctum Filii tui Corpus et Sanguinem sumpserimus, omni benedictione caelesti et gratia repleamur. (Per Christum Dominum nostrum. Amen.)*

Almighty God, *we pray* that your *angel may take this sacrifice* to your altar *in heaven. Then, as we* receive *from this altar* the *sacred body* and *blood* of your Son, *let us* be filled with every grace and blessing. [Through Christ our Lord. Amen.]

In humble prayer we ask you, almighty God: *command* that *these gifts be borne by the hands of* your *holy Angel* to your altar *on high in the sight of your divine majesty, so that all of us, who through this participation at the altar* receive the *most holy Body* and *Blood* of your Son, *may* be filled with every grace and *heavenly* blessing. [Through Christ our Lord. Amen.]

---

95. *Memento etiam, Domine, famulorum famularumque tuarum N. et N., qui nos praecesserunt cum signo fidei, et dormiunt in somno pacis. Ipsis, Domine, et omnibus in Christo quiescentibus, locum refrigerii, lucis et pacis, ut indulgeas, deprecamur. (Per Christum Dominum nostrum. Amen.)*

Remember, Lord, *those who have died and* have gone before us *marked* with the sign of faith, *especially those for whom* we *now* pray, N. and N. *May these*, and all who sleep in Christ, *find in your presence* light, *happiness* and peace. [Though Christ our Lord. Amen.]

Remember *also*, Lord, *your servants* N. and N., who have gone before us with the sign of faith *and rest in the sleep of peace. Grant them,* O Lord, we pray, and all who sleep in Christ, *a place of refreshment*, light and peace. [Through Christ our Lord. Amen.]

---

96. Nobis quoque peccatoribus famulis tuis, de multitudine miserationum tuarum sperantibus, partem aliquam et societatem donare digneris cum tuis sanctis Apostolis et Martyribus: cum Ioanne, Stephano, Matthia, Barnaba, (Ignatio, Alexandro, Marcellino, Petro, Felicitate, Perpetua, Agatha, Lucia, Agnete, Caecilia, Anastasia) et omnibus Sanctis tuis: intra quorum nos consortium, non aestimator meriti, sed veniae, quaesumus, largitor admitte. Per Christum Dominum nostrum.

For ourselves, too, we ask some share *in the* fellowship *of your apostles* and *martyrs*, with John the Baptist, Stephen, Matthias, Barnabas, [Ignatius, Alexander, Marcellinus, Peter, Felicity, Perpetua, Agatha, Lucy, Agnes, Cecilia, Anastasia] and all *the saints. Though we are sinners, we trust in your mercy and love. Do not consider what we truly deserve,* but *grant* us your *forgiveness*. Through Christ our Lord.

To us, also, your servants, who, though sinners, hope in your abundant mercies, graciously grant some share *and* fellowship *with* your *holy Apostles* and *Martyrs*: with John the Baptist, Stephen, Matthias, Barnabas, [Ignatius, Alexander, Marcellinus, Peter, Felicity, Perpetua, Agatha, Lucy, Agnes, Cecilia, Anastasia] and all *your Saints; admit us, we beseech you, into their company, not weighing our merits*, but *granting* us your *pardon*, through Christ our Lord.

---

97. Per quem haec omnia, Domine, semper bona creas, sanctificas, vivificas, benedicis, et praestas nobis.

Through *him* you *give us* all these *gifts*. You fill them with life *and goodness, you* bless them and *make* them *holy*.

Through *whom* you *continue to create* all these *good things, O Lord;* you *sanctify* them, fill them with life, bless them, and *bestow* them *upon us*.

---

98. Per ipsum, et cum ipso, et in ipso, est tibi Deo Patri omnipotenti, in unitate Spiritus Sancti, omnis honor et gloria per omnia saecula saeculorum.

Through him, with him, in him, in the unity of the Holy Spirit, all glory and honour is yours, almighty Father, for ever and ever.

Through him, *and* with him, *and* in him, *O God*, almighty Father, in the unity of the Holy Spirit, all glory and honour is yours, for ever and ever.

C.2 Eucharistic Prayer 2

99. V. Dominus vobiscum.
R. Et cum spiritu tuo.
V. Sursum corda.
R. Habemus ad Dominum.
V. Gratias agamus Domino Deo nostro.
R. Dignum et iustum est.

Vere dignum et iustum est, aequum et salutare, nos tibi, sancte Pater, semper et ubique gratias agere per Filium dilectionis tuae Iesum Christum, Verbum tuum per quod cuncta fecisti: quem misisti nobis Salvatorem et Redemptorem, incarnatum de Spiritu Sancto et ex Virgine natum. Qui voluntatem tuam adimplens et populum tibi sanctum acquirens extendit manus cum pateretur, ut mortem solveret et resurrectionem manifestaret. Et ideo cum Angelis et omnibus Sanctis gloriam tuam praedicamus, una voce dicentes: Sanctus, Sanctus, Sanctus Dominus Deus Sabaoth. Pleni sunt caeli et terra gloria tua. Hosanna in excelsis. Benedictus qui venit in nomine Domini. Hosanna in excelsis.

Priest: The Lord be with you.	**Priest:** The Lord be with you.
People: And *also* with *you*.	**People:** And with *your spirit*.
Priest: Lift up your hearts.	**Priest:** Lift up your hearts.
People: We lift them up to the Lord.	**People:** We lift them up to the Lord.
Priest: Let us give thanks to the Lord our God.	**Priest:** Let us give thanks to the Lord our God.
People: It is right *to give him thanks and praise.*	**People:** It is right *and just.*

Father, *it is* our duty and *our* salvation always and everywhere to give you thanks through your beloved Son, Jesus Christ. *He is the* Word through whom you made *the universe, the* Saviour you sent *to redeem us.* By *the power of* the Holy Spirit, *he took flesh* and *was* born of the Virgin *Mary. For our sake* he *opened* his *arms on the cross; he put an end to* death and *revealed* the resurrection. *In this he fulfilled* your will and *won* for you a holy people. And so *we join* the *angels* and the *saints in proclaiming* your glory as we *sing* (say): Holy, *holy, holy* Lord, God of *power and might.* Heaven and earth are full of your glory. Hosanna in the highest. Blessed is he who comes in the name of the Lord. Hosanna in the highest.

It is truly right and just, our duty and our salvation, always and everywhere to give you thanks, Father *most holy,* through your beloved Son, Jesus Christ, *your* Word through whom you made *all things, whom* you sent *as our* Saviour *and Redeemer, incarnate* by the Holy Spirit and born of the Virgin. *Fulfilling* your will and *gaining* for you a holy people, he *stretched out* his *hands as he endured his Passion, so as to break the bonds* of death and *manifest* the resurrection. And so, *with the Angels* and *all the Saints we declare* your glory, as *with one voice we acclaim:* Holy, *Holy, Holy* Lord God of *hosts.* Heaven and earth are full of your glory. Hosanna in the highest. Blessed is he who comes in the name of the Lord. Hosanna in the highest.

100. Vere Sanctus es, Domine, fons omnis sanctitatis.

Lord, you are *holy* indeed, the *fountain* of all holiness.

You are indeed *Holy,* O Lord, the *fount* of all holiness.

---

101. Haec ergo dona, quaesumus, Spiritus tui rore sanctifica, ut nobis Corpus et Sanguis fiant Domini nostri Iesu Christi.

Let your Spirit *come* upon these gifts to make them holy, so that they may become for us the *body* and *blood* of our Lord, Jesus Christ.

Make holy, *therefore*, these gifts, we *pray, by sending down* your Spirit upon them *like the dewfall,* so that they may become for us the *Body* and *Blood* of our Lord, Jesus Christ.

---

102. Qui cum Passioni voluntarie traderetur, accepit panem et gratias agens fregit, deditque discipulis suis, dicens: ACCIPITE ET MANDUCATE EX HOC OMNES: HOC EST ENIM CORPUS MEUM, QUOD PRO VOBIS TRADETUR.

Before he was *given up to death, a death he freely accepted*, he took bread and *gave you* thanks. *He* broke the *bread,* gave it to his disciples, *and said*: TAKE THIS, ALL OF YOU, AND EAT IT: THIS IS MY BODY WHICH WILL BE GIVEN UP FOR YOU.

At the time he was *betrayed and entered willingly into his Passion*, he took bread and, *giving thanks*, broke *it,* and gave it to his disciples, *saying*: TAKE THIS, ALL OF YOU, AND EAT *OF* IT, *FOR* THIS IS MY BODY, WHICH WILL BE GIVEN UP FOR YOU.

---

103. Simili modo, postquam cenatum est, accipiens et calicem iterum tibi gratias agens dedit discipulis suis, dicens: ACCIPITE ET BIBITE EX EO OMNES: HIC EST ENIM CALIX SANGUINIS MEI NOVI ET AETERNI TESTAMENTI, QUI PRO VOBIS ET PRO MULTIS EFFUNDETUR IN REMISSIONEM PECCATORUM. HOC FACITE IN MEAM COMMEMORATIONEM.

When supper was ended, he took the *cup. Again he gave you* thanks *and praise*, gave *the cup* to his disciples, *and said*: TAKE THIS, ALL OF YOU, AND DRINK FROM IT: THIS IS THE *CUP* OF MY BLOOD, THE BLOOD OF THE NEW AND *EVERLASTING* COVENANT. *IT* WILL BE *SHED* FOR YOU AND FOR *ALL SO THAT* SINS *MAY BE FORGIVEN*. DO THIS IN MEMORY OF ME.

In a similar way, when supper was ended, he took the *chalice and, once more giving* thanks, *he* gave *it* to his disciples, *saying:* TAKE THIS, ALL OF YOU, AND DRINK FROM IT, *FOR* THIS IS THE *CHALICE* OF MY BLOOD, THE BLOOD OF THE NEW AND *ETERNAL* COVENANT, *WHICH* WILL BE *POURED OUT* FOR YOU AND FOR *MANY FOR THE FORGIVENESS OF* SINS. DO THIS IN MEMORY OF ME.

---

104. Mysterium fidei
Mortem tuam annuntiamus, Domine, et tuam resurrectionem confitemur, donec venias.
Vel: *Quotiescumque manducamus panem hunc et calicem bibimus, mortem tuam annuntiamus, Domine, donec venias.*
Vel: *Salvator mundi, salva nos, quia per crucem et resurrectionem tuam liberasti nos.*

Priest: Let us proclaim the mystery of faith:
People: A – Christ has died, Christ is risen, Christ will come again.

or C – When we eat this bread and drink this cup, we proclaim your death, Lord Jesus, until you come in glory.
or D – Lord, by your cross and resurrection, you have set us free. You are the Saviour of the World.

Priest: The mystery of faith.
People: A – We proclaim your Death, O Lord, and profess your Resurrection until you come again.

or B – When we eat this Bread and drink this Cup, we proclaim your Death, O Lord, until you come again.
or C – Save us, Saviour of the world, for by your Cross and Resurrection, you have set us free.

---

105. Memores igitur mortis et resurrectionis eius, tibi, Domine, panem vitae et calicem salutis offerimus, gratias agentes quia nos dignos habuisti astare coram te et tibi ministrare.
Et supplices deprecamur ut Corporis et Sanguinis Christi participes a Spiritu Sancto congregemur in unum.
Recordare, Domine, Ecclesiae tuae toto orbe diffusae, ut eam in caritate perficias una cum Papa nostro N. et Episcopo nostro N. et universo clero.
In Missis pro defunctis addi potest:
Memento famuli tui [famulae tuae] N., quem [quam] [hodie] ad te ex hoc mundo vocasti. Concede, ut, qui [quae] complantatus [complantata] fuit similitudini mortis Filii tui, simul fiat et resurrectionis ipsius.
Memento etiam fratrum nostrorum, qui in spe resurrectionis dormierunt, omniumque in tua miseratione defunctorum, et eos in lumen vultus tui admitte.
Omnium nostrum, quaesumus, miserere, ut cum beata Dei Genetrice Virgine Maria, beatis Apostolis et omnibus Sanctis, qui tibi a saeculo placuerunt, aeternae vitae mereamur esse consortes, et te laudemus et glorificemus per Filium tuum Iesum Christum.

In memory of his *death* and *resurrection*, we offer you, *Father, this life-giving bread, this saving cup. We thank* you *for counting* us worthy to *stand* in your presence and *serve* you.

May *all of us who share* in the *body* and *blood* of Christ be *brought together in unity* by the Holy Spirit.

Lord, remember your Church throughout the world; *make us grow in love,* together with N. our Pope, N. our *bishop*, and all the clergy.

In Masses for the dead:
Remember N., whom you have called from this *life. In baptism* he [she] *died with Christ:* may he [she] *share* his resurrection.

Remember our brothers and sisters who have *gone to their rest* in the hope of *rising again; bring* them and all *the departed* into the light of your *presence*. Have mercy on us all; *make us worthy to share* eternal life with Mary, *the virgin* Mother of God, with the *apostles*, and *with* all the *saints* who have *done your will* throughout the ages. May we praise you *in union with them*, and give you *glory* through your Son, Jesus Christ.

Therefore, as we celebrate the memorial of his *Death* and *Resurrection*, we offer you, *Lord, the Bread of life and the Chalice of salvation, giving thanks that* you *have held* us worthy to *be* in your presence and *minister to* you.

Humbly we pray that, partaking of the *Body* and *Blood* of Christ, we may be *gathered into one* by the Holy Spirit.

Remember, Lord, your Church, *spread* throughout the world, and *bring her to the fullness of charity*, together with N. our Pope *and* N. our *Bishop* and all the clergy.

In Masses for the Dead:
Remember *your servant* N., whom you have called [*today*] from this *world to yourself. Grant that* he [she] *who was united with your Son in a death like his*, may *also be one with him* in his Resurrection.

Remember also our brothers and sisters who *have fallen asleep* in the hope of *the resurrection* and all *who have died in your mercy: welcome* them into the light of your *face*. Have mercy on us all, we *pray, that* with *the Blessed Virgin* Mary, Mother of God, with the *blessed Apostles*, and *all* the *Saints* who have *pleased you* throughout the ages, *we may merit to be co-heirs* to eternal life, *and* may praise and *glorify* you through your Son, Jesus Christ.

---

106. Per ipsum, et cum ipso, et in ipso, est tibi Deo Patri omnipotenti, in unitate Spiritus Sancti, omnis honor et gloria per omnia saecula saeculorum.

Through him, with him, in him, in the unity of the Holy Spirit, all glory and honour is *yours*, almighty Father, for ever and ever.

Through him, *and* with him, *and* in him, O God, almighty Father, in the unity of the Holy Spirit, all glory and honour is yours, for ever and ever.

C.3 Eucharistic Prayer 3

107. V. Dominus vobiscum.
R. *Et cum spiritu tuo.*
V. *Sursum corda.*
R. *Habemus ad Dominum.*
V. *Gratias agamus Domino Deo nostro.*
R. *Dignum et iustum est.*
Sanctus, Sanctus, Sanctus Dominus Deus Sabaoth. Pleni sunt caeli et terra gloria tua. Hosanna in excelsis. Benedictus qui venit in nomine Domini. Hosanna in excelsis.

Priest: The Lord be with you.	*Priest:* The Lord be with you.
People: And *also* with *you*.	*People:* And with *your spirit*.
Priest: Lift up your hearts.	*Priest:* Lift up your hearts.
People: We lift them up to the Lord.	*People:* We lift them up to the Lord.
Priest: Let us give thanks to the Lord our God.	*Priest:* Let us give thanks to the Lord our God.
People: It is right to *give him thanks and praise*.	*People:* It is right *and just*.
Holy, *holy, holy* Lord, God of *power and might*. Heaven and earth are full of your glory. Hosanna in the highest. Blessed is he who comes in the name of the Lord. Hosanna in the highest.	Holy, *Holy, Holy* Lord God of *hosts*. Heaven and earth are full of your glory. Hosanna in the highest. Blessed is he who comes in the name of the Lord. Hosanna in the highest.

---

108. Vere Sanctus es, Domine, et merito te laudat omnis a te condita creatura, quia per Filium tuum, Dominum nostrum Iesum Christum, Spiritus Sancti operante virtute, vivificas et sanctificas universa, et populum tibi congregare non desinis, ut a solis ortu usque ad occasum oblatio munda offeratur nomini tuo.

Father, you are holy indeed, and all *creation* rightly gives you praise. *All life, all holiness comes from you* through your Son, Jesus Christ our Lord, by the working of the Holy Spirit. *From age to age* you gather a people to yourself, so that from *east to west* a *perfect offering* may be *made* to *the glory of* your name.	You are indeed Holy, *O Lord*, and all *you have created* rightly gives you praise, *for* through your Son our Lord Jesus Christ, by the *power and* working of the Holy Spirit, *you give life to all things and make them* holy, and you *never cease* to gather a people to yourself, so that from *the rising of the sun to its setting* a *pure sacrifice* may be *offered* to your name.

---

109. Supplices ergo te, Domine, deprecamur, ut haec munera, quae tibi sacranda detulimus, eodem Spiritu sanctificare digneris ut Corpus et Sanguis fiant Filii tui Domini nostri Iesu Christi, cuius mandato haec mysteria celebramus.

And so, Father, we *bring* you these gifts. We *ask you to make them holy* by the *power of your* Spirit, that they may become the *body* and *blood* of your Son, our Lord Jesus Christ, at whose command we celebrate *this eucharist.*

Therefore, O Lord, we *humbly implore* you: by the *same* Spirit *graciously make holy* these gifts we *have brought* to you *for consecration*, that they may become the *Body* and *Blood* of your Son our Lord Jesus Christ, at whose command we celebrate *these mysteries.*

110. Ipse enim in qua nocte tradebatur accepit panem et tibi gratias agens benedixit, fregit, deditque discipulis suis, dicens: ACCIPITE ET MANDUCATE EX HOC OMNES: HOC EST ENIM CORPUS MEUM, QUOD PRO VOBIS TRADETUR.

On the night he was betrayed, he took bread and *gave* you thanks *and praise*. He broke the bread, gave it to his disciples, *and said*: TAKE THIS, ALL OF YOU, AND EAT IT: THIS IS MY BODY WHICH WILL BE GIVEN UP FOR YOU.

For on the night he was betrayed he *himself* took bread, and, *giving* you thanks, *he said the blessing*, broke the bread *and* gave it to his disciples, *saying*: TAKE THIS, ALL OF YOU, AND EAT *OF* IT, *FOR* THIS IS MY BODY, WHICH WILL BE GIVEN UP FOR YOU.

111. Simili modo, postquam cenatum est, accipiens calicem, et tibi gratias agens benedixit, deditque discipulis suis, dicens: ACCIPITE ET BIBITE EX EO OMNES: HIC EST ENIM CALIX SANGUINIS MEI NOVI ET AETERNI TESTAMENTI, QUI PRO VOBIS ET PRO MULTIS EFFUNDETUR IN REMISSION E M PECCATORUM. HOC FACITE IN MEAM COMMEMORATIONEM.

When supper was ended, he took the *cup. Again he gave you* thanks *and praise,* gave the *cup* to his disciples, *and said:* TAKE THIS, ALL OF YOU, AND DRINK FROM IT: THIS IS THE *CUP* OF MY BLOOD, THE BLOOD OF THE NEW AND *EVERLASTING* COVENANT. IT WILL BE *SHED* FOR YOU AND *FOR ALL SO THAT* SINS *MAY* BE FORGIVEN. DO THIS IN MEMORY OF ME.

In a similar way, when supper was ended, he took the *chalice, and, giving* you thanks, *he said the blessing, and* gave the *chalice* to his disciples, *saying:* TAKE THIS, ALL OF YOU, AND DRINK FROM IT, *FOR* THIS IS THE *CHALICE* OF MY BLOOD, THE BLOOD OF THE NEW AND *ETERNAL* COVENANT, *WHICH* WILL BE *POURED OUT* FOR YOU AND *FOR MANY FOR THE FORGIVENESS OF* SINS. DO THIS IN MEMORY OF ME.

112. Mysterium fidei
Mortem tuam annuntiamus, Domine, et tuam resurrectionem confitemur, donec venias.
Vel: *Quotiescumque manducamus panem hunc et calicem bibimus, mortem tuam annuntiamus, Domine, donec venias.*
Vel: *Salvator mundi, salva nos, quia per crucem et resurrectionem tuam liberasti nos.*

Priest: Let us *proclaim* the mystery of faith:
People: A – *Christ has died, Christ is* risen, *Christ will* come again.

or C – When we eat this *bread* and drink this *cup*, we proclaim your death, Lord *Jesus*, until you come *in glory.*
or D – *Lord*, by your *cross* and *resurrection*, you have set us free. *You are the* Saviour of the World.

Priest: The mystery of faith.
People: A – *We proclaim your Death, O Lord, and profess your Resurrection until you* come again.

or B – When we eat this *Bread* and drink this *Cup*, we proclaim your *Death*, O Lord, until you come *again.*
or C – *Save us*, Saviour of the world, *for* by your *Cross* and *Resurrection*, you have set us free.

---

113. Memores igitur, Domine, eiusdem Filii tui salutiferae passionis necnon mirabilis resurrectionis et ascensionis in caelum, sed et praestolantes alterum eius adventum, offerimus tibi, gratias referentes, hoc sacrificium vivum et sanctum.
Respice, quaesumus, in oblationem Ecclesiae tuae et, agnoscens Hostiam, cuius voluisti immolatione placari, concede, ut qui Corpore et Sanguine Filii tui reficimur, Spiritu eius Sancto repleti, unum corpus et unus spiritus inveniamur in Christo.
Ipse nos tibi perficiat munus aeternum, ut cum electis tuis hereditatem consequi valeamus, in primis cum beatissima Virgine, Dei Genetrice, Maria, cum beatis Apostolis tuis et gloriosis Martyribus (cum Sancto N.: Sancto diei vel patrono) et omnibus Sanctis, quorum intercessione perpetuo apud te confidimus adiuvari.
Haec Hostia nostrae reconciliationis proficiat, quaesumus, Domine, ad totius mundi pacem atque salutem. Ecclesiam tuam, peregrinantem in terra, in fide et caritate firmare digneris cum famulo tuo Papa nostro N. et Episcopo nostro N., cum episcopali ordine et universo clero et omni populo acquisitionis tuae. Votis huius familiae, quam tibi astare voluisti, adesto propitius. Omnes filios tuos ubique dispersos tibi, clemens Pater, miseratus coniunge.
Fratres nostros defunctos et omnes qui, tibi placentes, ex hoc saeculo transierunt, in regnum tuum benignus admitte, ubi fore speramus, ut simul gloria tua perenniter satiemur, per Christum Dominum nostrum, per quem mundo bona cuncta largiris.

Father, calling to mind the *death* your Son *endured for our salvation*, his *glorious resurrection* and *ascension* into heaven, and *ready to greet him when he comes again*, we offer you in thanksgiving this holy and living sacrifice.

Look *with favour* on your Church's *offering*, and *see* the Victim whose death *has reconciled* us to yourself. Grant that we, who are nourished by his *body* and *blood*, may *be* filled with his Holy Spirit, and become one body, one spirit in Christ.

May he make us an *everlasting gift* to you *and enable us to share in the* inheritance *of* your *saints*, with Mary, the *virgin* Mother of God, with t*he apostles*, the *martyrs*, (Saint N. – *the s*aint of the day or the patron saint*) and all *your saints*, on whose constant intercession we rely for help.

Lord, may this *sacrifice, which has made our peace with you*, advance the peace and salvation of all the world. *Strengthen* in faith and *love* your pilgrim Church on earth; your servant, Pope N., our Bishop N., *and all* the *bishops, with* the clergy and the entire people *your Son has* gained for *you*. Father, *hear* the prayers of *the* family you have *gathered here* before you. In *mercy and love unite* all your children wherever they may be.

Welcome into your kingdom our departed brothers and sisters, and all who *have left* this *world in your friendship*. We hope to enjoy for ever the *vision* of your glory, through Christ our Lord, *from* whom all good *things come*.

Therefore, O Lord, as we celebrate the memorial of the *saving Passion of* your Son, his *wondrous Resurrection* and *Ascension* into heaven, and *as we look forward to his second coming*, we offer you in thanksgiving this holy and living sacrifice.

Look, *we pray, upon the oblation of* your Church and, *recognising* the *sacrificial* Victim *by* whose death *you willed to reconcile* us to yourself, grant that we, who are nourished by *the Body* and *Blood of your Son and* filled with his Holy Spirit, may become one body, one spirit in Christ.

May he make of us an *eternal offering* to you, *so that we may obtain an* inheritance *with* your *elect, especially* with the *most blessed Virgin* Mary, Mother of God, with *your blessed Apostles and glorious Martyrs* [*with* Saint N.: *the Saint of the day or Patron Saint*] and *with* all the Saints, on whose constant intercession *in your presence* we rely for *unfailing* help.

May this *Sacrifice of our reconciliation, we pray, O Lord*, advance the peace and salvation of all the world. *Be pleased to confirm* in faith and *charity* your pilgrim Church on earth, *with* your servant N. *our* Pope and N. our Bishop, the *Order of Bishops*, all the clergy, and the entire people *you have gained* for *your own*.

Listen graciously to the prayers of *this* family, *whom* you have *summoned* before you: *in your compassion, O merciful* Father, *gather to yourself* all your children *scattered throughout the world.*

To our departed brothers and sisters and *to* all who *were pleasing to you at their passing from* this *life, give kind admittance to* your kingdom. *There* we hope to enjoy for ever the *fullness* of your glory through Christ our Lord, *through* whom *you bestow on the world* all *that is* good.

114. Per ipsum, et cum ipso, et in ipso, est tibi Deo Patri omnipotenti, in unitate Spiritus Sancti, omnis honor et gloria per omnia saecula saeculorum.

Through him, with him, in him, in the unity of the Holy Spirit, all glory and honour is *yours*, almighty Father, for ever and ever.

Through him, *and* with him, *and* in him, *O God*, almighty Father, in the unity of the Holy Spirit, all glory and honour is yours, for ever and ever.

115. Memento famuli tui [famulae tuae] N., quem [quam] [hodie] ad te ex hoc mundo vocasti. Concede, ut, qui [quae] complantatus [complantata] fuit similitudini mortis Filii tui, simul fiat et resurrectionis ipsius, quando mortuos suscitabit in carne de terra et corpus humilitatis nostrae configurabit corpori claritatis suae. Sed et fratres nostros defunctos, et omnes qui, tibi placentes, ex hoc saeculo transierunt, in regnum tuum benignus admitte, ubi fore speramus, ut simul gloria tua perenniter satiemur, quando omnem lacrimam absterges ab oculis nostris, quia te, sicuti es, Deum nostrum videntes, tibi similes erimus cuncta per saecula, et te sine fine laudabimus, per Christum Dominum nostrum, per quem mundo bona cuncta largiris.

Remember N. *In baptism* he (she) *died with Christ,* may he (she) also *share* his resurrection, when *Christ* will raise *our mortal bodies* and *make them like* his own *in glory. Welcome* into your kingdom our departed brothers and sisters, and all who *have left* this world *in your friendship.* There we hope to *share in* your glory when every tear *will be wiped* away. *On that day we shall see* you, our God, as you are. We shall *become* like you and praise you *for ever* through Christ our Lord, *from* whom all good *things* come.

Remember *your servant* N. *whom you have called [today] from this world to yourself. Grant that* he [she] *who was united with your Son in a death like his,* may also *be one with him in* his Resurrection, when *from the earth he* will raise *up in the flesh those who have died,* and *transform our lowly body after the pattern* of his own *glorious body.* To our departed brothers and sisters, too, and *to* all who *were pleasing to you at their passing from* this *life, give kind admittance to* your kingdom. There we hope to *enjoy for ever the fullness* of your glory, when *you will wipe* away every tear *from our eyes. For seeing* you, our God, as you are, we shall *be* like you *for all the ages* and praise you *without end,* through Christ our Lord, through whom *you bestow on the world* all *that is good.*

C.4 Eucharistic Prayer 4

116. V. Dominus vobiscum.
R. Et cum spiritu tuo.
V. Sursum corda.
R. Habemus ad Dominum.
V. Gratias agamus Domino Deo nostro.
R. Dignum et iustum est.
Vere dignum est tibi gratias agere, vere iustum est te glorificare, Pater sancte, quia unus es Deus vivus et verus, qui es ante saecula et permanes in aeternum, inaccessibilem lucem inhabitans; sed et qui unus bonus atque fons vitae cuncta fecisti, ut creaturas tuas benedictionibus adimpleres multasque laetificares tui luminis claritate. Et ideo coram te innumerae astant turbae angelorum, qui die ac nocte serviunt tibi et, vultus tui gloriam contemplantes, te incessanter glorificant. Cum quibus et nos et, per nostram vocem, omnis quae sub caelo est creatura nomen tuum in exsultatione confitemur, canentes:
Sanctus, Sanctus, Sanctus Dominus Deus Sabaoth. Pleni sunt caeli et terra gloria tua. Hosanna in excelsis. Benedictus qui venit in nomine Domini. Hosanna in excelsis.

Priest: The Lord be with you.
People: And *also* with *you.*
Priest: Lift up your hearts.
People: We lift them up to the Lord.
Priest: Let us give thanks to the Lord our God.
People: It is right to *give him thanks and praise.*

Father *in heaven*, it is right *that we should* give you thanks *and* glory:
you are the one God, living and
true. *Through* all eternity *you live* in
unapproachable light. Source of life *and goodness*, you *have created* all *things*,
to fill your creatures with *every blessing*
and *lead all men to the joyful vision* of
your light. Countless hosts of *angels stand before you to do your will; they look* upon your *splendour and praise*
you, night and day. *United* with them,
and in the name of every creature under
heaven, we too *praise your glory* as we
say:

Priest: The Lord be with you.
People: And with *your spirit.*
Priest: Lift up your hearts.
People: We lift them up to the Lord.
Priest: Let us give thanks to the Lord our God.
People: It is right *and just.*

It is *truly* right *to* give you thanks, *truly just to give you* glory, Father *most holy, for you* are the one God living and true, *existing before all ages and abiding for* all eternity, *dwelling* in unapproachable light; *yet* you, *who alone are good, the* source of life, *have made* all *that is,* so *that you might* fill your creatures with *blessings* and *bring joy to many of them by the glory* of your light. *And so, in your presence are* countless hosts of Angels, *who serve* you day and night *and, gazing* upon *the glory of* your *face,* glorify you *without ceasing*. With them we, *too, confess* your name *in exultation, giving voice to* every creature under heaven as we *acclaim:*

Holy, *holy, holy* Lord, God of *power and might*. Heaven and earth are full of your glory. Hosanna in the highest. Blessed is he who comes in the name of the Lord. Hosanna in the highest.

Holy, *Holy, Holy* Lord God of *hosts*. Heaven and earth are full of your glory. Hosanna in the highest. Blessed is he who comes in the name of the Lord. Hosanna in the highest.

---

117. Confitemur tibi, Pater sancte, quia magnus es et omnia opera tua in sapientia et caritate fecisti. Hominem ad tuam imaginem condidisti, eique commisisti mundi curam universi, ut, tibi soli Creatori serviens, creaturis omnibus imperaret. Et cum amicitiam tuam, non oboediens, amisisset, non eum dereliquisti in mortis imperio. Omnibus enim misericorditer subvenisti, ut te quærentes invenirent. Sed et foedera pluries hominibus obtulisti eosque per prophetas erudisti in exspectatione salutis.

Et sic, Pater sancte, mundum dilexisti, ut, completa plenitudine temporum, Unigenitum tuum nobis mitteres Salvatorem. Qui, incarnatus de Spiritu Sancto et natus ex Maria Virgine, in nostra condicionis forma est conversatus per omnia absque peccato; salutem evangelizavit pauperibus, redemptionem captivis, maestis corde lætitiam. Ut tuam vero dispensationem impleret, in mortem tradidit semetipsum ac, resurgens a mortuis, mortem destruxit vitamque renovavit. Et, ut non amplius nobismetipsis viveremus, sed sibi qui pro nobis mortuus est atque surrexit, a te, Pater, misit Spiritum Sanctus primitias credentibus, qui, opus suum in mundo perficiens, omnem sanctificationem compleret.

Father, *we acknowledge your greatness:* all your *actions show your* wisdom and love. You formed man in your own *likeness* and *set him over* the whole world to *serve* you, *his creator, and to rule* over all creatures. *Even* when *he disobeyed you and* lost your friendship you did not abandon him to the *power* of death, *but helped* all *men* to seek *and* find you. *Again* and again you offered *a covenant to man*, and through the prophets taught *him* to *hope for* salvation.

We give you praise, Father *most holy, for you are great and you have fashioned* all your *works* in wisdom and *in* love. You formed man in your own *image* and *entrusted* the whole world to *his care, so that in serving* you alone, *the Creator, he might have dominion* over all creatures. *And* when *through disobedience he* had lost your friendship, you did not abandon him to the *domain* of death. *For you came in mercy to the aid of* all, *so that those who* seek *might* find you. *Time* and again you offered *them covenants* and through the prophets taught *them* to *look forward* to salvation.

Father, you so loved the world that in the fullness of time you sent your *only* Son to be our Saviour. *He was conceived through the power of* the Holy Spirit, and born of the Virgin Mary, *a man like us* in all things but sin. To the poor he proclaimed the good news of salvation, to prisoners, freedom, and to *those in sorrow, joy. In fulfilment of your will* he gave himself up to death; *but by* rising from the dead, he destroyed death and restored life. And that we might live no longer for ourselves but for him, he sent the Holy Spirit from you, Father, as *his* first *gift* to those who believe, to *complete* his work *on earth and bring us the fullness of grace.*

And you so loved the world, Father *most holy*, that in the fullness of time you sent your *Only Begotten* Son to be our Saviour. *Made incarnate by* the Holy Spirit and born of the Virgin Mary, *he shared our human nature* in all things but sin. To the poor he proclaimed the good news of salvation, to prisoners, freedom, and to *the sorrowful of heart*, joy. *To accomplish your plan*, he gave himself up to death, *and*, rising from the dead, he destroyed death and restored life. And that we might live no longer for ourselves but for him *who died and rose for us*, he sent the Holy Spirit from you, Father, as the first *fruits for* those who believe, *so that, bringing to perfection* his work *in the world, he might sanctify creation to the full.*

---

118. *Quæsumus igitur, Domine, ut idem Spiritus Sanctus hæc munera sanctificare dignetur, ut Corpus et Sanguis fiant Domini nostri Iesu Christi ad hoc magnum mysterium celebrandum, quod ipse nobis reliquit in foedus æternum.*

Father, may this Holy Spirit sanctify these offerings. *Let them* become the *body* and *blood* of Jesus Christ our Lord *as we celebrate the* great mystery which he left us as an *everlasting* covenant.

Therefore, O Lord, we pray: may this *same* Holy Spirit *graciously* sanctify these offerings, *that they may* become the *Body* and *Blood* of our Lord Jesus Christ *for the celebration of this* great mystery, which he *himself* left us as an *eternal* covenant.

---

119. Ipse enim, cum hora venisset ut glorificaretur a te, Pater sancte, ac dilexisset suos qui erant in mundo, in finem dilexit eos: et cenantibus illis accepit panem, benedixit ac fregit, deditque discipulis suis, dicens: ACCIPITE ET MANDUCATE EX HOC OMNES: HOC EST ENIM CORPUS MEUM, QUOD PRO VOBIS TRADETUR.

He *always* loved those who were his own in the world. When the *time came* for him to be glorified by you, *his heavenly* Father, he *showed the depth of his love*. While they were at supper, he took bead, *said the blessing*, broke *the bread*, and gave it to his disciples, saying: TAKE THIS, ALL OF YOU, AND EAT IT: THIS IS MY BODY WHICH WILL BE GIVEN UP FOR YOU.

For when *the hour had come* for him to be glorified by you, Father *most holy*, *having* loved his own who were in the world, *he loved them to the end: and* while they were at supper, he took bread, *blessed and* broke *it*, and gave it to his disciples, saying: TAKE THIS, ALL OF YOU, AND EAT *OF* IT, *FOR* THIS IS MY BODY, WHICH WILL BE GIVEN UP FOR YOU.

---

120. Simili modo, accipiens calicem, ex genimine vitis repletum, gratias egit, deditque discipulis suis, dicens: ACCIPITE ET BIBITE EX EO OMNES: HIC EST ENIM CALIX SANGUINIS MEI NOVI ET AETERNI TESTAMENTI, QUI PRO VOBIS ET PRO MULTIS EFFUNDETUR IN REMISSIONEM PECCATORUM. HOC FACITE IN MEAM COMMEMORATIONEM.

In *the same* way, *he took* the *cup*, filled with *wine*. He gave *you* thanks, and *giving* the *cup* to his disciples, *said*: TAKE THIS ALL OF YOU AND DRINK FROM IT: THIS IS THE *CUP* OF MY BLOOD, THE BLOOD OF THE NEW AND *EVERLASTING* COVENANT. *IT* WILL BE *SHED* FOR YOU AND FOR *ALL SO THAT* SINS *MAY BE FORGIVEN*. DO THIS IN MEMORY OF ME.

In *a similar way, taking* the *chalice* filled with *the fruit of the vine*, he gave thanks, and *gave* the *chalice* to his disciples, *saying*: TAKE THIS, ALL OF YOU, AND DRINK FROM IT, *FOR* THIS IS THE *CHALICE* OF MY BLOOD, THE BLOOD OF THE NEW AND *ETERNAL* COVENANT, *WHICH* WILL BE *POURED OUT* FOR YOU AND FOR *MANY FOR THE FORGIVENESS OF* SINS. DO THIS IN MEMORY OF ME.

---

121. Mysterium fidei

Mortem tuam annuntiamus, Domine, et tuam resurrectionem confitemur, donec venias.

Vel: *Quotiescumque manducamus panem hunc et calicem bibimus, mortem tuam annuntiamus, Domine, donec venias.*

Vel: *Salvator mundi, salva nos, quia per crucem et resurrectionem tuam liberasti nos.*

Priest: *Let us proclaim* the mystery of faith:

People: A – *Christ has died, Christ is risen, Christ will* come again.

or C – When we eat this *bread* and drink this *cup*, we proclaim your death, Lord Jesus, until you come *in glory.*

or D – *Lord,* by your *cross* and *resurrection*, you have set us free. *You are the* Saviour of the World.

Priest: The mystery of faith.

People: A – *We proclaim your Death, O Lord, and profess your Resurrection until you* come again.

or B – When we eat this *Bread* and drink this *Cup*, we proclaim your *Death*, O Lord, until you come *again.*

or C – *Save us*, Saviour of the world, *for* by your *Cross* and *Resurrection*, you have set us free.

---

122. Unde et nos, Domine, redemptionis nostræ memoriale nunc celebrantes, mortem Christi eiusque descensum ad inferos recolimus, eius resurrectionem et ascensionem ad tuam dexteram profitemur, et, exspectantes ipsius adventum in gloria, offerimus tibi eius Corpus et Sanguinem, sacrificium tibi acceptabile et toti mundo salutare.

Respice, Domine, in Hostiam, quam Ecclesiæ tuæ ipse parasti, et concede benignus omnibus qui ex hoc uno pane participabunt et calice, ut, in unum corpus a Sancto Spiritu congregati, in Christo hostia viva perficiantur, ad laudem gloriae tuæ.

Nunc ergo, Domine, omnium recordare, pro quibus tibi hanc oblationem offerimus: in primis famuli tui, Papæ nostri N., Episcopi nostri N., et Episcoporum ordinis universi, sed et totius cleri, et offerentium, et circumstantium, et cuncti populi tui, et omnium, qui te quaerunt corde sincero.

Memento etiam illorum, qui obierunt in pace Christi tui, et omnium defunctorum, quorum fidem tu solus cognovisti.

Nobis omnibus, filiis tuis, clemens Pater, concede, ut cælestem hereditatem consequi valeamus cum beata Virgine, Dei Genetrice, Maria, cum Apostolis et Sanctis tuis in regno tuo, ubi cum universa creatura, a corruptione peccati et mortis liberata, te glorificemus per Christum Dominum nostrum, per quem mundo bona cuncta largiris.

Father, we now celebrate *this* memorial of our redemption. We *recall* Christ's death, his descent *among* the dead, his *resurrection*, and his *ascension* to your right hand; and, *looking forward to* his coming in glory, we offer you his *body* and *blood*, the acceptable sacrifice which brings salvation to the whole world.

Lord, look upon *this sacrifice* which you have *given* to your Church; and by *your* Holy Spirit, *gather* all who *share* this one *bread* and one *cup* into the one body of *Christ*, a living sacrifice of praise.

Lord, remember *those* for whom we *offer* this sacrifice, especially N. our Pope, N., our bishop, and *bishops and* clergy *everywhere. Remember* those who *take part* in this offering, those *here present* and *all* your people, and all who seek you with a sincere heart.

Remember those who have died in the peace of Christ and all the dead whose faith *is* known *to you* alone.

Father, *in your mercy* grant *also* to us, your children, *to* enter into *our* heavenly inheritance *in the company of* the Virgin Mary, *the* Mother of God, and your *apostles* and *saints. Then*, in your kingdom, freed from the corruption of sin and death, we *shall sing your glory* with *every creature* through Christ our Lord, through whom you *give us everything* that is good.

Therefore, O Lord, as we now celebrate *the* memorial of our redemption, we *remember* Christ's death *and* his descent *to the realm* of the dead, *we proclaim* his *Resurrection* and his *Ascension* to your right hand, and, *as we await* his coming in glory, we offer you his *Body* and *Blood*, the sacrifice acceptable *to you* which brings salvation to the whole world.

Look, *O* Lord, upon *the Sacrifice* which you *yourself* have *provided for* your Church, and *grant in your loving kindness to* all who *partake of* this one *Bread* and one *Chalice that, gathered* into one body by *the* Holy Spirit, *they may truly become* a living sacrifice *in Christ to the* praise of *your glory*.

Therefore, Lord, remember *now all* for whom we *offer this sacrifice*: especially *your servant*, N. our Pope, N. our Bishop, and *the whole Order of Bishops, all the* clergy, those who *take part in* this offering, those *gathered here before you, your entire* people, and all who seek you with a sincere heart.

Remember *also* those who have died in the peace of *your* Christ and all the dead, whose faith you alone *have* known.

To *all* of us, your children, grant, *O merciful* Father, *that we may* enter into *a* heavenly inheritance *with the Blessed* Virgin Mary, Mother of God, and *with* your *Apostles* and *Saints* in your kingdom. *There*, with *the whole of* creation, freed from the corruption of sin and death, *may* we *glorify you* through Christ our Lord, through whom you *bestow on the world all* that is good.

123. Per ipsum, et cum ipso, et in ipso, est tibi Deo Patri omnipotenti, in unitate Spiritus Sancti, omnis honor et gloria per omnia saecula saeculorum.

Through him, with him, in him, in the unity of the Holy Spirit, all glory and honour is *yours*, almighty Father, for ever and ever.

Through him, *and* with him, *and* in him, *O God*, almighty Father, in the unity of the Holy Spirit, all glory and honour is yours, for ever and ever.

D. Communion and Concluding Rites

124. Praeceptis salutaribus moniti, et divina institutione formati, audemus dicere:

Let us pray with confidence to the Father in the words our Saviour gave us.

At the Saviour's command and formed by divine teaching, we dare to say:

125. Libera nos, quaesumus, Domine, ab omnibus malis, da propitius pacem in diebus nostris, ut, ope misericordiae tuae adiuti, et a peccato simus semper liberi et ab omni perturbatione securi: exspectantes beatam spem et adventum Salvatoris nostri Iesu Christi.

Deliver us, Lord, from every evil, and grant *us* peace in our day. *In your* mercy *keep us* free from sin and *protect us* from all *anxiety* as we *wait in joyful* hope *for* the coming of our Saviour, Jesus Christ.

Deliver us, Lord, *we pray,* from every evil, *graciously* grant peace in our *days, that, by the help of* your mercy, *we may be always* free from sin and *safe* from all *distress,* as we *await the blessed* hope *and the* coming of our Saviour, Jesus Christ.

126. Domine Iesu Christe, qui dixisti Apostolis tuis: Pacem relinquo vobis, pacem meam do vobis: ne respicias peccata nostra, sed fidem Ecclesiae tuae; eamque secundum voluntatem tuam pacificare et coadunare digneris. Qui vivis et regnas in saecula saeculorum.

Lord Jesus Christ, *you* said to your *apostles*: I leave you peace, my peace I give you. Look not on our sins, but on the faith of your Church, and grant *us the* peace and unity of *your kingdom, where you* live for ever and ever.

Lord Jesus Christ, *who* said to your *Apostles*: Peace I leave you, my peace I give you, look not on our sins, but on the faith of your Church, and *graciously* grant *her* peace and unity in *accordance with your will. Who* live and reign for ever and ever.

127. Pax Domini sit semper vobiscum
Et cum spiritu tuo.

Priest: The peace of the Lord be with you always.
People: And *also* with *you.*

Priest: The peace of the Lord be with you always.
People: And with *your spirit.*

---

131. Domine Iesu Christe, Fili Dei vivi, qui ex voluntate Patris, cooperante Spiritu Sancto, per mortem tuam mundum vivificasti: libera me per hoc sacrosanctum Corpus et Sanguinem tuum ab omnibus iniquitatibus meis et universis malis: et fac me tuis semper inhaerere mandatis, et a te numquam separari permittas. Vel: Perceptio Corporis et Sanguinis tui, Domine Iesu Christe, non mihi proveniat in iudicium et condemnationem: sed pro tua pietate prosit mihi ad tutamentum mentis et corporis, et ad medelam percipiendam.

Lord Jesus Christ, Son of the living God, by the will of the Father and the work of the Holy Spirit your death *brought* life to the world. By your holy *body* and *blood* free me from all my sins, and from every evil. Keep me faithful to your *teaching,* and never let me be parted from you.

Or: Lord Jesus Christ, *with faith in your love and mercy I eat* your *body* and *drink your blood. Let it* not bring me condemnation, but *health* in mind and body.

Lord Jesus Christ, Son of the living God, *who,* by the will of the Father and the work of the Holy Spirit, *through* your *Death gave* life to the world, free me by *this,* your *most* holy *Body* and *Blood,* from all my sins and from every evil; keep me *always* faithful to your *commandments,* and never let me be parted from you.

Or: May the receiving of your *Body* and *Blood,* Lord Jesus Christ, not bring me to *judgment and* condemnation, but *through your loving mercy be for me protection* in mind and body *and a healing remedy.*

---

132. Ecce Agnus Dei, ecce qui tollit peccata mundi. Beati qui ad cenam Agni vocati sunt.
Domine, non sum dignus ut intres sub tectum meum: sed tantum dic verbo, et sanabitur anima mea.

This is the Lamb of God who takes away the sins of the world. *Happy* are those *who are* called to *his* supper.

Lord, I am not worthy to *receive* you, but only say the word, and *I* shall be healed.

Behold the Lamb of God, *behold him* who takes away the sins of the world. *Blessed* are those called to *the* supper *of the Lamb.*

Lord, I am not worthy *that you should enter under my roof,* but only say the word and *my soul* shall be healed.

---

133. Corpus Christi custodiat me in vitam aeternam. Sanguis Christi custodiat me in vitam aeternam.

May the *body* of Christ *bring me* to *everlasting* life. May the *blood* of Christ *bring me to everlasting* life.

May the *Body* of Christ *keep me safe for eternal* life. May the *Blood* of Christ *keep me safe for eternal* life.

---

137. Quod ore sumpsimus, Domine, pura mente capiamus, et de munere temporali fiat nobis remedium sempiternum.

Lord, *may I receive these gifts* in purity of heart. *May they bring me* healing *and strength, now and* for ever.

What has passed our lips as food, O Lord, *may we possess* in purity of heart, *that what has been given to us in time may be* our healing for *eternity.*

---

141. Dominus vobiscum
Et cum spiritu tuo.

Priest: The Lord be with you.
People: And *also* with *you.*

Priest: The Lord be with you.
People: And *with your spirit.*

---

144. Ite, missa est.
[Ite ad Evangelium Domini nuntiandum.
Ite in pace, glorificando vita vestra Dominum.
Ite in pace.]

The Mass is ended, go *in peace.*

Go *forth*, the Mass is ended.
Go and announce the Gospel of the Lord.
Go in peace, *glorifying the Lord by your life.*
Go in peace.

E. A Selection of Extracts from the Prefaces

I. Preface I of Lent: *Quia fidélibus tuis dignánter concédis quotánnis paschália sacraménta in gáudio purificátis méntibus exspectáre: ut, pietátis offícia et ópera caritátis propénsius exsequéntes, frequentatióne mysteriórum, quibus renáti sunt, ad grátiae filiórum plenitúdinem perducántur.*

Each year you *give us this joyful season when we prepare to celebrate* the paschal *mystery* with *mind and heart renewed. You give us a spirit of loving reverence for you, our Father, and of willing service to our neighbour. As we recall the great events that gave us new life in Christ, you bring the image of your Son to perfection within us.*

For by your gracious gift each year *your faithful await the sacred* paschal *feasts with the joy of minds made pure, so that, more eagerly intent on prayer and on the works of charity, and participating in the mysteries by which they have been reborn, they may be led to the fullness of grace that you bestow on your sons and daughters.*

II. Preface II of Lent: *Qui fíliis tuis ad reparándam méntium puritátem, tempus praecípuum salúbriter statuísti, quo, mente ab inordinátis afféctibus expedíta, sic incúmberent transitúris ut rebus pótius perpétuis inhaerérent.*

This great season of grace is your gift to your family to renew us in spirit. You give us strength to purify our hearts, to control our desires, and so to serve you in freedom. You teach us how to live in this passing world with our heart set on the world that will never end.

For you have given your children a sacred time for the renewing and purifying of their hearts, that, freed from disordered affections, they may so deal with the things of this passing world as to hold rather to the things that eternally endure.

III. Preface IV of Lent: *Qui corporáli ieiúnio vítia cómprimis, mentem élevas, virtútem largíris et praemia: per Christum Dóminum nostrum.*

Through *our observance of Lent you correct* our faults *and* raise our minds *to you, you* help us grow in holiness, and offer us the reward of everlasting life through *Jesus* Christ our Lord.

For through *bodily fasting* you *restrain* our faults, raise *up* our minds, *and bestow both virtue and its rewards,* through Christ our Lord.

IV. Preface VI of Sundays of Ordinary Time: *In quo vívimus, movémur et sumus, atque in hoc córpore constitúti non solum pietátis tuae cotidiános experímur efféctus, sed aeternitátis étiam pígnora iam tenémus.*

In you we live and move and have our being. *Each day you show us a Father's love; your Holy Spirit, dwelling within us, gives us on earth the hope of unending joy.*

For in you we live and move and have our being, *and while in this body we not only experience the daily effects of your care, but even now possess the pledge of life eternal.*

V. Preface I for the Dead: *In quo nobis spes beátae resurrectiónis effúlsit, ut, quos contrístat certa moriéndi condício, eósdem consolétur futúrae immortalitátis promíssio. Tuis enim fidélibus, Dómine, vita mutátur, non tóllitur, et, dissolúta terréstris huius incolátus domo, aetérna in caelis habitátio comparátur.*

In him, *who rose from the dead, our* hope of resurrection dawned. *The sadness of death gives way to the bright* promise of immortality. Lord, for your faithful *people* life is changed, not ended. When the *body of our* earthly dwelling *lies in death we gain* an *everlasting* dwelling *place* in heaven.

In him *the* hope of *blessed* resurrection *has* dawned, *that those saddened by the certainty of dying might be consoled by* the promise of immortality *to come. Indeed* for your faithful, Lord, life is changed not ended, *and,* when *this* earthly dwelling *turns to dust,* an *eternal* dwelling *is made ready for them* in heaven.

F. A Selection from the Collects, Prayers over the Offerings and Prayers after Communion

VI. Collect, Fourth Sunday of Advent: *Gratiam tuam, quaesumus, Domine, mentibus nostris infunde, ut qui, Angelo nuntiante, Christi Filii tui incarnationem cognovimus, per passionem eius et crucem ad resurrectionis gloriam perducamur. Per Dóminum.*

Lord, *fill* our hearts *with* your love, *and as you revealed to us* by an *angel the coming of* your Son as *man, so lead us through his suffering and death* to the glory of his resurrection, *for he* lives and reigns with you *and* the Holy Spirit, one God, for ever and ever.

Pour forth, we beseech you, O Lord, your *grace* into our hearts, *that we, to whom the Incarnation of Christ* your Son was made known by the *message of* an *Angel, may by his Passion and Cross be brought* to the glory of his Resurrection. Who lives and reigns with you *in the unity of* the Holy Spirit, one God, for ever and ever.

VII. Prayer over the Offerings, The Nativity of the Lord, At the Mass of Dawn: *Múnera nostra, quaesumus, Dómine, nativitátis hodiérnae mystériis apta provéniant, ut sicut homo génitus idem praefúlsit et Deus, sic nobis haec terréna substántia cónferat quod divínum est. Per Christum.*

Father, may *we follow the example of* your Son who became man and *lived among us.* May *we receive the gift of* divine *life through* these *offerings here on earth. We ask this in the name of* Jesus the Lord.

May *our offerings be worthy, we pray, O* Lord, of the mysteries of the Nativity this day, that, just as Christ was born a man and *also shone forth as God, so* these earthly gifts may *confer on us what is* divine. *Through Christ our* Lord.

VIII. Alternative Collect, The Baptism of the Lord: *Deus, cuius Unigénitus in substántia nostrae carnis appáruit, praesta, quaesumus, ut, per eum, quem símilem nobis foris agnóvimus, intus reformári mereámur. Qui tecum.*

Father, your only Son revealed *himself to us by becoming man. May* we *who share his humanity come to share his divinity, for he* lives and reigns with you and the Holy Spirit, one God, for ever and ever.

O God, whose Only Begotten Son has appeared in our very flesh, grant, we pray, that we may be inwardly transformed through him whom we recognise as outwardly like ourselves. Who lives and reigns with you in the unity of the Holy Spirit, one God, for ever and ever.

IX. Prayer over the Offerings, Second Sunday of Lent: *Haec hostia, Domine, quaesumus, emundet nostra delicta, et ad celebranda festa paschalia fidelium tuorum corpora mentesque sanctificet. Per Christum.*

Lord, *make us holy.* May this Eucharist *take away* our *sins that we may be prepared to celebrate the Resurrection. We ask this in the name of Jesus the* Lord.

May this *sacrifice, O* Lord, *we pray, cleanse us of* our *faults and sanctify your faithful in body and mind for the celebration of the paschal festivities. Through Christ our* Lord.

X. Prayer after Communion, Fourth Sunday of Lent: *Deus, qui illuminas omnem hominem venientem in hanc mundum, illumina, quaesumus, corda nostra gratiae tuae splendore, ut digna ac placita maiestati tuae cogitare semper, et te sincere diligere valeamus. Per Christum.*

Father, you enlighten *all* who *come* into *the* world. *Fill our hearts with the light of your Gospel, that our thoughts may please you, and our* love *be sincere. Grant this* through Christ our Lord.

O God, who enlighten *everyone* who comes into *this* world, illuminate our hearts, *we pray,* with *the splendour of your grace, that we may always ponder what is worthy and pleasing to your majesty and love you in all sincerity.* Through Christ our Lord.

XI. Collect, Passion (Palm) Sunday: *Omnipotens sempiterne Deus, qui humano generi ad imitandum humilitatis exemplum, Salvatorem nostrum carnem sumere, et crucem subire fecisti: concede propitius; ut et patientiae ipsius habere documenta, et resurrectionis consortia mereamur. Per eumdem Dominum.*

Almighty, ever-living God, *you have given* the human race *Jesus Christ* our Saviour as *a model* of humility. *He fulfilled your will by becoming man* and *giving his life* on the cross. *Help us to bear witness to you by following* his *example* of suffering and *make us worthy* to share in his resurrection. *We ask this through our Lord Jesus Christ, your Son,* who lives and reigns with you in the unity of the Holy Spirit, one God,

for ever and ever.
Almighty ever-living God, *who* as an *example* of humility *for* the human race to *follow* caused our Saviour to *take* flesh and *submit* to the Cross, *graciously grant that we may heed* his *lesson* of *patient* suffering and *so merit* a share in his Resurrection. Who lives and reigns with you in the unity of the Holy Spirit, one God, for ever and ever.

XII. Prayer after Communion, Second Sunday of Easter: *Concede, quaesumus, omnipotens Deus, ut paschalis perceptio sacramenti continua in nostris mentibus perseveret. Per Christum.*

Almighty God, *may the Easter sacraments we have received live forever* in our minds and hearts. *We ask this* through Christ our Lord.

Grant, we pray, almighty God, *that our reception of this paschal Sacrament may have a continuing effect* in our minds and hearts. Through Christ our Lord.

XIII. Collect, Third Sunday of Easter: *Semper exsultet populus tuus, Deus, renovata animae iuventute, ut, qui nunc laetatur in adoptionis se gloriam restitutum, resurrectionis diem spe certae gratulationis exspectet. Per Dóminum.*

God *our Father*, may we look forward *with* hope *to our* resurrection, for *you have made us your sons and daughters, and restored the joy of our youth. We ask this* through our Lord Jesus Christ, your Son, who lives and reigns with you *and* the Holy Spirit, one God, for ever and ever.

May your people exult for ever, O God, in renewed youthfulness of spirit, so that, rejoicing now in the restored glory of our adoption, we may look forward *in confident* hope *to the rejoicing of the day of* resurrection. Through our Lord Jesus Christ, your Son, who lives and reigns with you *in the unity of* the Holy Spirit, one God, for ever and ever.

XIV. Prayer after Communion, Third Sunday of Easter: *Populum tuum, quaesumus, Domine, intuere benignus, ut, quem aeternis dignatus es renovare mysteriis, ad incorruptibilem glorificandae carnis resurrectionem penvenire concede. Per Christum.*

Lord, look on your people with kindness and by *these Easter* mysteries *bring us to* the glory of the *Resurrection. We ask this in the name of Jesus the* Lord.

Look with kindness upon your people, O Lord, and *grant, we pray, that those you were pleased to renew by eternal* mysteries *may attain in their flesh* the *incorruptible* glory of the r*esurrection. Through Christ our* Lord.

XV. Alternative Collect, Pentecost Sunday, At the Vigil Mass: *Praesta, quaesumus, omnípotens Deus, ut claritátis tuae super nos splendor effúlgeat, et lux tuae lucis corda eórum, qui per tuam grátiam sunt renáti, Sancti Spíritus illustratióne confírmet. Per Dóminum.*

God *our Father, you have given us new birth. Strengthen us with your* Holy Spirit *and fill us with* your light. *Grant this* through our Lord Jesus Christ, your Son, who lives and reigns with you *and* the Holy Spirit, one God for ever and ever.

Grant, we pray, almighty God, *that the splendour of your glory may shine forth upon* us *and that, by the bright rays of the* Holy Spirit, *the light of your* light *may confirm the hearts of those born again by your grace.* Through our Lord Jesus Christ, your Son, who lives and reigns with you *in the unity* of the Holy spirit, one God, for ever and ever.

XVI. Prayer after Communion, Second Sunday in Ordinary Time: *Spiritum nobis, Domine, tuae caritatis infunde, ut, quos uno caelesti pane satiasti, una facias pietate concordes. Per Christum.*

Lord, you have nourished *us with bread from heaven. Fill* us *with your* Spirit, and make *us* one in *peace and love. We ask this* through Christ our Lord.

Pour on us, O Lord, the Spirit *of your* love, and *in your kindness* make *those* you have nourished *by this one heavenly Bread* one in *mind and heart.* Through Christ our Lord.

XVII. Collect, Fourth Sunday: *Concede nobis, Domine Deus noster, ut tota mente veneremur, et omnes homines rationabili diligamus affectu. Per Dóminum.*

Lord our God, *help us to love* you with all our *hearts* and *to* love *all men as you love them. Grant this* through our Lord Jesus Christ, your Son, who lives and reigns with you *and* the Holy Spirit, one God, for ever and ever.

Grant us, Lord our God, *that we may honour* you *with all our mind*, and love *everyone in truth of heart.* Through our Lord Jesus Christ, your Son, who lives and reigns with you *in the unity* of the Holy Spirit, one God, for ever and ever.

XVIII. Prayer over the Offerings, Eleventh Sunday: *Deus, qui humani generis utramque substantiam praesentium munerum et alimento vegetas et renovas sacramento, tribue, quaesumus, ut eorum et corporibus nostris subsidium non desit et mentibus. Per Christum.*

Lord God, in *this bread and wine you give us* food *for body and spirit. May the Eucharist renew our strength and bring us health of mind and body. We ask this* through Christ our Lord.

O God, *who in* the offerings presented here provide for the twofold needs of human nature, nourishing *us with* food and renewing us with your Sacrament, grant, we pray, that the sustenance they provide may not fail us in body or in spirit. Through Christ our Lord.

XIX. Prayer over the Offerings, Twenty-Third Sunday: *Deus, auctor sincerae devotionis et pacis, da, quaesumus, ut et maiestatem tuam convenienter hoc munere veneremur, et sacri participatione mysterii fideliter sensibus uniamur. Per Christum.*

God *of peace and love, may our* offering *bring you true worship and make us one with you. We ask this in the name of* Christ our Lord.

O God, *who give us the gift of true prayer and of peace, graciously grant that, through this* offering, *we may do fitting homage to your divine majesty and, by partaking of the sacred mystery, we may be faithfully united in mind and heart. Through* Christ our Lord.

XX. Prayer after Communion, Twenty-Fourth Sunday: *Mentes nostras et corpora possideat, quaesumus, Domine, doni caelestis operatio, ut non noster sensus in nobis, sed eius praeveniat semper effectus. Per Christum.*

Lord, *may the Eucharist you have given us influence our thoughts and actions. May your Spirit guide and direct us in your way. We ask this in the name of* Christ our Lord.

May the working of this heavenly gift, O Lord, *we pray, take possession of our minds and bodies, so that its effects, and not our own desires, may always prevail in us. Through* Christ our Lord.

XXI. Prayer after Communion, Twenty-Sixth Sunday: *Sit nobis, Domine, reparatio mentis et corporis caeleste mysterium, ut simus eius in gloria coheredes, cui, mortem ipsius annuntiando, compatimur. Qui vivit et regnat in saecula saeculorum, Amen.*

Lord, may this *Eucharist in which we proclaim the death of* Christ *bring us salvation and make us one with him* in glory, *for he is Lord* for ever and ever, Amen.

May this *heavenly mystery, O* Lord, *restore us in mind and body, that we may be coheirs* in glory *with* Christ, *to whose suffering we are united whenever we proclaim his Death. Who lives and reigns* for ever and ever. Amen.

XXII. Prayer after Communion, The Most Holy Trinity: *Proficiat nobis ad salutem corporis et animae, Domine Deus noster, huius sacramenti susceptio, et sempiternae sanctae Trinitatis eiusdemque individuae Unitatis confessio.*

Lord God, *we worship you, a* Trinity *of Persons, one eternal God.* May *our faith and the sacrament we receive* bring us health of *mind* and body.

May *receiving this Sacrament, O* Lord our God, bring us health of body and soul, *as we confess your eternal holy* Trinity *and undivided Unity.*

XXIII. Collect, The Most Holy Body and Blood of Christ: *Deus, qui nobis sub sacraménto mirábili passiónis tuae memóriam reliquísti, tríbue, quaesumus, ita nos Córporis et Sánguinis tui sacra mystéria venerári, ut redemptiónis tuae fructum in nobis iúgiter sentiámus. Qui vivis et regnas cum Deo Patre in unitáte Spíritus Sancti, Deus, per ómnia saecula saeculórum.*

Lord Jesus Christ, *you gave* us *the eucharist* as the memorial of your *suffering and death. May our worship of this sacrament* of your *body* and *blood help* us to experience *the salvation you won for us and the peace of the kingdom where you* live with the Father and the Holy Spirit, one God for ever and ever.

O God, who in this wonderful Sacrament have *left* us a memorial of your *Passion, grant us, we pray, so to revere the sacred mysteries* of your Body and Blood *that we may always* experience *in ourselves the fruits of your redemption. Who* live *and reign* with God the Father *in the unity of* the Holy Spirit, one God, for ever and ever.

XXIV. Prayer after Communion, The Most Holy Body and Blood of Christ:

Fac nos, quaesumus, Dómine, divinitátis tuae sempitérna fruitióne repléri, quam pretiósi Córporis et Sánguinis tui temporális percéptio praefigúrat. Qui vivis et regnas in saecula saeculórum.

Lord *Jesus Christ, you give us* your *body* and *blood in the eucharist as a sign that even now we* share your life. *May we come to possess it completely in the kingdom where you* live for ever and ever.

Grant, O Lord, *we pray, that we may delight for all eternity in that* share *in* your *divine* life, *which is foreshadowed in this present age by our reception of* your *precious Body* and *Blood. Who* live *and reign* for ever and ever.

Notes

Introduction

1. Charlton T. Lewis, *A Latin Dictionary* (Oxford: Clarendon Press, 1987), 1892.

2. See Samuel Johnson, *A Dictionary of the English Language*, 2 vols. (London, 1755).

3. A. M. Roguet and Lancelot Sheppard, 'Translation of the Roman Canon', in *The New Liturgy*, ed. Lancelot Sheppard (London: Darton, Longman & Todd, 1970), 161–73 at 161.

4. Sr Teresia de Spiritu Sancto Posselt OCD, *Edith Stein*, trans. Cecily Hastings and Donald Nicholl (London; New York: Sheed and Ward, 1952), 14.

5. Edith Stein, *Übersetzungen V. Alexandre Koyré*, Descartes und die Scholastik. Einführung, Bearbeitung und Anmerkungen von H.-B. Gerl-Falkovitz, Gesamtausgabe, 25 (Freiburg: Herder, 2002), 1.

6. Edith Stein, *Selbstbildnis in Briefen III: Briefe an Roman Ingarden*, 2 ed., Edith Stein Gesamtausgabe, 4 (Freiburg: Herder, 2004), n. 83.

7. Edith Stein, *Übersetzungen II. John Henry Newman, Briefe und Texte zur ersten Lebenshälfte (1801–1846). Einführung, Bearbeitung und Anmerkungen von H.-B. Gerl-Falkovitz*, Gesamtausgabe, 22 (Freiburg: Herder, 2002), 1; Edith Stein, *Übersetzungen I. John Henry Newman, Die Idee der Universität. Einführung, Bearbeitung und Anmerkungen von H.-B. Gerl-Falkovitz*, Gesamtausgabe, 21 (Freiburg: Herder, 2004), 1; Edith Stein, *Übersetzungen III-IV. Thomas von Aquin, Über die Wahrheit 1-2*, Gesamtausgabe, 23-24 (Freiburg: Herder, 2008), 1:1, 2:1, 928; Edith Stein, *Übersetzungen VI. Thomas von Aquin, Über das Seiende und das Wesen*, Gesamtausgabe, 26 (Freiburg: Herder, 2010), 1.

8. See Sarah R. Borden, *Edith Stein*, Outstanding Christian Thinkers series (London; New York: Continuum, 2003), 8.

9. Roguet and Sheppard, 162.

10. See Ronald Knox, *On Englishing the Bible* (London: Burns and Oates, 1949), 4.

11. Roguet and Sheppard, 163–4.

12. A Missal is 'a book that contains all the prayers and instructions for the celebration of the Mass'; see the leaflet: Irish Catholic Bishops' Conference, ed., *Introducing the New Missal* (Dublin: Veritas, 2011).

13. See Pope Paul VI, 'Allocutio Summi Pontificis ad participantes "Conventum de popularibus interpretationibus textuum liturgicorum" (Address to translators of liturgical texts into vernacular languages)', *Notitiae 1* (1965), 377–81 at 379.

14. The terms 'dynamic equivalence' and 'functional equivalence' are generally attributed to the essay 'Principles of Correspondence' by Eugene A. Nida (1914–2011); see Eugene Nida, 'Principles of Correspondence', in *The Translation Studies Reader*, ed. Lawrence Venuti (New York: Routledge, 2004), 153–67. Nida played a significant role in the joint effort by the Vatican and the United Bible Societies to produce inter-denominational translations of the Bible in the years following Vatican II.

15. Roguet and Sheppard, 161, 165–6.

16. Keith Pecklers, *The Genius of the Roman Rite: On the Reception and Implementation of the New Missal* (London: Burns & Oates, 2009), 36.

17. Klaus Gamber, *The Modern Rite: Collected Essays on the Reform of the Liturgy* (Farnborough: St Michael's Abbey Press, 2002), 7.

18. Pecklers, *The Genius of the Roman Rite*, 37.

19. See Robert F. Taft, 'Translating Liturgically', *Jogos: A Journal of Eastern Christian Studies* 39/2-4 (1988), 155–90 at 157–9.

20. See Liturgical Books, ed., *The Roman Missal* (Dublin: Liturgical Books, 1974).

21. An earlier revised edition of the Paul IV Latin Missal of 1970 was published in 1975 (no English translation of this edition was issued) and an amended reprint of the 2002 version was issued in 2008.

22. Bishop John McAreavey of Dromore has been the Irish bishop-member of ICEL since 2002.

23. See Congregation for Divine Worship and the Discipline of the Sacraments, ed., *Ratio translationis for the English Language* (Vatican City: Congregation for Divine Worship and the Discipline of the Sacraments, 2007). For an online version of this document, see the following website consulted on 12 November 2011: https://wikispooks.com/wiki/File:Ratio_translationis_-_for_the_English_Language_II.pdf

24. See Jorge Teixeira da Cunha, 'A Eucaristia e a Missao da Igreja: Uma reflexao subre a *Sacramentum caritatis* de Bento XVI', *Didaskalia* 38/2 (2008), no. 2, 311–26.

25. See Benedict XVI, *Sacramentum Caritatis*, n. 51 on the following website, accessed on 13 February 2012: http://vatican.va/holy_father/benedict_xvi/apost_exhortations/documents/hf_ben-xvi_exh_20070222_sacramentum-caritatis_en.html

26. See Maurizio Barba, 'Le formule alternative per il congedo della messa', *Rivista Liturgica* 96 (2009), 147–59; Pecklers, The Genius of the Roman Rite, 109.

27. See Libreria Editrice Vaticana, *The Roman Missal* (Dublin: Veritas, 2011). For a timeline summarising the developments between 1963 and 2010 leading up to the promulgation of the new translation, see Edward Foley et al., eds., *A Commentary on the Order of Mass of the Roman Missal* (Collegeville, Minnesota: Liturgical Press, 2011), xxiii–xxviii. For a more detailed outline and analysis of the process, see Keith Pecklers and Gilbert Ostdiek, 'The History of Vernaculars and Role of Translation', in *A Commentary on the Order of Mass of the Roman Missal*, ed. Foley et al., 35–72 at 51–72.

28. See *Introducing the New Missal*.

29. Pecklers, *The Genius of the Roman Rite*, 47.

30. Anscar J. Chupungco, 'The Translation of Liturgical Texts', in *Handbook for Liturgical Studies: Introduction to the Liturgy*, ed. Anscar J. Chupungco (Collegeville, Minnesota: Liturgical Press, 1997), 381–97 at 388. See also Anscar J. Chupungco, 'Excursus on Translating OM2008', in *A Commentary on the Order of Mass of the Roman Missal*, ed. Foley et al., 133–41 at 133.

31. See Chupungco, 'Excursus on Translating OM2008', at 133–4.

Chapter I. *Comme le prévoit* and the 1973 Translation

1. Literally 'place of cooling'.

2. See Raymond Moloney, *The Eucharistic Prayers in Worship, Preaching and Study* (Dublin: Dominican Publications, 1985), 49.

3. See Anscar J. Chupungco, 'The ICEL2010 Translation', in *A Commentary on the Order of Mass of the Roman Missal*, ed. Foley et al. (Collegeville, Minnesota: Liturgical Press, 2011), 137–41, 181–5, 219–20 at 138.

4. See the Appendix n. 4.

5. In the Appendix, see Baruch 3:2 (*miserere nostri, quia peccavimus ante te*) and the omission of *quia* in 'we have sinned against you' in n. 5. See also Hebrews 1:3 (*sedet ad dexteram*) and the omission of *Qui sedes* in 'You plead for us at the right hand of the Father' in n. 6.

6. In the Appendix, see *vobis* in n. 2, *Per* in n. 16, *et* [*Incarnatus*] and *et* [*resurrexit*] in n. 18, *et* [*in Iesum Christum*] and *Dei* in n. 19, *accepimus, quem tibi* and *fructum* in n. 23 and *quod tibi* and *et* [*adventum*] in n. 25.

7. In the Appendix, see *Ideo* in n. 4, *corde* in n. 6, *magnam* in n. 8, *et competenter* and *valeam* in n. 14, *ante omnia saecula* in n. 18, *a mortuis, omnipotentis* and *inde* in n. 19, *quia* in n. 23, *quia* in n. 25, *spiritu* and *in conspectu tuo hodie* in n. 26, *sanctae* in n. 29, *et iustum* in n. 83, 99, 107 and 116, *quaesumus, propitius, semper* and *beatam* in n. 125, *digneris* and *secundum voluntatem tuam* in n. 126, *hoc sacrosanctum* and *semper* in n. 131, *Beati* and *Agni* in n. 132 and *temporali* in n. 137.

8. In the Appendix, see the repeat of *qui tollis peccata mundi* in n. 8, *et divina institutione formati* in n. 124, and *pro tua pietate prosit mihi ad tutamentum* in n. 131.

9. See the Appendix n. 5.

10. In the Appendix, see 'by the power of the Holy Spirit (*de Spiritu Sancto*)' in n. 18, 'and born of the Virgin Mary (*natus ex Maria Virgine*)' and 'he suffered under (*passus sub*)' in n. 19, 'this bread (*panem*)' in n. 23, 'It is right to give him thanks and praise (*Dignum et iustum est*)' in n. 83, 99, 107 and 116, 'Let us proclaim the mystery of faith (*Mysterium fidei*)' and 'Lord ... Saviour (*Salvator*)' in n. 91, 104, 112 and 121, 'Let us pray with confidence to the Father (*audemus dicere*)' in n. 124, 'Lord, Jesus Christ with faith in your love and mercy (*Domine Iesu Christe*)' in n. 131, 'healing and strength (*remedium*)' in n. 137 and 'The Mass is ended, go in peace (*Ite, missa est*)' in n. 144.

11. 5.3 or 16 in 302 Latin words.

12. 7.88 or 19 in 241 Latin words.

13. 7.58 or 15 in 198 Latin words.

14. 7.38 or 9 in 122 Latin words.

15. See the Appendix n. 2, 127 and 141.

16. See, for example, the 1662 edition at the following website, accessed on 10 October 2010: http://vulcanhammer.org/anglican/bcp-1662.pdf

17. See, for example, the French *Et avec votre esprit,* the German *Und mit deinem Geiste,* the Italian *E con il tuo spirito*, the Continental Portuguese *E com teu espirito* and the Spanish *Y con tu espiritu.* Zulu has *Ibe nomoya wakho futhi* ('Let it be with your spirit as well'); see Nicholas King, 'Lost, and found, in translation', *The Tablet,* 19 November 2011, S1.

18. See the National Centre for Liturgy, ed., *The New Missal: Explaining the Changes* (Dublin: Veritas, 2011), 28.

19. See the following websites, accessed on 10 October 2010: http://justus.anglican.org/ resources/bcp/euchr3.rtf; http://ireland.anglican.org/cmsfiles/files/worship/rtf/HC2.rtf

20. Ronald Knox, *The Mass in Slow Motion* (London: Sheed and Ward, 1948), 10.

21. In the Appendix n. 5, see the translation of *Miserere nostri, Domine* and *Quia peccavimus tibi* as 'Lord, we have sinned against you' and 'Lord, have mercy' rather than as 'Lord, have mercy' and 'Lord, we have sinned against you'.

22. See the Appendix n. 4.

23. In the Appendix, see 'let us call to mind (*agnoscamus*)' and 'to prepare ourselves (*ut apti simus*)' in n. 4, 'You plead for us at the right hand of the Father (*Qui ad dexteram Patris sedes, ad interpellandum pro nobis*)' in n. 6 and 'his people (*hominibus bonae voluntatis*)', 'we worship you, we give you thanks, we praise you for your glory (*Laudamus te, benedicimus te, adoramus te, glorificamus te, gratias agimus tibi propter magnam gloriam tuam*)' and 'Lord Jesus Christ, only Son of the Father, Lord God, Lamb of God (*Domine Fili Unigenite, Iesu Christe, Domine Deus, Agnus Dei, Filius Patris*)' in n. 8.

24. See 'The Lord be (*Dominus sit*)' in n. 14, 'wipe away (*deleantur*)' in n. 16, 'eternally begotten (*natum ante omnia saecula*)', 'one in Being (*consubstantialem*)', 'was born (*incarnatus*)', 'suffered, died (*passus*)', 'in fulfilment of (*secundum*)', 'he (*qui*)', 'is

worshipped (*adoratur*)', He (*qui*)', 'We acknowledge (*Confiteor*)' and 'We look for (*expecto*)' in n. 18 and 'He (*qui*)' in n. 19.

25. In the Appendix, see 'which earth has given and human hands have made (*fructrum terrae et operis manuum hominum*)' in n. 23, 'we ask you to receive us (*suscipiamur a te*)' and 'be pleased with (*placeat tibi*)' in n. 26, 'and work of human hands (*et operis manuum hominum*)' in n. 25 and 'our sacrifice (*meum ac vestrum sacrificium*)' in n. 29. Patrick Regan has noted that the translation of 'our sacrifice' in n. 29 'was criticised for seeming to blur the distinction between the ministerial priesthood and that of the baptised'; see Patrick Regan, 'Theology of the Latin Text and Rite', in *A Commentary on the Order of Mass of the Roman Missal,* ed. Foley et al., 211–17 at 217.

26. In the Appendix, see 'Let us pray with confidence to the Father (*audemus dicere*)' and 'in the words our Saviour gave us (*Praeceptis salutaribus moniti*)' in n. 124, 'we may be always free (*simus semper liberi*)', 'in our day (*diebus*)', 'In your mercy (*ope misericordiae tuae adiuti*)', 'we may always be … safe from all distress (*ab omni perturbatione securi*)' and 'as we wait in joyful hope for the coming (*exspectantes beatam spem et adventum*)' in n. 125, 'you (*qui*)', 'and … us (*eamque*)', 'of your kingdom (*secundum voluntatem tuam*)' and 'where you (*Qui*)' in n. 126, 'your death brought life to the world (*qui … per mortem tuam mundum vivificasti*)', 'faithful to your teaching (*tuis simper inhaerere mandatis*)', 'I eat your Body and Blood (*Perceptio Corporis et Sanguinis tui*)' and 'with faith in your love and mercy … Let it not bring me condemnation, but health in mind and body (*pro tua pietate prosit mihi ad tutamentum mentis et Corporis, et ad medelam percipiendam*)' in n. 131, 'This is the Lamb of God who (*Ecce Agnus Dei, ecce qui*)' and 'to receive you (*ut intres*)' in n. 132 and 'Lord, may I receive these gifts in purity of heart. May they bring me healing and strength, now and for ever (*Quod ore sumpsimus, Domine, … capiamus, et de munere temporali fiat nobis remedium sempiternum*)' in n. 137.

27. See Tom Elich, 'The ICEL2010 Translation', in *A Commentary on the Order of Mass of the Roman Missal,* ed. Foley et al., 327–33, 375–82, 607–14, 639–44 at 607–9.

28. See Charles C. Butterworth, *The English Primers (1529–1545),* (New York: Octagon, 1971), 8–9, 301–3; Herbert Thurston, *Familiar Prayers: Their Origins and History* (London: Burns & Oates, 1953), 22–37.

29. See the Appendix n. 2.

30. See 1 Cor 1:3; 2 Cor 1:2; 2 Th 1:2; Eph 1:2; Gal 1:3; Phil 1:2, Phm 3, Rm 1:7.

31. See the Appendix n. 2.

32. In the Appendix, see Hebrews 7:25 (*ad interpellandum pro eis*) and the paraphrase of *ad interpellandum pro nobis* as 'plead for us' rather than 'intercede for us' and Psalm 146:3 and Isaiah 61:1 and the paraphrase of *contritus corde* as 'the contrite' in n. 6, Luke 2:14 and the paraphrase of *et in terra pax hominibus bonae voluntatis* as 'and peace to his people on earth', John 3:16 (*ut Filium suum unigenitum daret*) and the paraphrase of *Filii Unigenite* as 'only Son' and John 1:29 (*peccatum mundi*) and the paraphrase of *peccata mundi* as 'the sin of the world' in n. 8.

33. In the Appendix, see the implicit reference to Colossians 1:16 (*visibilia, et invisibilia*) and the paraphrase of *visibilium omnium et invisibilium* as 'of all that is seen and unseen' and John 3:16 (*ut Filium suum unigenitum daret*) and the paraphrase of *Filium Dei Unigenitum* as 'the only Son of God' in n. 18.

34. In the Appendix, see the implicit citation of Daniel 3:39-40 (*sed in anima contrita et spiritu humilitatis suscipiamur … sic fiat sacrificium nostrum in conspectu tuo hodie*) and the paraphrase of *In spiritu humilitatis et in animo contrito suscipiamur a te, Domine; et sic fiat sacrificium nostrum in conspectu tuo hodie, ut placeat tibi, Domine* as 'Lord God, we ask you to receive us and be pleased with the sacrifice we offer you with humble and contrite hearts' in n. 26, the implicit citation of Psalm 51:4 and the paraphrase of *Lava me, Domine, ab iniquitate mea, et a peccato meo munda me* as 'Lord, wash away my iniquity; cleanse me from my sin' in n. 28, the implicit citation of Revelation 19:9 and the paraphrase of

Beati qui ad cenam Agni vocati sunt as 'Happy are those who are called to his supper' and the implicit citation of Matthew 8:8 (*ut intres sub tectum meum … sanabitur puer meum*) and the paraphrase of *ut intres sub tectum meum … sanabitur anima mea* as 'to receive you … I shall be healed' in n. 132.

35. See the Appendix n. 18 and 117.

36. See the Appendix n. 4, 29, 105 and 115.

37. In the Appendix, see n. 11, 14 (second sentence), 18 (the sentence beginning *Qui cum Patre*), 126 (first sentence), 131 and 137.

38. In the Appendix, see n. 23, 25 and 131.

39. See the first Latin sentence of the Apostles' Creed in the Appendix n. 19.

40. In the Appendix, see n. 126 and the sentences beginning with *Et in unum*, with *Deum de Deo*, with *Qui propter nos* and with *Et incarnatus* in n. 18.

41. In the Appendix, see n. 14, 18 [twice], 124 and 131 [twice].

42. In the Appendix, see n. 8, 18, 131 and 132.

43. In the Appendix, see n. 6 [twice] and 126.

44. In the Appendix, see n. 4, 14 and 125.

45. In the Appendix, see n. 5 and 8.

46. In some cases, the Latin capitalisations are somewhat ambiguous since they occur at the beginning of a sentence; see Lamb (*Agni*) and 'May the body … May the blood' (*Corpus … Sanguis*) in nn. 132–133.

47. See the Appendix n. 131. See also 'apostles' (*Apostolis*) in n. 126.

48. In the Appendix, see 'virgin … angels and saints' (*Virginem … Angelos et Sanctos*) in n. 4 and 'only Son (*Unigenite*)' in n. 8.

49. In the Appendix, see 'only Son' (*Unigenitum*) in n. 18 and 'creator' (*Creatorem*) in n. 19.

50. See 'Holy, holy, holy' (*Sanctus, Sanctus, Sanctus*) in Appendix n. 83, 99, 107 and 116.

51. See the Appendix n. 14 and 144.

52. See the Appendix n. 18.

53. Roguet and Sheppard, 'Translation of the Roman Canon', 167.

54. Ibid., at 169–70.

55. Ibid., at 170–2.

56. See Moloney, 105–16.

57. See ibid., 52–4.

58. See ibid., 140–5.

59. See ibid., 76–81.

60. In the Appendix, see n. 92, 94 and 96 and the first stanza of n. 105.

61. See King, 'Lost, and found, in translation', S2, S4-S5, S7.

62. See ibid., S2, S4.

63. He is referring, presumably, to '*beatissima Virgine, Dei Genetrice*'.

64. See King, 'Lost, and found, in translation', S9.

65. See the Appendix, n. 117.

66. See Ostdiek, 'The ICEL2010 Translation', in *A Commentary on the Order of Mass of the Roman Missal,* ed. Foley et al., 279–92, 417–23 at 279.

67. See *[vel qui tibi offerunt hoc sacrificium laudis, pro se suisque omnibus]* in n. 85.

68. In the Appendix, see *clementissime … Dominum nostrum … supplices … sancta … illibata … toto … famulo tuo … orthodoxies … apostolicae* in n. 84, *aeterno* in n. 85, *gloriosae*

... beati ... beatorum ... tuorum ... tuorum ... protectionis in n. 86, *servitutis nostrae ... aeterna* in n. 87, *rationabilem ... dilectissimi* in n. 88, *quam pateretur ... sanctas ac venerabiles* in n. 89 and *praeclarum ... sanctas ac venerabiles* in n. 90.

69. In the Appendix, see *beatae ... gloriosae ... Domini nostri ... sancta ... praeclarae ... tuae ... puram ... immaculatam ... sanctam ... aeternae* in n. 92, *iusti ... summus ... sanctum sacrificium, immaculatam hostiam* in n. 93, *Supplices ... sancti ... ex hac altaris participatione ... sacrosanctum ... sumpserimus ... caelesti* in n. 94, *et dormiunt in somno pacis ... refrigerii* in n. 95, *peccatoribus famulis tuis, de multitudine miserationum tuarum sperantibus ... sanctis ... tuis* in n. 96 and *bona* in n. 97.

70. In the Appendix, see *igitur* and *in primis* in n. 84, *pro spe salutis et incolumitatis suae: tibique reddunt vota sua* in n. 85, *Communicantes, et memoriam venerantes, in primis, eiusdem Virginis Sponsi, in omnibus* in n. 86, *igitur* and *placatus* in n. 87, *in omnibus* in n. 88, *pridie* and *et elevatis oculis in caelum* in n. 89, *Simili modo* and *in sanctas ac venerabiles manus suas* in n. 90, *Unde* and *in caelos* in n. 92, *propitio ac sereno vultu* in n. 93, *sublime* and *in conspectus divinae maiestatis tuae* in n. 94 and *digneris, intra quorum nos consortium* and *non aestimator meriti, sed veniae* in n. 96.

71. In the Appendix, see *haec munera, quae, digneris, cum* and *et Antistite* in n. 84, *et omnium* in n. 85, *muniamur* in n. 86, *quaesumus, disponas, atque* and *in electorum tuorum iubeas grege* in n. 87, *tu, Deus ... quaesumus* and *digneris* in n. 88, *Deum, deditque, enim* and *ex hoc* in n. 89, *deditque* and *enim* in n. 90, *Domine, annuntiamus, confitemur* and *salva* in n. 91, *digneris* and *dignatus es* in n. 93, *iube* in n. 94, *famulorum famularumque tuarum* and *locum refrigerii* in n. 95, *et societatem, cum tuis, quaesumus* and *admitte* in n. 96, *Domine* in n. 97 and *et cum ipso, et in ipso* and *Deo* in n. 98, 106, 114 and 123.

72. In the Appendix, see *in sanctas ac venerabiles manus suas* in nn. 89–90.

73. In the Appendix, see *vere dignum et iustum, sancte, tuum, Redemptorem* and *omnibus* in n. 99 and *vitae, salutis, diffusae, famuli tui [famulae tuae], qui [quae] complantatus [complantata] fuit similitudini mortis Filii tui* and *qui in spe resurrectionis dormierunt, in tua miseratione defunctorum, beata, beatis, omnibus* and *qui tibi ... placuerunt* in n. 105.

74. In the Appendix, see *Vere dignum et iustum, cum pateretur* and *una voce* in n. 99, *ergo* and *rore* in n. 101, *cum ... traderetur* and *cum Passioni voluntarie* in n. 102, *Simili modo* and *iterum* in n. 103 and *igitur, supplices, in unum, toto orbe diffusae, [hodie]* and *ad te* in n. 105.

75. In the Appendix, see *nobis, et* and *cum* in n. 99, *quaesumus* in n. 101, *ex hoc* in n. 102, *enim* in nn. 102–103, *et* in nn. 103–105, *Domine, annuntiamus, confitemur* and *salva* in n. 104 and *Et, deprecamur ut, diffusae, et, Concede, ut* and *et* in n. 105.

76. In the Appendix, see *munda* in n. 108, *eodem* and *quae tibi sacranda detulimus* in n. 109, *Ipse* in n. 110, *salutiferae, mirabilis, alterum eius, Filii tui, beatissima, beatis ... tuis, gloriosis, nostrae reconciliationis, Papa nostro, huius familiae, clemens, ubique dispersos, qui, tibi placentes, ex hoc saeculo transierunt* and *benignus* in n. 113 and *famuli tui [famulae tuae] N., quem [quam] [hodie] ad te ex hoc mundo vocasti, qui [quae] complantatus [complantata] fuit similitudini mortis Filii tui, mortuos, humilitatis, claritatis, qui, tibi placentes, ex hoc saeculo transierunt* and *benignus* in n. 115.

77. In the Appendix, see *a te [condita]* and *operante virtute* in n. 108, *Supplices, ergo* and *digneris* in 109, *Simili modo* in n. 111, *igitur, in primis, apud te, propitius, miseratus* and *ubi* in n. 113 and *in carne de terra, corpori claritatis suae, perenniter, ab oculis nostris, cuncta per saecula* and *sine fine* in n. 115.

78. In the Appendix, see *quia* in 108, *deditque, ex hoc* and *enim* in n. 110, *et tibi, deditque* and *enim* in n. 111, *Domine, annuntiamus, confitemur* and *salva* in n. 112, *quaesumus, voluisti, cum, et gloriosis Martyribus, cum, quaesumus, et Episcopo nostro, digneris, cum, largiris* and *per quem* in n. 113 and *complantatus [complantata] fuit, quia, per quem* and *largiris* in n. 115.

79. In the Appendix, see *iustum, qui es ante saecula et permanens in aeternum* and *qui unus bonus* in n. 116, *sancte, sancte, Unigenitum* and *qui pro nobis mortuus est atque surrexit* in n. 117, *idem* and *ipse* in n. 118, *simili* in n. 120 and *ipse, in Christo, famuli tui, ordinis universi ... totius, cuncti, tui, omnibus, clemens* and *beata* in n. 122.

80. In the Appendix, see *Vere ... vere iustum, ideo, coram te, incessanter, in exsultatione* and *per nostram vocem, omnis quae sub caelo est creatura* in n. 116, *soli, misericorditer, corde* and *vero* in n. 117, *igitur* and *dignetur* in n. 118 and *Unde, tibi, benignus, a Sancto Spiritu, perficiantur, gloriae tuae, Nunc ergo, tibi, etiam, ubi, cum universa creatura* and *mundo* in n. 122.

81. In the Appendix, see *es ante saecula et, quia, Et ideo, et, vultus* and *et nos* in n. 116, *quia, et, Et, enim, Et, est conversatus* and *ac* in n. 117, *Quæsumus* in n. 118, *et cenantibus, ac fregit, ex hoc* and *enim* in n. 119, *enim* in n. 120, *Domine, annuntiamus, confitemur* and *salva* in n. 121 and *eiusque descensum, profitemur, concede, perficiantur, sed et* and *cum* in n. 122.

82. In the Appendix, see *ex* and *enim* in n. 89, 102, 110 and 119 and *enim* in n. 90, 103, 111 and 120.

83. In the Appendix, see 'we honour' in n. 86 and 'may' in n. 105.

84. In the Appendix, see 'Lord' in n. 84, 'especially', 'of us' and 'before you' in n. 85, 'many gifts (*donis*)' in n. 92 and 'marked with the sign (*cum signo*)' in n. 94.

85. In the Appendix, see 'the power of', 'Mary', 'For our sake' and 'In this' in n. 99, 'and praise' in 103 and 'all of us' in n. 105.

86. In the Appendix, see 'the glory of your name (*nomini tuo*)' in n. 108, the 'power of your Spirit (*eodem Spiritu*)' in n. 109, 'and all your Saints (*et omnibus Sanctis*)', 'your Son has gained for you (*acquisitionis tuae*)' and 'mercy and love (*clemens*)' in n. 113 and 'On that day' in n. 115.

87. In the Appendix, see '*every* blessing (*benedictionibus*)' in n. 116, 'your actions show your wisdom (*opera tua in sapientia ... fecisti*)', '*his* creator (*Creatori*)', 'all *men* (*Omnibus*)', '*power of the* Holy Spirit (*de Spiritu Sancto*)' and '*his* first gift (*primitias*)' in n. 117, '*always* love (*dilexxisset*)' in n. 119, 'he gave *you* thanks (*gratias egit*)' in n. 120 and '*this* memorial (*memoriale*)', '*this* sacrifice (*Hostiam*)', 'one body *of Christ* (*unum corpus*), 'your Holy Spirit (*a Sancto Spiritu*)', 'grant *also* (*concede*)' and '*our* heavenly inheritance (*caelestem hereditatem*)' in n. 122.

88. The word *Sabaoth* is a Latin transliteration of the word used in the Greek Septuagint text of Isaiah 6:3 (σαβαωθ) to translate the similarly sounding Hebrew plural noun. That Hebrew noun, meaning hosts or armies, is translated as *exercituum* in the Vulgate text of Isaiah 6:3.

89. See the Appendix n. 83, 99, 107 and 116.

90. In the Appendix, see the translation of *donec veniat* as 'until you come in glory', rather than according to the implicit citation of 1 Corinthians 11:26, and the inappropriate influence of John 4:42 (*hic est vere Salvator mundi*) on the translation of *Salvator mundi, Salva nos* as 'You are the Saviour of the world' in n. 91, 104, 112 and 121. See also the influence of Jesus being described as both using, and specifically referring to, a ποτηριον (*potérion*) or cup in 1 Corinthians 11:25-27 and in many other New Testament texts on the translation of the Latin noun *calix*, which denoted a cup with a foot that was generally used for drinking wine at banquets, as 'cup' in nn. 90–92, 103–105, 111 and 120. Similarly, there appears to be some influence of 1 Timothy 2:6, where St Paul says that Jesus gave himself as a ransom 'for all (*huper pantón / pro omnibus*)', on the paraphrase of *qui pro vobis et pro multis effundetur in remissionem peccatorum* as 'It will be shed for you and for all so that sins may be forgiven' in n. 90, 103, 111 and 120.

91. In the Appendix, see n. 87, 92, 105, 108–109, 113, 118 and 122.

92. In the Appendix, see n. 91, 104, 112 and 121.

93. In the Appendix, see *supplices rogamus ac petimus* in n. 84 and *Supplices te rogamus* in n. 94.

94. In the Appendix, see the oversimplified paraphrase 'all who hold and teach' and the use of the pronoun 'it' rather than 'her' as translations of *omnibus orthodoxis atque ... cultoribus* and *quam* in n. 84, the clash between the translation of *famulorum* as 'people' and *famulo* as 'servant' in n. 84 and 85, the interpretation of the relative pronouns *quibus, qui, suarum, suae* and *sua* as referring specifically to those gathered for Mass in n. 85, the possible ambiguity of 'mother of Jesus Christ our Lord and God (*Genitricis Dei et Domini nostri Iesu Christi*)' in relation to the implicit affirmation of the doctrine of the Theotokos and the obscuring of the instrumental ablative in 'May their merits and prayers grant (*quorum meritis precibusque*)' in n. 86 and the obscuring of the service nature of the offering in the paraphrase 'this offering from your whole family (*oblationem servitutis nostrae, sed et cunctae familiae tuae*)' in n. 87.

95. In the Appendix n. 90, see 'Again (*item*)', which could be understood as implying that there had been no verbal thanksgiving since the one over the bread, but the context of a Passover meal makes this uncertain, and the translation of *aeterni* as 'everlasting' rather than 'eternal'.

96. In the Appendix, the translation 'ministers (*servi*)' rather than 'servants' seems unusual and anachronistic in n. 92, the paraphrase *munera pueri tui iusti Abel* as 'the gifts of your servant Abel' in n. 93 seems to ignore the implicit citation of Hebrews 11:4 (*Abel ... justus*) and the paraphrase 'you give us all these gifts ... you fill them with [life] and goodness (*haec omnia ... semper bona creas ...et praestas nobis*)' in n. 97 hardly reflects the emphasis on the goodness of created things that is found in the Latin.

97. In the Appendix, see the translation of *cuncta* as 'the universe' and of *incarnatum* as 'he took flesh' in n. 99, of *fons* as 'fountain' in n. 100, of *aeterni* as 'everlasting' in n. 103, and of *ministrare* as 'serve', of *eam* as 'us', of *caritate* as 'love' and of *mundo* as 'life' in n. 105.

98. In the Appendix, see the translation of *aeterni* as 'everlasting' in n. 111, of *oblationem Ecclesiae tuae* as 'your Church's offering', of *nos tibi perficiat munus aeternum* as 'make us an everlasting gift to you', of *electis* as 'saints', of *caritate* as 'love' in n. 113, of *satiemur* as 'enjoy the vision of' and 'share in' in n. 113 and 115 and of *erimus* as 'become' in n. 115.

99. In the Appendix, see the translation of *Pater sancte* as 'Father in heaven' and of *sed et ... cuncta fecisti* as 'you have created all things' in n. 116, of *imperaret* as 'rule over', of *imperio* as 'power', of *subvenisti* as 'helped', of *incarnatus* as 'He was conceived' and of *primitias* as 'first gift' in n. 117, of *aeternum* as 'everlasting' in n. 118, of *hora venisset* as 'the time came' and of *Pater sancte* as 'his heavenly Father' in n. 119, of *genimine vitis* as 'wine' and of *aeterni* as 'everlasting' in n. 120 and of *ad inferos* as 'to the realm the dead', of *recolimus* as 'recall', of *exspectantes* as 'looking forward to', of *parasti* as 'you have given to', of *participabunt* as 'share' and of *omnium* as 'those' in n. 122.

100. The difference between a variation and a paraphrasing would seem to be that a variation represents a meaning fundamentally different from that of the original context while a paraphrasing represents a meaning fundamentally similar to that of the original context.

101. The text has often been described as the Canon of Hippolytus, an early third-century Roman presbyter, but Baldovin points out that the document may not be Roman at all, that it is 'fairly clear' that Hippolytus was not the author and that there is 'a growing consensus that the institution narrative in this prayer was a fourth-century addition'; see John F. Baldovin, 'History of the Latin Text and Rite', in *A Commentary on the Order of Mass of the Roman Missal*, ed. Foley et al., 247–54, 311–16, 401–6, 593–600 at 311.

102. See the Appendix n. 99, 101 and 105.

103. See Moloney, 29, 32.

104. See ibid., 55–6.

105. See Baldovin, 'History of the Latin Text and Rite', 250.

106. See Moloney, 9, 83.

107. See Cipriano Vagaggini, *The Canon of the Mass and Liturgical Reform* (London: Chapman, 1967), 123.

108. Here, the number of words in Latin refers to the number of words in the texts cited in the Appendix.

109. In the Appendix, see 'And also with you (*Et cum spiritu tuo*)' in n. 107, 'all creation (*omnis a te condita creatura*)', 'All life, all holiness comes from you (*vivificas et sanctificas universa*)', 'From age to age (*non desinis*)', 'from east to west (*a solis ortu usque ad occasum*)' and 'a perfect offering may be made to the glory of your name (*oblatio munda offeratur nomini tuo*)' in n. 108, 'We ask you (*Supplices … deprecamur*)', 'to make them holy (*sanctificare digneris*)' and 'this eucharist (*haec mysteria*)' in n. 109, 'gave you thanks and praise (*tibi gratias agens benedixit*)' and 'and said (*dicens*)' in n. 110, 'and said (*dicens*)' in n. 111, 'Christ has died, Christ is risen, Christ will come again (*Mortem tuam annuntiamus, Domine, et tuam resurrectionem confitemur, donec venias*)' in n. 112, 'calling to mind (*memores*)', 'ready to greet him when he comes again (*praestolantes alterum eius adventum*)', 'Look with favour on your Church's offering (*Respice … in oblationem Ecclesiae tuae*)', 'see (*agnoscens*)', 'may be filled with his Holy Spirit (*Spiritu eius Sancto repleti*)', 'and enable us to share in (*ut … consequi valeamus*)', 'Strengthen in faith and love (*in fide et caritate firmare digneris*)', 'hear (*adesto propitius*)', 'you have gathered here before you (*tibi astare voluisti*)' and 'in your friendship (*tibi placentes*)' in n. 113 and 'when Christ will raise our mortal bodies (*quando mortuos suscitabit in carne de terra*)', 'in your friendship (*tibi placentes*)', 'every tear will be wiped away (*omnem lacrimam absterges*)' and 'shall see (*videntes*)' in n. 115.

110. Thirty-one in 588 words of Latin.

111. Twenty-six in 437 words of Latin.

112. In the Appendix, see 'And also with you (*Et cum spiritu tuo*)', 'It is our duty and our salvation (*Vere dignum et iustum est, aequum et salutare*)', 'In this he fulfilled (*adimplens*)', 'won (*aquirens*)', 'he put an end to death and revealed the resurrection (*ut mortem solveret et resurrectionem manifestaret*)', 'in proclaiming (*praedicamus*)' and 'sing (say) [*dicentes*]' in n. 99, 'to make holy (*sanctifica*)' in n. 101, 'Before he was given up to death, a death he freely accepted (*Qui cum Passioni voluntarie traderetur*)', 'gave you thanks (*tibi gratias agens*)', 'and said (*dicens*)' in n. 102, 'gave you thanks and praise (*tibi gratias agens*)', 'and said (*dicens*)' in n. 103, 'Christ has died, Christ is risen, Christ will come again (*Mortem tuam annuntiamus, Domine, et tuam resurrectionem confitemur, donec venias*)' in n. 104 and 'In memory of (*memores*)', 'We thank you (*gratias agentes*)', 'share in (*participes*)', 'be brought together in unity (*congregemur in unum*)', 'make us grow in (*perficias*)', 'bring them … into the light of your presence (*eos in lumen vultus tui admitte*)' and 'May we praise you in union with them, and give you glory (*aeternae vitae mereamus esse consortes, et te laudemus et glorificemus*)' in n. 105.

113. Forty-eight in 676 words of Latin.

114. In the Appendix, see 'And also with you (*Et cum spiritu tuo*)', 'that we should give you thanks and glory (*tibi gratias agere … te glorificare*)', 'through all eternity (*qui es ante saecula et permanes in aeternum*)', 'you live (*inhabitans*)', 'every blessing (*benedictionibus*)', 'to fill (*ut … adimpleres*)', 'and lead all men to the joyful vision (*multasque laetificares claritate*)', 'stand before you to do your will (*coram te … astant … serviunt tibi*)', 'they look upon your splendour (*vultus tui gloriam contemplantes*)', 'and praise you (*te incessanter glorificant*)' and 'praise your glory as we say (*nomen tuum in exsultatione confidemur canentes*)' in n. 116, 'we acknowledge your greatness (*Confitemur tibi … quia magnus es*)', 'all your actions show your wisdom and love (*omnia opera tua in sapientia et caritate fecisti*)', 'and set him over the whole world (*eique commisisti mundi curam universi*)', 'to serve you (*tibi soli Creatori serviens*)', 'to rule (*ut … imperaret*)', 'through disobedience he had lost (*non oboediens, amisisset*)', 'to seek and find you (*ut te quaerentes invenirent*)', 'a covenant (*foedera*)', 'a man like us (*in nostra condicionis forma est conversatus*)', 'those in

sorrow (*maestis corde*)', 'In fulfilment of your will (*Ut tuam vero dispensationem impleret*)', 'to complete (*perficiens*)' and 'bring us the fullness of grace (*omnem sanctificationem compleret*)' in n. 117, 'for the celebration of this great mystery (*ad hoc magnum mysterium celebrandum*)' and 'Let them become (*ut ... fiant*)' in n. 118, 'always loved (*ac dilexisset*)' in n. 119, 'heavenly (*sancte*)', 'showed the depth of his love (*in finem dilexit eos*)', 'said the blessing, broke the bread (*benedixit ac fregit*)', 'and giving (*deditque*)' and 'said (*dicens*)' in n. 120, 'Christ has died, Christ is risen, Christ will come again (*Mortem tuam annuntiamus, Domine, et tuam resurrectionem confitemur, donec venias*)' in n. 121 and 'looking forward to (*expectantes*)', 'by your Holy Spirit, gather (*a Sancto Spiritu congregati*)', 'we offer this sacrifice (*hanc oblationem offerimus*)', 'those who take part in this offering (*et offerentium*)', 'those here present (*circumstantium*)', 'is known to you alone (*tu solus cognovisti*)', 'Father, in your mercy (*clemens Pater*)', 'that we may enter (*consequi valeamus*)' and 'we shall sing your glory (*te glorificemus*)' in n. 122.

115. Twenty-nine in 701 words of Latin.

116. In the Appendix, see 'And also with you (*Et cum spiritu tuo*)' in n. 83, 'to accept and bless (*uti accepta habeas et benedicas*)', 'these gifts we offer you in sacrifice (*haec dona, haec menera, haec sancta sacrificia illibata*)' and 'watch over it, Lord, and guide it; grant it peace and unity (*quam pacificare, custodire, adunare et regere digneris*)' in n. 84, 'You know how firmly we believe in you and dedicate ourselves to you (*quorum tibi fides cognita est et nota devotio*)' in n. 85, 'In union with the whole Church, we honour (*Communicantes, et memoriam venerantes*)' and 'we may be defended by your protecting help (*protectionis tuae muniamur auxilio*)' in n. 86, 'Grant us your peace in this life (*diesque nostros in tua pace disponas*)', 'save us (*nos eripi*)', 'final (*aeterna*)' and 'count us (*numerari*)' in n. 87, 'our offering (*quam oblationem*)' and 'Let it become (*ut ... fiat*)' in n. 88, 'with eyes raised to heaven (*et elevatis oculis in caelum*)', 'gave you thanks and praise (*gratias agens benedixit*)' and 'and said (*dicens*)' in n. 89, 'gave you thanks and praise (*gratias agens benedixit*)', 'and said (*dicens*)' and 'so that sins may be forgiven (*in remissionem peccatorum*)' in n. 90, 'Christ has died, Christ is risen, Christ will come again (*Mortem tuam annuntiamus, Domine, et tuam resurrectionem confitemur, donec venias*)' in n. 91, 'we celebrate the memorial of (*memores*)' and 'this holy and perfect sacrifice (*hostiam puram, hostiam sanctam, hostiam immaculatam*)' in n. 92, 'the bread and wine offered by (*quod tibi obtulit*)' in n. 93, 'we pray that your angel may take (*Supplices te rogamus ... iube haec perferri per manus sancti Angeli tui*)', 'as we receive (*ut, quotquot ... sumpserimus*)' and 'let us be filled (*repleamur*)' in n. 94, 'May these ... find in your presence ... happiness (*Ipsis ... locum refrigerii ... ut indulgeas*)' in n. 95, 'For ourselves ... we ask (*Nobis ... donare digneris*)' in n. 96 and 'Through him (*Per quem*)' in n. 97.

117. See the Appendix n. 88.

118. See the Appendix n. 117.

119. See the Appendix n. 117.

120. In the Appendix, see 2 Chronicles 6:12 (*extendit manus*) and the translation of *extendit manus* as 'he opened his arms' in n. 99 and John 6:35 and 6:48 (*panis vitae*) and the paraphrase of *panem vitae* as 'life-giving bread', Psalm 116:13 (*calicem salutaris*) and the paraphrase of *calicem salutis* as 'saving cup', Romans 6:5 (*Si ... complantati facti sumus similitudini mortis eius, sed et resurrectionis erimus*) and the paraphrase of *complantatus [complantata] fuit similitudini mortis Filii tui* as 'In baptism he [she] died with Christ' and Psalm 89:16 (*in lumine vultus tui*) and the paraphrase of *in lumen vultus tui* as 'into the light of your presence' in n. 105.

121. In the Appendix, see Malachi 1:11 (*Ab ortu enim solis usque ad occasum ... et offertur nomini meo oblatio munda*) and the paraphrase of *ut a solis ortu usque ad occasum oblatio munda offeratur nomini tuo* as 'so that from east to west a perfect offering may be made to the glory of your name' in n. 108, 1 Peter 2:9 (*populus in acquisitionem*) and the paraphrase *et omni populo acquisitionis tuae* as 'and the entire people your Son has gained for you' in n. 113 and Romans 6:5 (*Si ... complantati facti sumus similitudini mortis eius, sed*

et resurrectionis erimus) and the paraphrase of *complantatus [complantata] fuit similitudini mortis Filii tui* as 'In baptism he [she] died with Christ', Philippians 3:21 (*transfigurabit corpus humilitatis nostrae, ut illud conforme faciat corpori gloriae suae*) and the translation of *et corpus humilitatis nostrae configurabit corpori claritatis suae* as 'and make them [our mortal bodies] like his own in glory' and Revelation 7:17 (*absterget Deus omnem lacrimam ex oculis eorum*) and the translation of *quando omnem lacrimam absterges ab oculis nostris* as 'when every tear will be wiped away' in n. 115.

122. In the Appendix, see Genesis 1:26 (*Faciamus hominem ad imaginem et similitudinem nostram*) and the paraphrase of *Hominem ad tuam imaginem condidisti* as 'You formed man in your own likeness' and Romans 8:23 (*primitias spiritus*) and the paraphrase of *misit Spiritum Sanctus primitias credentibus* as 'he sent the Holy Spirit ... as his first gift to those who believe' in n. 117, Genesis 17:13 (*in carne vestra in foedus aeternum*) and the paraphrase of *quod ipse obis reliquit in foedus aeternum* as 'which he left us as an everlasting covenant' in n. 118, the phrase from John 13:1, *dilexisset suos qui erant in mundo, in finem dilexit eos*, which is paraphrased as 'He always loved those who were his own in the world ... he showed the depth of his love', n. 119 and 1 Corinthians 10:17 (*Quoniam unus panis, unum corpus multi sumus, omnes enim de uno pane participamur*) and the paraphrase of *qui ex hoc uno pane participabunt et calice, ut, in unum corpus a Sancto Spiritu congregati* as 'by your Holy Spirit gather all who share this one bread and one cup into the one body of Christ' and Ephesians 1:12 (*in laudem gloriæ ejus*) and the paraphrase of *in Christo hostia viva perficiantur, ad laudem gloriae tuae* as 'into the one body of Christ, a living sacrifice of praise' in n. 122.

123. In the Appendix, see n. 84, 89–90, 92, 94, 96–97; 102, 105 (sentences beginning *Memores igitur* and *Omnium nostrum*); 109–110, 113, 122.

124. In the Appendix, see n. 86, 103, 108, 111, 115 (final sentence) and 116 (first sentence).

125. See the Appendix n. 85.

126. In the Appendix, see the sentences beginning with *Memento famuli tui* and *Concede* in n. 115 and beginning with *Et cum* and *Omnibus enim* in n. 117.

127. In the Appendix, see n. 89, 90, 99, 102, 103, 110, 111, 116, 119 and 120.

128. In the Appendix, see n. 84, 85, 86, 87, 88, 96, 119 and 122.

129. In the Appendix, see n. 84, 94 and 96.

130. In the Appendix, see n. 86 and 92.

131. In the Appendix, see n. 113 and 93.

132. In the Appendix, see n. 91, 104, 112 and 121.

133. *Hic est enim Calix Sanguinis mei, novi et aeterni testamenti: mysterium fidei: qui pro vobis et pro multis effundetur in remissionem peccatorum.*

134. *Ratio translationis*, 115.

135. In the Appendix, see *Antistite nostro N.* in n. 84, *Virginis Mariae, Genetricis* and *Apostolorum ... Martyrum ... Sanctorum* in n. 86, *Corpus ... Sanguis* in n. 88, *Panem ... Calicem* in n. 92, *Patriarchae* in n. 93, *Angeli ... Corpus et Sanguinem* in n. 94 and *Apostolis ... Martyribus ... Sanctis* in n. 96.

136. In the Appendix, see 'holy (*Sanctus*)' in n. 100, 'body and blood (*Corpus et Sanguis*)' in n. 101, 'death (*Passioni*)' in n. 102 and 'body and blood (*Corporis et Sanguinis*)', 'bishop (*Episcopo*)', 'virgin (*Vergine*)', 'apostles (*Apostolis*)' and saints (*Sanctis*) in n. 105.

137. In the Appendix, see 'body and blood (*Corpus et Sanguis*)' in n. 109 and 'body and blood (*Corpore et Sanguine*)', 'virgin ... apostles ... martyrs ... saint ... saints (*Virgine ... Apostolis ... Martyribus ... Sancto ... Sanctis*)' and 'sacrifice (*Hostia*)' in n. 113.

138. In the Appendix, see 'creator (*Creatori*)' and 'only Son (*Unigenitum*)' in n. 117, 'body and blood (*Corpus et Sanguis*)' in n. 118 and 'body and blood (*Corpus et Sanguinem*)', 'sacrifice (*Hostiam*)', 'bishops (*Episcoporum*)' and 'apostles and saints (*Apostolis et Sanctis*)' in n. 122.

139. These particular prayers have been chosen because they include some of the terms associated with our common humanity that will be the focus of the next chapter.

140. See *Quia ... dignánter* in n. I, *atque in hoc córpore constitúti non solum* in n. IV *and nobis ... beatae ... ut ... futúrae ... enim ... et* in n. V.

141. In the Appendix, see n. XVI.

142. See *quaesumus* and *nuntiante, Christi* in the Appendix n. VI.

143. In the Appendix, see *nativitátis hodiérnae mystériis apta provéniant ... idem praefúlsit et Deus* in n. VII, *patientiae* and the transposition of *carnem sumere* so that it is no longer part of our Saviour's example of humility in n. XI and *Fac nos ... divinitátis tuae sempitérna fruitióne ... temporális percéptio* in n. XXIV.

144. In the Appendix, see *quaesumus* in n. VII, VIII, IX, X, XII, XIV, XV, XVIII, XIX, XX, XXIII and XXIV, *nostra* in n. VII, *praesta* in n. VIII, *corpora mentesque* in n. IX, *propitius* in n. XI, *Concede* in n. XII, *Semper exsultet populus tuus ... certae* in n. XIII, *quem ... dignatus es renovare ... ad incorruptibilem glorificandae carnis resurrectionem pervenire concede* in n. XIV, *omnipotens, ut claritátis tuae super nos splendor effúlgeat, corda* and *illustratióne* in n. XV, *renovas sacramento* in n. XVIII, *da ... maiestatem tuam ... sacri participatione mysterii fideliter sensibus* in n. XIX, *compatimur* in n. XXI, *noster ... sempiternae sanctae* in n. XXII, *tríbue ... fructum in nobis iúgiter ... in unitáte* in n. XXIII and *pretiósi* in n. XXIV.

145. In the Appendix, see 'our Father' in n. I and 'who rose from the dead, our ... bright ... people ... the body of our' in n. V.

146. In the Appendix, see 'Jesus Christ', 'He fulfilled your will by', 'giving his life on' and 'bear witness to you' in n. XI, 'these' in n. XIV and 'Jesus Christ' and 'in the eucharist' in n. XXIV.

147. In the Appendix, see 'our Father' in n. XIII, 'Lord' in n. XVIII, 'of Christ' in n. XXI, 'of Persons ... our faith and' in n. XXII and 'in the kingdom where' in n. XXIV.

148. See 'us this joyful season ... prepare to celebrate ... mystery with mind and heart renewed. You give us a spirit of loving reverence for you ... and of willing service to our neighbour ... the image of your Son' in n. I, 'great season of grace ... renew us in spirit ... your gift to your family ... teach us how to live ... with our heart set on the world' in n. II and 'Each day you show us a Father's love' in n. IV.

149. In the Appendix, see 'you give us a spirit of' in n. I, 'You give us strength to purify our hearts, to control our desires, and so to serve you in freedom' in n. II, 'observance of Lent' in n. III and 'we gain' in n. V.

150. See 'your Holy Spirit, dwelling within us, gives us on earth the hope of unending joy' in n. IV.

151. See 'correct ... help us grow in holiness, and offer us the reward of eternal life' in n. III and 'sadness of death gives way to' in n. V.

152. See 'As we recall the great events that gave us new life in Christ' in n. I.

153. In the Appendix, see n. XVII.

154. In the Appendix, see 'fill ... hearts ... love ... you revealed to us ... coming ... as man ... his suffering and death' in n. VI, 'who became man and lived among us' in n. VII, 'Father ... only Son' in n. VIII, 'Eucharist take away our sins that we ... Resurrection' in n. IX, 'Father ... Fill ... with the light of your Gospel ... that our thoughts may please you, and our love be sincere' in n. X, 'as a model ... and giving his life on ... bear witness to you by following his example of' in n. XI, 'we have received ... live forever ... minds and hearts' in n. XII, 'to our resurrection ... for you have made us your sons and daughters, and restored the joy of our youth' in n. XIII, 'nourished ... Fill ... with ... one in peace and love' in n. XVI, 'this bread and wine ... May the Eucharist renew our strength and bring ... health' in n. XVIII, 'of peace and love ... with you' in n. XIX, 'Eucharist you have given us influence our thoughts and actions' in n. XX, 'this Eucharist ... make us one with him' in n. XXI, 'one eternal God ... mind and body' in n. XXII and 'the eucharist ... suffering and death ... our worship ... this sacrament ... the salvation you won for us and the peace of the kingdom' in n. XXIII.

155. In the Appendix, see 'may we follow the example of your Son' and 'May we receive the gift of divine life through these offerings here on earth' in n. VII, 'May we who share his humanity come to share his divinity' in n. VIII, 'sacraments' in n. XII, 'Easter' in n. XIV, 'you have given us new birth' in n. XV, 'your Spirit' in n. XVI, 'May your Spirit guide and direct us in your way' in n. XX, 'bring us salvation' in n. XXI and 'you give us … as a sign that even now we share your life' in n. XXIV.

156. See the Appendix n. VIII.

157. 'The origins of both his substances display him as man and as God (*utriusque substantiae … hominem et Deum exhibuit*): from the one, born, and from the other, not born; from the one, flesh (*carneum*), and from the other, spiritual.' See Tertullian, *The Flesh of Christ*, 5.7 in Jacques-Paul Migne, ed., *Patrologia Latina*, 221 vols. (Paris: Vrayet, 1844–91), 2:761.

158. See the Appendix n. X.

159. See 'that the splendour of his grace (*gratiae tuae splendor*) should gleam there', St Ambrose, *De Mysteriis* 4 (n. 23) in Migne, ed., *PL*, 16:395.

160. In the Appendix, see 'God (*Deus*)' in n. XI, XII, XVII, XIX and XXII and 'Lord God (*Deus*)' in n. XVIII.

161. In the Appendix, see 'Father (*Deus*)' in n. X, 'God the Father (*Deus*)' in n. XIII and 'God our Father (*omnipotens Deus*)' in n. XV.

162. Pecklers, *The Genius of the Roman Rite,* 102.

163. See 'Lord Jesus Christ (*Deus*)' in the Appendix n. XXIII.

164. See the Appendix n. VII and XXIV.

165. In the Appendix, see *in adoptionis* in n. XIII, *pietátis* in n. IV, *fidélibus* in n. V, in *substántia nostrae carnis* in n. VIII and *incarnationem* in n. VI.

166. In the Appendix, see 'the image of your Son … within us (*ad grátiae filiórum*)' in n. I.

167. In the Appendix, see 'your family (*filiis tuis*)' in n. II.

168. In the Appendix, see 'all (*omnem hominem*)' in n. X.

169. In the Appendix, see 'became man (*homo génitus*)' in n. VII.

170. In the Appendix, see 'all men (*omnes homines*)' in n. XVII.

171. In the Appendix, see n. V (both Latin sentences), VII, VIII, X, XV, XVI, XVIII, XX and XXII.

172. In the Appendix, see n. I, II and XI.

173. In the Appendix, see n. VIII and XXI.

174. See the Appendix n. XXIII.

175. In the Appendix, see n. I.

176. In the Appendix, see n. III.

177. See 'angel (*Angelo*)' in n. VI, 'only Son (*Unigénitus*)' in n. VIII, 'body and blood (*Corporis et Sanguinis*)' in n. XXIII and 'body and blood (*Corporis et Sanguinis*)' in n. XXIV.

178. King, 'Lost, and found, in translation', S1.

179. The Introductory Rite, the Liturgy of the Word, the Liturgy of the Eucharist, Eucharistic Prayers 1 and 2, and the Communion and Concluding Rites.

180. 5.70 or 114 in 2001 Latin words.

Chapter II. *Liturgiam authenticam* and the 2011 Translation

1. The two translations are given side by side in the Appendix.

2. For the official Latin version, see Congregation for Divine Worship and the Discipline of the Sacraments, 'Instruction *Liturgiam authenticam*, on the use of vernacular languages in the publication of the liturgical books of the Roman Rite', *Acta Apostolicae Sedis* 93 (2001) 91–134.

3. Taft, 'Translating Liturgically', 157–9.

4. The *Nova Vulgata Editio* may be accessed at the following website, consulted on 10 October 2011: http://vatican.va/archive/bible/nova_vulgata/documents/nova-vulgata_index_lt.html.

5. See articles 37–45 of *Liturgiam authenticam*.

6. *Liturgiam authenticam* 37.

7. Presumably, examples of what the text has in mind here might be the automatic replacement of 'man' by 'person', 'people', 'men and women' or 'humanity' when translating *homo*.

8. *Ratio translationis,* 1.

9. See Congregation for Divine Worship and the Discipline of the Sacraments, 'Instruction *Varietates legitimae*, on Inculturation in the Roman Liturgy', *Acta Apostolica Sedis* 87 (1995), 288–314.

10. *Ratio translationis,* 95.

11. Ibid., 97.

12. Ibid., 101.

13. Ibid., 105, 107.

14. Ibid., 108–109.

15. Citing *Liturgiam authenticam,* n. 8, the *Ratio translationis* notes that 'As first characteristics of liturgical vernacular, intelligibility and accessibility of expression are vital for the Church's prayer' (n. 74).

16. King, 'Lost, and found, in translation', S1.

17. See Chupungco, 'The ICEL2010 Translation', 138.

18. See Catherine Vincie, 'The Mystagogical Implications', in *A Commentary on the Order of Mass of the Roman Missal,* ed. Foley et al. (Collegeville, Minnesota: Liturgical Press, 2011), 143–50, 187–94, 221–7, 148.

19. See Chupungco, 'The ICEL2010 Translation', 140–1.

20. Pecklers, *The Genius of the Roman Rite*, 106.

21. See Chupungco, 'The ICEL2010 Translation', 181.

22. In n. 124, 'we dare' is a 'strong' rendering of the Latin; in n. 125, despite its length, the Embolism 'reads well' and 'all distress' is a good translation because it can be 'external as well as internal'; in n. 126, the prayer is unified 'into a single sentence' by the change from 'you' to 'who', the Lord's greeting 'is given greater emphasis by beginning with the word "peace"' and 'in accordance with your will' has been 'rightfully restored'; in n. 132, the repeated 'behold' is 'a strong and compelling invitation', 'supper of the Lamb' should 'lay to rest the common misunderstanding, often vocalised by the priest, that the people are invited to "this supper", i.e., just to communion here and now', 'my soul' is 'rich enough to evoke the depth of healing enjoyed when the sins of the world are taken away'; in n. 137, the new translation 'is well balanced and memorable'; see Elich, 609–14.

23. In n. 124, 'Taught by the Saviour's command and formed by the word of God' spoils 'the balance between *moniti-formati*' and the decision to follow the 1973 translation in using a text of the Our Father that employs 'the archaic second-person singular pronoun ("Thy")' is regretted; in n. 125, the introduction of 'and' before 'the coming of our Saviour' could leave the reader 'somewhat mystified about the nature of the 'blessed hope', and 'sustained (*adiuti*)' should not have been omitted before 'by the help of your mercy'; in n. 126, 'and graciously grant her peace and unity' is 'disappointing ... redundant' and 'uninspired', 'the feminine pronoun for the church sits uneasily in the contemporary ear', 'Who live and reign for ever and ever' is 'problematic' since 'a relative pronoun after "your will" would have to refer to "will" not "your"'; in n. 131, the new translation 'follows the

structure of the Latin more closely' and time 'will tell' if these prayers 'become as familiar and well loved' as the texts of the 1973 translation; in n. 132, 'enter under my roof' may lead people to think of 'the roof of my mouth'; in n. 137, the new translation 'is something of an elaboration on the Latin text; see ibid., 607, 609–14.

24. See ibid., 614.

25. The 'rendering of the concluding rites is simple and straightforward' and it 'serves well the purpose of the dismissal "that each may go out to do good works, praising and blessing God"', the new forms of the dismissal 'are suitably concise and enjoy crisp alliterations', the 'missionary sense of *ite* is strongly expressed in the phrase, "Go forth"', the 'final spoken words of the Mass, voiced by the assembly, express the eucharistic motif of thanksgiving' and 'Mass' and 'Eucharist' are both referenced in the words of the dismissal; see ibid., 642–43.

26. The alternative forms of the dismissal in the older translation, particularly 'Go in peace to love and serve the Lord', 'will be missed' and the juxtaposition representing *ad* in 'Go and announce' would have been better expressed by 'Go out to announce'; see ibid.

27. 'Go forth, the Mass is ended' or 'Go and announce the Gospel of the Lord' or 'Go in peace, glorifying the Lord by your life' or 'Go in peace'.

28. King, 'Lost, and found, in translation', S1.

29. See the Appendix n. 4.

30. See the *Ordo Romanus XIV*, 71 in Jean Mabillon, *Museum Italicum*, 2 vols. (Paris: Montalant, 1724), 2:329.

31. See the Appendix n. 4.

32. In the Appendix, see Baruch 3:2 (*miserere nostri, quia peccavimus ante te*) and the translation of *quia peccabimus tibi* as 'For we have sinned against you' in n. 5, Psalm 146:3 (*contritus corde*) and Isaiah 61:1 and the translation 'contrite of heart (*contritus corde*)' and Hebrews 1:3 (*sedet ad dexteram*) and the translation 'You are seated at the right hand of the Father (*Qui ad dexteram Patris sedes*)' in n. 6 and John 3:16 and the translation of *Filii Unigenite* as 'Only Begotten Son' in n. 8.

33. In the Appendix, see John 3:16 and the translation of *Filium Dei Unigenitum* as 'Only Begotten Son of God' in n. 18.

34. See Chupungco, 'The ICEL2010 Translation', 140.

35. As in the 1973 translation, *valeam* is again left untranslated in Appendix n. 14. See ibid., 182.

36. In the Appendix, see 'therefore (*Ideo*)' in n. 4, 'of good will (*bonae voluntatis*)', 'great (*magnam*)' in n. 8, 'and well (*et competenter*)' in n. 14, 'before all ages (*ante omnia saecula*)' in n. 18, 'from the dead (*a mortuis*)', 'almighty (*omnipotentis*)' and 'from there (*inde*)' in n. 19, 'for (*quia*)' in n. 23, 'for (*quia*)' in n. 25, 'spirit (*spiritu*)' and 'in your sight this day (*in conspectu tuo hodie*)' in n. 26, 'holy (*sanctae*)' in n. 29, 'and just (*et iustum*)' in n. 83, 99, 107 and 116, 'we pray (*quaesumus*)', 'graciously (*propitius*)', 'always (*semper*)' and 'blessed (*beatam*)' in n. 125, 'graciously (*digneris*)' and 'in accordance with your will (*secundum voluntatem tuam*)' in n. 126, 'this … most holy (*hoc sacrosanctum*)' and 'always (*semper*)' in n. 131, 'Blessed (*Beati*)' and 'of the Lamb (*Agni*)' in n. 132 and 'in time (*temporali*)' in n. 137.

37. In the Appendix, see 'to you (*vobis*)' in n. 2, 'therefore (*Ideo*)' in n. 4, 'are seated (*sedes*)' in n. 6, 'Through (*Per*)' in n. 16, 'and (*et* [*Incarnatus*])' and 'and (*et* [*resurrexit*])' in n. 18, 'and (*et* [*in Iesum Christum*])' and 'of God (*Dei*)' in n. 19, 'have received (*accepimus*)', 'we [offer] you (*quem tibi*)' and 'fruit (*fructum*)' in n. 23 and 'we [offer] you (*quod tibi*)' and 'and (*et* [*adventum*])' in n. 25.

38. In the Appendix, see the repeat of 'you take away the sins of the world (*qui tollis peccata mundi*)' in n. 8, 'and formed by divine teaching (*et divina institutione formati*)' in n. 124 and 'through your loving mercy be for me protection (*pro tua pietate prosit mihi ad tutamentum*)' in n. 131.

39. See Vincie, 'The Mystagogical Implications', 226.

40. In the Appendix, see 'mercy (*misericordiam*)' in n. 5, 'by the Holy Spirit (*de Spiritu Sancto*)' in n. 18, 'born of the Virgin Mary (*natus ex Maria Virgine*)' and 'suffered under (*passus sub*)' in n. 19, 'the bread (*panem*)' in n. 23, 'It is right and just (*Dignum et iustum est*)' in n. 83, 99, 107 and 116, 'The mystery of faith (*Mysterium fidei*)', 'Saviour (*Salvator*)' in n. 91, 104, 112 and 121, 'we dare to say (*audemus dicere*)' in n. 124, 'Lord Jesus Christ (*Domine Iesu Christe*)' in n. 131 and 'healing (*remedium*)' in n. 137.

41. See King, 'Lost, and found, in translation', S1.

42. See Pecklers, *The Genius of the Roman Rite*, 109.

43. See the Appendix n. 144.

44. King, 'Lost, and found, in translation', S1.

45. See the letter by Stephen Hough in *The Tablet* (17 September 2011), 18. See also the following website, accessed on 17 September 2011: http://catholicexchange.com/2010/05/22/130549/?utm_source=feedburner&utm_medium=feed&utm_campaign=Feed%3A+catholicex+%28Catholic+Exchange%29.

46. See the following website, accessed on 17 September 2011: http://blog.adw.org/2010/05/and-with-your-spirit-its-not-what-you-think.

47. See 'The grace of our Lord Jesus Christ be with your [pl.] spirit brethren' (Gal 6:18), 'The grace of the Lord Jesus Christ be with your [pl.] spirit' (Phil 4:23) and 'The grace of the Lord Jesus Christ be with your [pl.] spirit' (Philemon 25).

48. The distinction between Timothy and those associated with him may reflect the 'gift' of leadership that Timothy 'was given ... by prophetic utterance when the council of elders laid their hands upon' him; see 1 Tm 4:14. See also see 2 Tm 1:6.

49. According to the *General Instruction of the Roman Missal* (n. 50), it is by means of this dialogue that the Priest 'signifies the presence of the Lord to the community gathered there'.

50. Jungmann interpreted the *et cum spiritu tuo* as 'a popular consensus in the work of the priest' who is celebrating the Mass; see Joseph A. Jungmann, *The Mass of the Roman Rite: its Origins and Development*, trans. F. A. Brunner (Westminster, MD: Christian Classics, 1986), 363.

51. The liturgical exchange translated into Latin as *Dominus vobiscum* and *et cum spiritu tuo* is first documented about 215 AD in *The Apostolic Tradition* 4; see Bernard Botte, ed., *Hippolyte de Rome: La tradition apostolique d'après les anciennes versions*, 2 ed., Sources chrétiennes 11 bis (Paris: Les éditions du Cerf, 1968), 48–9.

52. See the *Didascalia Apostolorum*, the *Apostolic Constitutions* and the liturgies of Jerusalem (Greek), Antioch (Greek), Rome (Latin), Milan (Latin), Alexandria (Greek), Constantinople (Greek) and Edessa (Syriac).

53. In 1988, for example, the Sacred Congregation for Sacraments and the Divine Liturgy's *Directory for Sunday Celebrations in the Absence of a Priest* (n. 39) laid down that the layperson who leads such celebrations 'is not to use words that are proper to a priest or deacon and is to omit rites that are too readily associated with the Mass, for example, greetings – especially "The Lord be with you" – and dismissals, since these might give the impression that the layperson is a sacred minister.'

54. John Chrysostom, *Homilies on the Holy Pentecost*, 1.4 in Jacques-Paul Migne, ed., *Patrologia Graeca*, 161 vols. (Paris: Vrayet, 1857–1866) at 50:458–459.

55. See Michael K. Magee, 'The Liturgical Translation of the Response *Et cum spiritu tuo*', *Communio* 29 (Spring 2002), 152–71; W. C. Van Unnik, '*Dominus Vobiscum*: The Background of a Liturgical Formula', in *New Testament Essays*, ed. A. J. B. Higgins (Manchester: University Press, 1959), 270–305.

56. See the Appendix n. 2, 127 and 141.

57. See the Appendix n. 5, 8, 15, 26, 28.'

58. See the Appendix n. 5 and 13.

59. The number of paraphrases per 100 Latin words fell from 6.84 to 1.16.

60. See 'Have mercy on us, O Lord (*Miserere nostri, Domine*)' and 'For we have sinned against you (*Quia peccavimus tibi*)' in Appendix n. 5.

61. See Pecklers, *The Genius of the Roman Rite*, 108.

62. *Ecce Agnus Dei, ecce qui*, see the Appendix n. 132.

63. In the Appendix, see 'that we may prepare (*ut apti simus*)' in n. 4, 'You are seated at the right hand of the Father to intercede for us (*Qui ad dexteram Patris sedes, ad interpellandum pro nobis*)' in n. 6 and 'Lord Jesus Christ, Only Begotten Son, Lord God, Lamb of God, Son of the Father (*Domine Fili Unigenite, Iesu Christe, Domine Deus, Agnus Dei, Filius Patris*)' in n. 8. Chupungco suggests 'that we may be worthy' as a more appropriate translation of *ut apti simus*; see Chupungco, 'The ICEL 2010 Translation', 138.

64. In the Appendix, see 'let us acknowledge (*agnoscamus*)' in n. 4, 'to people of good will (*hominibus bonae voluntatis*)' and 'We praise you, we bless you, we adore you, we glorify you, we give you thanks for your great glory (*Laudamus te, benedicimus te, adoramus te, glorificamus te, gratias agimus tibi propter magnam gloriam tuam*)' in n. 8, 'At the Saviour's command (*Praeceptis salutaribus moniti*)' in n. 124, 'in our days (*diebus*)' in n. 125 and 'What has passed our lips as food, O Lord, may we possess ... that what has been given to us in time may be our healing for eternity (*Quod ore sumpsimus, Domine, ... capiamus, et de munere temporali fiat nobis remedium sempiternum*)' in n. 137.

65. In the Appendix, see 'May the Lord be (*Dominus sit*)' in n. 14, 'be wiped away (*deleantur*)' in n. 16, 'I believe (*Credo*)', 'born ... before all ages (*natum ante omnia saecula*)', 'consubstantial (*consubstantialem*)', 'incarnate (*incarnatus*)', 'suffered death (*passus*)', 'in accordance with (*secundum*)', 'who (*Qui*)', 'is adored (*adoratur*)', who (*qui*)', 'I confess (*Confiteor*)' and 'I look forward to (*expecto*)' in n. 18 and 'who (*qui*)' in n. 19.

66. In the Appendix, see 'fruit of the earth (*fructrum terrae*)' in n. 23, 'be accepted by you (*suscipiamur a te*)' and 'be pleasing to you (*placeat tibi*)' in n. 26 and 'my sacrifice and yours (*meum ac vestrum sacrificium*)' in n. 29.

67. In the Appendix, see 'we dare to say (*audemus dicere*)' in n. 124, 'keep us free (*simus semper liberi*)', 'by the help of your mercy (*ope misericordiae tuae adiuti*)', 'protect us from all anxiety (*ab omni perturbatione securi*)' and 'as we await the blessed hope and the coming (*exspectantes beatam spem et adventum*)' in n. 125, 'who (*qui*)', 'and ... her (*eamque*)', 'in accordance with your will (*secundum voluntatem tuam*)' and 'Who (*Qui*)' in n. 126, 'who ... through your death gave life to the world (*qui ... per mortem tuam mundum vivificasti*)', 'always faithful to your commandments (*tuis semper inhaerere mandatis*)', 'the receiving of your Body and Blood (*Perceptio Corporis et Sanguinis tui*)' and 'through your loving mercy be for me protection in mind and body, and a healing remedy (*pro tua pietate prosit mihi ad tutamentum mentis et corporis, et ad medelam percipiendam*)' in n. 131 and 'that you should enter (*ut intres*)' in n. 132. Elich regards the translation of *perturbatione* as 'anxiety' in n. 124 as an example of a 'psychologizing tendency that is to be avoided'; see Elich, 610.

68. In the Appendix, see n. 14 and compare n. 87 and n. 94.

69. In the Appendix, see n. 23 and 25. On this point, see also Chupungco, 'The ICEL2010 Translation', 219.

70. In the Appendix, see n. 29.

71. Catherine Vincie comments that 'There is only one sacrifice, although there are differences in the ministers and their liturgical functions'; see Vincie, 'The Mystagogical Implications', 225.

72. See Chupungco, 'The ICEL2010 Translation', 220; Vincie, 'The Mystagogical Implications', 226.

73. See Chupungco, 'The ICEL2010 Translation', 183.

74. See Peter Jeffery, *Translating Tradition: A Chant Historian Reads Liturgiam Authenticam* (Collegeville, Minnesota: Liturgical Press, 2005), 18–19.

75. See Pecklers, *The Genius of the Roman Rite*, 63.

76. See the following website, accessed on 29 October 2011: http://romanmissalchanges.com/2011/01/what-consubstantial-with-father-means.html.

77. See Chupungco, 'The ICEL 2010 Translation', 184.

78. The Apostles' Creed had been permitted in Masses for children since 1973 and it became an option for all Masses only in the 2002 edition of the Roman Missal; see Michael Witczak, 'History of the Latin Text and Rite', in *A Commentary on the Order of Mass of the Roman Missal,* ed. Foley et al. (Collegeville, Minnesota: Liturgical Press, 2011), 161–70 at 169.

79. See Appendix n. 122. The phrase *ad inferos* is used in the *Nova Vulgata Editio* to translate the words Sheol or Hades in many Old Testament texts; cf. Gn 42:38; 44:29, 31; Job 7:9; Prov 5:5; Is 14:11; 57:9; Ezek 31:15; Tob 3:10; 4:19; 13:2; Est 3:13.7.

80. See Chupungco, 'The ICEL2010 Translation', 184.

81. See Butterworth, *The English Primers*, 8–9, 301–3; Thurston, *Familiar Prayers*, 22–37.

82. See Pecklers, *The Genius of the Roman Rite*, 105.

83. See the Appendix n. 86.

84. See, for example, the article on excommunication in the online version of the *Catholic Encyclopedia*, consulted on 10 October 2011: http://newadvent.org/cathen/05678a.htm.

85. See 1 Cor 1:3; 2 Cor 1:2; 2 Th 1:2; Eph 1:2; Gal 1:3; Phil 1:2, Phlm 3, Rm 1:7.

86. See *Catechism of the Catholic Church* (Dublin: Veritas, 1994), p. 48. See also the following websites, all accessed on 10 October 2011: http://solochristo.org/info_apostlescreed.asp; http://elca.org/What-We-Believe/Statements-of-Belief/The-Apostles-Creed.aspx; http://anglicansonline.org/basics/apostles.html; http://gbgm-umc.org/umw/bible/apcreed.html.

87. In the Appendix, see n. 19.

88. The omission of the definite article before 'everlasting life' was probably because no further qualification was deemed necessary when the 'life' in question was already qualified by the adjective 'everlasting'.

89. See the translation of *vitam aeternam* in John 3:16 as 'eternal life'.

90. See the Appendix n. 85, 87, 90, 92, 103, 105, 111, 113, 120 and 133. On the two occasions where the 1973 text translates *aeternus,* it uses the English adjectives 'final' and 'everlasting'; see the Appendix n. 19, 87, 90, 103, 111, 113, 120 and 133.

91. In the Appendix, see Hebrews 7:25 (*ad interpellandum pro eis*), which is translated as 'to intercede for' in the Lectionary for Sunday 31 of Year B, and 'to intercede for us (*ad interpellandum pro nobis*)' in n. 6. See also Luke 2:14 and the translation of *et in terra pax hominibus bonae voluntatis* as 'and on earth peace to people of good will' and the literal translation of *peccata mundi* as 'the sins of the world' rather than following John 1:29 in n. 8.

92. In the Appendix, see Colossians 1:16 (*visibilia, et invisibilia*), which is translated in the Catechism (n. 331) as 'all things … visible and invisible', and the translation of *visibilium omnium et invisibilium* as 'of all things visible and invisible' in n. 18.

93. In the Appendix, see Daniel 3:39-40 (*sed in anima contrita et spiritu humilitatis suscipiamur … sic fiat sacrificium nostrum in conspectu tuo hodie*) and Isaiah 57:15 (*spiritum humilium et … cor contritorum*) and the translation of *In spiritu humilitatis et in animo contrito suscipiamur a te, Domine; et sic fiat sacrificium nostrum in conspectu tuo hodie, ut placeat tibi, Domine Deus* as 'With humble spirit and contrite heart may we be accepted by you, O Lord, and may our sacrifice in your sight this day be pleasing to you, Lord God' in n. 26. See also Psalm 51:4 and the translation of *Lava me, Domine, ab iniquitate mea, et a*

peccato meo munda me as 'Wash me, O Lord, from my iniquity and cleanse me from my sin' in n. 28.

94. In the Appendix n. 132, see Revelation 19:9 (*Beati qui ad coenam nuptiarum Agni vocati sunt*) and the translation of *Beati qui ad cenam Agni vocati sunt* as 'Blessed are those called to the supper of the Lamb', and also Matthew 8:8, which is recognised in n. 1386 of the *Catechism of the Catholic Church* (1992) as the basis of this response, and the translation of *intres sub tectum meum ... sanabitur anima mea* as 'that you should enter under my roof ... and my soul shall be healed'.

95. See the Appendix n. 18 and 117.

96. See the Appendix n. 4, 29, 105 and 115.

97. *Ratio translationis,* 108.

98. In the Appendix, see n. 11, 14 (second sentence), 18 (the sentence beginning *Qui cum Patre*), 126 (first sentence), 131 and 137.

99. In the Appendix, see n. 23, 25 and 131.

100. See the first seven sentences of the Apostles' Creed in Appendix n. 19.

101. See the sentences beginning *Qui propter nos* and *Et incarnatus* in Appendix n. 18.

102. In the Appendix, see the sentences beginning with *Et in Spiritum Sanctum*, with *Qui cum Patre*, with *Confiteor* and with *Et Exspecto* in n. 18.

103. *Ratio translationis*, 109–110.

104. See ibid., at 110–111,and see the Appendix n. 86 and 93.

105. In the Appendix, see n. 6 [twice], 8, 14, 18, 131 and 132.

106. In the Appendix, see n. 18 and 131 [twice].

107. In the Appendix, see n. 4, 8, 14, 18 [twice], 125, 126, 131 and 132.

108. In the Appendix, see n. 6 [twice], 14 and 124.

109. See Chupungco, 'The ICEL2010 Translation', 138–9.

110. In the Appendix, see 'Virgin ... Angels and Saints (*Virginem ... Angelos et Sanctos*)' in n. 4 and 'Only Begotten (*Unigenite*)' in n. 8.

111. In the Appendix, see 'Only Begotten (*Unigenitum*)' in n. 18 and 'Creator (*Creatorem*)' in n. 19.

112. See 'Holy, Holy, Holy (*Sanctus, Sanctus, Sanctus*)' in Appendix n. 83, 99, 107 and 116.

113. In the Appendix, see 'Apostles (*Apostolis*)' in n. 126 and 'Body and Blood (*Corpus et Sanguinem*) and 'Body and Blood (*Corporis et Sanguinis*)' in n. 131. In one case, the Latin capitalisations are somewhat ambiguous since they occur at the beginning of a sentence; see 'Lamb (*Agni*)' and 'Body ... Blood (*Corpus ... Sanguis*)' in nn. 132–133.

114. See the Appendix n. 18.

115. See *Ratio translationis*, 117–118.

116. See the Appendix n. 14 and 144.

117. See 'words of the Gospel (*evangelica dicta*)' in Appendix n. 16.

118. King says that the first part of n. 84 is 'far harder to pronounce, especially for a priest operating in his second or third language' than the 1973 translation, that translating n. 92, 94 and 96 as one sentence rather than two, as in the 1973 text, makes them, respectively, 'harder to say', 'difficult to pronounce' and 'almost impossible to say in English' and that, by keeping the order of the Latin in n. 92, 'the English becomes much harder to say'; see King, 'Lost, and found, in translation', S2, S4–S5.

119. King says that the second part of n. 84 'comes fairly easily off the lips', that the second part of n. 85 'is perhaps an improvement on' the previous translation, that the translation 'with eyes raised to heaven' in n. 89 'works quite well in English' and that the translation

'holy and venerable' in nn. 89–90 'works'. He comments that '*benedixit* is well captured by … "said the blessing"', that 'Victim' is 'a good shot at *hostia*, and captures more of the Old Testament resonance of the word than … "sacrifice"' in n. 92, that n. 93 'manages the translation well' and that 'In humble prayer' for *Supplices* is 'not bad'. He also says that 'every grace and heavenly blessing', rather than the more literal 'every heavenly blessing and grace' protects 'the natural rhythms of English' and avoids 'the inappropriately heavy sound of that final monosyllable' in n. 94 and that 'continue to make' for *semper … creas* 'is neat' and that 'bestow' is 'a good English *praestas*' in n. 97; see ibid., S2–S6.

120. See Ostdiek, 279.

121. In n. 83, 'It is right and just' is 'a more exact' translation and, in 'God of hosts', which 'reads well', the translators 'wisely chose to leave the word "hosts" unspecified'; in n. 84, the 'delicate grammatical rearrangement' that produced 'we make humble prayer and petition' follows the Latin 'more closely', translating *igitur* preserves 'the full meaning of the connection between thanksgiving and the offering that follows', the contrast between *clementissime* and *supplices* is 'well drawn', restoring the triple Latin designation of the gifts in 'to accept and bless these gifts we offer you in sacrifice' recognises 'a Latin rhetorical device to add stress', translating *illibata* as 'unblemished' could 'evoke a resonance with the Passover lamb (Exod 12:5)' and priests will 'be pleased' that the long paragraph 'has been broken into two sentences midway through'; in n. 86, 'blessed Joseph, her Spouse' reads 'more felicitously' than a strictly literal translation; in n. 87, inverting the sequence of the Latin at the beginning produces 'a more pleasing English phrasing'; in n. 89, 'O' has been added to the phrase 'to you, O God' for 'euphony'; in n. 92, translating *unde* as 'therefore' has the effect of making the text 'more pleasing for proclamation'; in n. 93, 'these offerings' is a 'shorthand' that 'makes proclamation less cumbersome' and 'once' is an addition that 'enhances the euphony'; see ibid., 280–1, 284–6, 288–9.

122. In n. 84, although the line in question 'reads well', translating 'in *primis* as "firstly" is not felicitous' and 'all those who, holding to the truth, hand on the catholic and apostolic faith' reads 'somewhat awkwardly' when compared to the translation used in 1973 or to 'and all faithful guardians of the catholic and apostolic faith'; in n. 85, people will find it hard to make sense of 'For them, we offer you this sacrifice of praise or they offer it for themselves and all who are dear to them' and the 1973 text had 'a simpler and clearer wording: "We offer you this sacrifice of praise for ourselves and those who are dear to us"' and, although 'paying their homage to you' 'may make the connection [between *offerunt* and *reddunt*] clearer to hearers' a 'more accurate' alternative would have been 'and offer you their desires'; in n. 86, a literal translation such as 'sharing in one holy fellowship and venerating the memory' would have preserved the parallel between *communicantes* and *venerantes* better than 'In communion with those whose memory we venerate', 'Mother of Jesus Christ, our God and Lord' would have flowed more naturally than 'Mother of our God and Lord, Jesus Christ', 'grant that through their merits and prayers we may be defended in all things' would have been preferable to 'we ask that through their merits and prayers, in all things we may be defended'; in n. 87, 'of our service, that of your whole family' does not 'fully' capture the contrast of the Latin, 'offering' might have been 'more readily understood' as a translation of *oblatio* and 'give birth of' is not the clearest translation of *regenerare ex*; in n. 90, the word 'chalice', which evokes 'images of medieval jeweled chalices', will 'sound strange, even archaic, to the faithful'; in n. 91, the translation of *calix* as 'cup' is 'inconsistent with the words of institution'; in n. 92, 'as we celebrate the memorial … of Christ, your Son, our Lord, we, your servants and your holy people' would have been 'rendered more felicitously' by 'we celebrate the memory of Christ, your Son. We, your holy people and your ministers, call to mind', 'splendour of your glory … sacrifice' is proposed as an alternative to 'glorious majesty … spotless victim'; in n. 93, 'kindly' is 'too weak and equivalent for *propitio*', 'your just servant, Abel' would have been better than 'Abel the just' and 'a spotless offering' would have been better than 'a spotless victim'; in n. 94, 'those of us who shall [have] received' would have been better than 'all

of us, who … receive', in n. 95, 'an implied verb, such as "sealed" or "marked," needs to be supplied' in 'with the sign of faith' and *locum refrigerii* might best have been translated as 'place of solace'; in n. 96, the opening line 'is fractured and does not flow well' and *quoque* should have been translated as 'especially'; in n. 97, *creas* should have been translated as 'create' rather than 'make'; in n. 98, *tibi Deo Patri* is translated as 'a vocative of address' rather than as 'an indirect object in the dative case'; see ibid., 281–5, 287–92.

123. See ibid., 292.

124. See Mark E. Wedig, 'The Mystagogical Implications', in *A Commentary on the Order of Mass of the Roman Missal*, ed. Foley et al., 293–300, 425–30, 575–82 at 295.

125. In the Appendix, see n. 96 and note that both the 1973 and 2011 texts leave *quoque* untranslated in n. 29.

126. He describes as 'confusing' the translation of *traderetur* both as 'betray' and 'hand over' in n. 102, notes the loss of 'flow in English' because the first stanza of n. 105 is translated as one sentence rather than two, and highlights the difficulties with the translation of *astare coram te* and *ministrare* in the same stanza. Commenting on 'merit to be co-heirs' in the final stanza, he says that it 'is practically impossible to say out loud' and 'does not sound like English'; see King, 'Lost, and found, in translation', S6–S7.

127. Noting that some had objected to 'dewfall' as a translation of *rore* in n. 101, King imagines 'that the translators wished to avoid the idea being misunderstood by hearers as either "due" or "Jew"'. Although, from a scientific point of view, dew does, as such, 'fall', the *Ratio translationis for the English Language* (2007) recommended that translators ensure that any anthropomorphisms, metaphors or images in the original text are fully included in any translation (nn. 62–63). King says that the translation of n. 102 is 'admirably brief', notes that the 2011 translation 'has it right, translating *congregemur in unum* as "we may be gathered into one"' in the second stanza of n. 105 and he describes 'fallen asleep' as 'slightly better than "gone to their rest"' and 'died in your mercy' as capturing the Latin 'quite well'; see ibid.

128. See Elich, 328, 334.

129. In n. 99, although 'just' does not 'correspond to English usage', the meanings of 'right' and just' are 'amplified by the beginning of the preface' when these words 'are juxtaposed with "duty" and "salvation"', the 'opening protocol of the preface' summarises 'Christ's role in creation, redemption, and incarnation' with 'admirable concision', 'he stretched out his hands as he endured his Passion' is better than the 1973 text, and 'incarnate' is 'a technical and accessible term' for ensuring that the flesh is 'clearly linked with the work of the Spirit'; in n. 100, 'You are indeed holy' is 'an emphatic beginning'; in n. 101, 'Make holy, therefore, these gifts, we pray' will 'encourage a staccato proclamation' and the 'beatiful poetic image of the settling dew' is an improvement on the 'matter of fact … "come upon"' of the 1973 translation; in n. 102, 'betrayed' reflects 'the common biblical translation of *tradere* in the passion arratives'; in n. 103, 'poured out' may refer to either the cup or the blood 'and so retains the ambiguity of the Latin'; in n. 104, 'The mystery of faith' is 'a straightforward announcement' that 'parallels the direct statements used at the end of the readings and in giving Holy Communion' and the acclamations 'are given in a crisp memorable translation'; in n. 105, 'as we celebrate the memorial' seems to be regarded as a reasonable compromise translation; 'we offer … giving thanks' is described as 'a rich expression of the church's offertory', '*Supplices deprecamur* is given its full force in … "Humbly we pray"', 'bring to fulness' is 'a good translation' and the word 'perfect' may have been rejected 'because it could be confused with the adjective with the stress placed on the wrong syllable'; in n. 106, the 'strong formal language of the doxology … will soon become well-loved and known by heart'; see ibid., 327–9, 331–4.

130. In n. 99, 'you made all things' is 'probably not an improvement' on the older translation 'since *cuncta* really has a collective sense of the whole', 'he stretched out his arms on the cross' would have painted the picture more 'vividly' than 'he stretched out his hands as he endured his Passion', and 'Lord God of hosts' is 'not quite transparent' and has the

'serious consequence' of abandoning 'the common ecumenical texts we have shared with other churches'; in n. 100, the translation of *vere* as 'indeed' does not 'retain the linguistic parallel with the beginning of the preface' where *vere* is translated as 'truly'; in n. 101, 'like the dewfall' is 'wordy and prosaic' and the 'crisp metaphor' of 'by the dew of your Spirit' would have been better; in n. 102 'two subordinate clauses ("At the time … and entered willingly …")' are 'allowed to intervene between the epiclesis and the subject of the institution narrative over the bread, "he"'; the 'significant verbal parallel between' being 'given up' to death and his body being 'given up' for you 'would have been worth preserving in translation'; in n. 103, *calix* should have been translated as 'cup' rather than 'chalice' and *pro multis* should have been translated as 'for the many' or 'for the multitude'; in n. 105, the capitalisation of 'Bread', 'Cup', 'Chalice', 'Cross', 'Death', 'Resurrection' is described as having 'no basis in the Latin' and as not being 'consistent', the change from the verbs 'deemed … stand … serve' to 'held … be … minister to' are 'unhelpful', translating *caritas* as 'charity' is 'a mistake' because the word 'is too narrow in its meaning and can be perceived as pejorative', describing the dead as being united with Christ 'in a death like his' is 'misleading' since 'they would not have died by crucifixion', 'who had found favour with you' would have been better than 'who have pleased you' and 'worthy to share eternal life' would have been better than 'merit to be coheirs to eternal life', which pushes 'the limits of intelligibility'; see ibid., 327–34.

131. See Joyce Ann Zimmerman, 'The Mystagogical Implications', in *A Commentary on the Order of Mass of the Roman Missal*, ed. Foley et al., 335–9, 383–8, 615–20, 645–50 at 335, 337.

132. See King, 'Lost, and found, in translation', S7.

133. See the Appendix n. 105.

134. The upright see the face of God (cf. Ps 10:7) and the Psalmist asks the Lord to 'lift up the light of your face upon us' (Ps 4:7) and to save his people by making his face to shine on them (cf. Ps 79:4, 8, 20). In Old Testament times, it was considered a privilege to look on the face of the King (cf. Esth 1:14), particularly if his face lit up in a welcoming smile (cf. Job 29:24), so that 'In the light of the king's face is life' (Prov 16:15).

135. King says that Eucharistic Prayer 3 'starts off very well indeed' in n. 108 where 'by the power and working of the Holy Spirit' is 'not bad', 'you give life to all things and make them holy' is to his liking, 'you never cease to gather' captures the Latin better than 'From age to age you gather', and 'a pure sacrifice' for *oblatio* 'works very nicely'. He comments that 'make holy' is 'more authentic English' than 'sanctify' and that he prefers 'these mysteries' to 'this Eucharist' in n. 109, and there is 'some good work' in the fourth stanza of n. 113, including 'sacrifice of reconciliation', 'which has made our peace with you', 'the entire people you have gained for your own' and the 'not too bad' translation 'Listen graciously' for *adesto propitius*. He also welcomes the decision to retain 'advance the peace and salvation of all the world' and 'your pilgrim Church on earth' from the 1973 translation in that stanza. In the final stanza, he speaks positively about 'all who were pleasing to you at their passing from this life' and 'give kind admittance'. See King, 'Lost, and found, in translation', S7–S9.

136. Commenting that something 'has gone horribly wrong with' the 2011 translation of the second stanza of n. 113, King seems to imply that the translation should have corrected what he describes as 'the slightly alarming theology of the Latin, suggesting a bad-tempered God demanding blood'; see ibid., S8.

137. King says that the translation of 'relatively unimportant words such as *igitur* seems 'slightly self-conscious' and he questions the translations of *memores*, *salutiferae* and *praestolantes* in the first stanza of n. 113. In the second stanza, he says that 'the hanging participle "recognising" simply cannot have the effect in English that *agnoscens* has in Latin' and, in the third, he questions the translations of *nos perficiat* and *valeamus* and the 'plethora of adjectives, taken lock, stock and barrel from the Latin' that 'does not really work well in English, and does not add anything to the meaning'. In stanza four, he again

questions the 'coyness about … the congregation standing during the Eucharistic Prayer' in the translation 'whom you have summoned before you (*quam tibi astare voluisti*)' and, concerning the final stanza, he says that putting 'departed brothers and sisters' at the beginning 'means that the English prepositional phrase is bearing an impossible weight, with "To" staggering under the immense burden of the rest of the sentence'; see ibid., S7–S9.

138. See Elich, 375.

139. In n. 108, three sentences from the 1973 translation are combined in a single sentence that 'is theologically powerful' but 'without becoming turgid', 'what was rather static has become more dynamic' thanks to replacing 'all creation' and 'all life, all holiness' with 'all you have created' and 'you give life to all things and make them holy', the reference to the Spirit is strengthened by the addition of 'power and'; in n. 109, the adjective 'same' before 'Spirit' links this paragraph with the previous paragraph but appreciating the connection may not be obvious 'because the idea spans half a dozen lines of text', 'humbly implore' and 'graciously' express due deference more strongly than the 'we ask you' of the 1973 translation, 'for consecration' indicates 'that the gifts are brought and set aside at this point but not yet offered' and the change from 'this eucharist' to 'these mysteries' reflects the distinction between 'the celebration actually taking place' and the fact that 'whenever and wherever we celebrate the Mass, we do so at Christ's command'; in n. 110, the addition of 'For' and 'himself' connects the institution narrative to the preceding paragraph and retaining 'the strong word "betrayed"' makes the word order 'a little more comfortable'; in n. 113, the translation of *igitur* as 'Therefore' connects the communal offering to the just completed acclamation by the assembly and 'may become one body, one spirit in Christ' connects the second epiclesis with the first, 'in your presence' and 'unfailing' are an addition that 'enriches the content and endows the phrase with a solemn cadence', drawing 'the "peace and salvation of all the world" within the scope of "this Sacrifice of our reconciliation"' is 'a useful conterbalance to any possible misunderstanding of … "for many for the forgiveness of sins"' and 'bestow on the world all that is good' and 'the rhetorical force of a repeated "though"' provides 'a strong conclusion'; in n. 114, the formal doxology 'provides a solemn ending with a clear rhetorical structure that builds to a forceful climax'; ibid., 375–82.

140. In n. 109, 'humbly implore' might have been better expressed as 'humbly pray' because 'excess quickly appears insincere in English'; in n. 113, the introduction of the verbs 'celebrate' and 'look forward' is described as 'a surprising lapse in the way the English is structured on the Latin model', the translations of *oblationem* as 'oblation', of *immolatio* as 'death' and of *Hostiam* as 'Victim' are criticised, and the introduction of 'may' after the mention of the Spirit 'means that the phrase no longer exactly constitutes an invocation of the Holy Spirit, 'Be pleased' is 'somewhat stiff', translating *firmare* as 'confirm' and *caritate* as 'charity' spoils the memorable 'strengthen in faith and love your pilgrim Church on earth' of the earlier translation, 'you make your own' would have been more straightforward than 'you have gained for your own', 'summoned before you' is 'somewhat stern' and 'whom you have called to stand before you' would have been preferable, 'give kind admittance to your kingdom' is 'disappointing' and 'their passing from this life' carries 'the burden of the euphemism "passing"'; see ibid., 377–9, 381–2.

141. See ibid., 376; King, 'Lost, and found, in translation', S7; Pecklers, *The Genius of the Roman Rite*, 102.

142. On n. 118 in the Appendix, he comments that '"for the celebration" works better' and that 'it also seems important that the new version has translated *ipse*' and, on n. 119, he says that 'the strength of the new version is that it preserves the all-important echo of the Johannine last Supper narrative (John 13:1; 17;1)' so that the 'overall effect, happily, is to safeguard the memory of the fourth gospel's unique presentation of the Passion of Jesus'. On n. 120, he welcomes the restoration of '"fruit of the vine", a reminder of the echo of the three Synoptic accounts of the institution of the Eucharist', and on n. 122, he describes 'realm of the dead' as 'slightly better than "among the dead"', 'we proclaim' as 'better …

than "we profess"', 'salvation to the whole world' as helping to clarify the true significance of 'for many' in n. 120, 'grant in your loving kindness' as showing 'some respect to the target language', the 'pleasing' translation of *filiis* as 'children' rather than as 'sons' and the translation 'bestow' as 'better for *largiris* than "give"'. See King, 'Lost, and found, in translation', S10–S12.

143. In the Appendix n. 117, see his comment on the inclusive language in the translations 'so that those who seek (*te quaerentes*) might find you' and 'taught them (*hominibus*) to look forward to salvation', the 'much better' translation 'entrusted the whole world to his care', the 'correct' translation of *ut tibi soli Creatori serviens* as 'so that serving you alone, the Creator, he might have dominion over all creatures' and his comment that '"when through disobedience" catches better the impact' of *non oboediens*. Noting the 'pleasing touch' of repeating 'the root "dominion ... domain" for the Latin cognates *imperaret ... imperio*', he says that '"shared our human nature in all things but sin" is excellent for catching the scriptural echoes of the Latin'. He approves the translation of *redemptionem* as 'freedom' rather than as 'redemption' and he describes the description of 'sorrowful of heart' as being 'closer to the original'. The description of 'To accomplish your plan' is 'better' and the restoration of 'him who died and rose again for us' is 'important'. He describes the description of 'first fruits' as 'better', 'bringing to perfection his work in the world' as 'an improvement' and 'sanctify creation to the full' as 'closer to the Latin'.

144. See his discussion of the translation of *hominem* as 'man', the criticism of the translation of *de* in *de Spiritu Sancto* and the preference for 'by rising' rather than 'rising' in n. 117 and the comment about n. 118 that 'this same' and 'graciously' sound 'otiose in English'. On n. 122, King describes "may truly become" as 'less convincing' than some of the other translations offered and he questions the translations of *circumstantium* and *offerentium*, the use of 'O', which he says 'is not really natural English', to translate the vocative and the translation of *caelestem hereditatem*. See King, 'Lost, and found, in translation', S10–S12.

145. See Ostdiek, 423.

146. In n. 16, translating *claritate* as 'glory' is not in keeping with the allowance for 'some variety' within consistency in *Liturgiam authenticam* 50d–51 and 'in your presence are countless hosts of Angels' is 'somewhat awkward'; in n. 117, *confitemur* might have been better translated as 'acclaim', the 'abrupt shift ... from "man" to "all/those/them"' will 'raise concerns on the pastoral level', 'more of the richness of the *conversatio morum* found in the Catholic tradition of spirituality might have been drawn in' when translating *conversatus*, '*nostra condicionis forma* embraces not only our "human nature" ... but also the concrete circumstances of human life' and 'he sent from you, Father, as the first fruits for those who believe, the Holy Spirit who, completing his work in the world would bring them [believers] to full holiness' would have been better than 'he sent the Holy Spirit from you, Father, as the first fruits for those who believe, so that, bringing to perfection his work in the world, he might sanctify creation to the full'; in n. 118, 'for the celebration' is 'ambiguous'; in n. 119, the 'parallel between *venisset ac dilexisset* has been lost', the translation of *benedixit* as 'blessed' (rather than 'said the blessing') may 'trip up' priests who proclaim the words from memory; in n. 120, *calix* and *effundetur* should have been translated as 'cup' and 'will be shed'; in n. 122, the sentence beginning 'Look, O Lord' is long and 'tests the skills of the priest', catechesis will be needed to ensure that 'offer you his Body and Blood' is 'not understood as a new act of offering separate from that of Christ himself', *parasti* and *participabunt* should have been translated as 'you have prepared' and 'will partake', 'all for whom we make this offering' would have been better than 'all for whom we offer this sacrifice', 'those who make this offering' would have been better than 'those who take part in this offering', 'that we may' would have been better than 'may we' and the parallel between *glorificemus* and *valeamus* has been lost; see ibid., 417–22.

147. In n. 16, the translation 'Father most holy' avoids the 'confusion the normal English word order, "Holy Father," would cause' and it 'heightens the solemnity and aids proclamation', adding 'of them' expresses the 'delimiting' implied in *creaturas ... multasque*, translating *claritate* as 'glory' echoes the other words associated with 'glory' at the beginning and

end of the preface; in n. 117, translating *caritate* as 'love' is 'appropriate', 'he might have dominion over all creatures' is a translation that 'captures well the pleasing resonance between *imperaret and imperio*'; in n. 119, 'For when the hour had come' expresses well 'the temporal sequence of the two verbs … and is better suited for proclamation'; in n. 122, *Hostia* and *hostia viva* are 'well translated as "Sacrifice" (of Christ) and "living sacrifice" (of Christians)', *circumstantium* is 'well translated as "those gathered here before you"' and the division at 'There, with the whole of creation' makes the text 'easier to proclaim'; see ibid., 417–8, 421–2.

148. See the Appendix n. 86. King comments that 'wisely but inconsistently' the 2011 text omitted 'the orotund expression, "of the same Virgin"' when describing Joseph as Mary's Spouse; see King, 'Lost, and found, in translation', S2.

149. See the Appendix n. 87 and King's comment that *placatus* 'does not really mean the same as "graciously"' in ibid.

150. In the Appendix, see 'our Lord' and 'these offerings' in n. 84, '[or they offer it for themselves and all who are dear to them]' in n. 85, 'those whose memory we venerate' in n. 86, 'in his holy and venerable hands' in n. 89, 'In a similar way' and 'in his holy and venerable hands' in n. 90, 'our Lord' in n. 92, 'a holy sacrifice, a spotless victim' in n. 93 and 'your servants, who, though sinners, hope in your abundant mercies' and 'admit us, we beg you, into their company' in n. 96.

151. In the Appendix, see 'most merciful', 'our Lord', 'humble', 'holy and unblemished', 'whole', 'your servant', 'holding to the truth' and 'apostolic' in n. 84, 'eternal' in n. 85, 'glorious', 'blessed', 'your blessed', 'your' and 'protecting' in n. 86, 'of our service' and 'eternal' in n. 87, 'spiritual' and 'most beloved' in n. 88, 'before he was to suffer' and 'holy and venerable' in n. 89, 'precious' and 'holy and venerable' in n. 90.

152. In the Appendix, see 'blessed', 'glorious', 'our Lord', 'holy', 'your glorious', 'pure', 'spotless', 'holy' and 'everlasting' in n. 92, 'high' and 'a holy sacrifice, a spotless victim' in n. 93, 'humble', 'holy', 'who through this participation at the altar', 'most holy' and 'heavenly' in n. 94, 'and rest in the sleep of peace' and 'of refreshment' in n. 95, 'your servants, who, though sinners, hope in your abundant mercies', 'holy' and 'your' in n. 96 and 'good' in n. 97.

153. In the Appendix, see 'therefore' and 'first of all' in n. 84, 'in hope of health and well-being, and fulfilling their vows to you' in n. 85, 'In communion with those whose memory we venerate, especially' and 'in all things' in n. 86, 'Therefore' in 87, 'in every respect' in n. 88, 'on the day before' and 'with eyes raised to heaven' in n. 89, 'In a similar way' and 'in his holy and venerable hands' in n. 90, 'Therefore' and 'into heaven', in n. 92, 'with serene and kindly countenance' in 93, 'on high' and 'in the sight of your divine majesty' in 94 and 'graciously', 'into their company' and 'not weighing our merits, but granting us your pardon' in n. 96.

154. In the Appendix, see 'these offerings', 'which we offer', 'Be pleased to', 'together with' and 'and N. our Bishop' in n. 84, 'and all gathered' in n. 85, 'we may be defended' in n. 86, 'we pray', 'order' and 'and command' in n. 87, 'O God' in nn. 88–89, 'Be pleased … to' and 'we pray' in n. 88, 'of' in n. 89, 'and gave' and 'for' in nn. 89–90, 'O Lord', 'proclaim', 'profess' and 'Save' in n. 91, 'Be pleased … to' and 'were pleased to' in n. 93, 'command (*iube*)' in n. 94, 'flock', 'servants' and 'place' in n. 95, 'with', 'and fellowship', 'admit' and 'we beg you' in n. 96, 'O Lord' in n. 97 and 'and with him, and' and 'O God' in n. 98, 106, 114 and 123.

155. See the Appendix n. 93.

156. Neither the 1973 nor the 2011 text translate the first word of *Et supplices* in Appendix n. 105.

157. In the Appendix, see 'truly right and just', 'most holy', 'your', 'Redeemer' and 'all' in n. 99 and 'of life', 'of salvation', 'spread', 'your servant', 'who was united with your Son in a death like his', 'who have fallen asleep in the hope of the resurrection', 'who have died in your mercy', 'blessed', 'blessed', 'all' and 'who have pleased you' in n. 105.

158. In the Appendix, see 'truly right and just', 'as he endured his Passion' and 'with one voice' in n. 99, 'therefore' and 'sending down ... like the dewfall' in n. 101, 'At the time he was betrayed' and 'and entered willingly into his Passion' in n. 102, 'In a similar way' and 'once more' in n. 103 and 'Therefore', 'Humbly', 'into one', 'spread throughout the world', 'today' and 'to yourself' in n. 105.

159. In the Appendix, see 'proclaim', 'profess' and 'Save' in n. 91, 'and Redeemer' and 'with' in n. 99, 'we pray' in n. 101, 'of' in n. 102, 'for' in nn. 102–103, 'chalice and' in n. 103, 'Save us' in n. 104 and 'and', 'Chalice', 'we pray that', 'spread', 'and', 'Grant that', 'we pray' and 'and' in n. 105.

160. In the Appendix, see 'pure' in n. 108, 'same' and 'we have brought to you for consecration' in n. 109, 'himself' in n. 110, 'saving', 'wondrous', 'his second', 'of your Son', 'most blessed', 'our Pope', 'your blessed', 'glorious', 'of our reconciliation', 'this family', 'merciful', 'scattered throughout the world', 'who were pleasing to you at their passing from this life' and 'kind' in n. 113 and 'your servant N. whom you have called [today] from this world to yourself', 'who was united with your Son in a death like his', 'who have died', 'lowly', 'glorious', 'who were pleasing to you at their passing from this life' and 'kind' in n. 115.

161. In the Appendix, see 'you have created' and 'by the power and working' in n. 108, 'Therefore', 'humbly' and 'graciously' in n. 109, 'In a similar way' in n. 111, 'therefore', 'especially', 'in your presence', 'graciously', 'in your compassion' and 'there' in n. 113 and 'from the earth ... in the flesh', 'after the pattern of his own glorious body', 'for ever', 'from our eyes', 'for all the ages' and 'without end' in n. 115.

162. In the Appendix, see 'our (*nobis*)' in n. 99, 'for through' in n. 108, 'and' and 'of' in n. 110, 'for' in nn. 110–111, 'and' in n. 111, 'O Lord', 'proclaim', 'profess' and 'Save' in n. 112, 'we pray', 'you willed', 'with', 'elect', 'and', 'with', 'we pray', 'Be pleased to', 'with', 'and', 'through whom' and 'you bestow on the world' in n. 113 and 'was united', 'for', 'through whom' and 'you bestow on the world' in n. 115.

163. In the Appendix, see 'sacrificial Victim (*Hostiam*)' and 'unfailing help (*adiuvari*)' in n. 113.

164. In the Appendix, neither the 1973 nor the 2011 text translate the *vero* in the sentence beginning *Ut tuam vero* in n. 117 or the *tibi* (in *pro quibus tibi*) and *sed et* in n. 122.

165. In the Appendix, see 'just', 'existing before all ages and abiding for all eternity' and 'who alone are good' in n. 116, 'most holy', 'most holy', 'Only Begotten' and 'who died and rose for us' in n. 117, 'same' and 'himself' in n. 118, 'same' in n. 120 and 'yourself', 'in Christ', 'of your glory', 'your servant', 'the whole Order', 'entire', 'your', 'all of', 'merciful' and 'blessed' in n. 122.

166. In the Appendix, see 'truly', 'truly just', 'so', 'in your presence', 'without ceasing', 'in exultation' and 'giving voice to every creature under heaven' in n. 116, 'alone', 'in mercy', 'of heart' in n. 117, 'Therefore' and 'graciously' in n. 118 and 'Therefore', 'to you', 'in your loving kindness', 'by the Holy Spirit', 'Therefore ... now', 'also', 'There', 'with the whole of creation' and 'on the world' in n. 122.

167. In the Appendix, see 'for', 'existing before all ages and', 'And so', 'and, gazing' and 'we, too' in n. 116, 'for', 'and', 'And', 'for', 'And' and 'he shared' in n. 117, 'we pray' in n. 118, 'and', 'and' and 'of' in n. 119, 'for' in nn. 119–120, 'O Lord', 'proclaim', 'profess' and 'Save' in n. 121 and 'and', 'we proclaim', 'grant', 'they may truly become' and 'with' in n. 122.

168. In the Appendix, see the translation of *confidimus adiuvari* as 'we rely for *unfailing* help' in n. 113.

169. The number of paraphrases per 100 Latin words fell from 5.54 to 0.77.

170. In the Appendix, compare the translations of *supplices rogamus ac petimus*, of *quam pacificare* and of *omnibus orthodoxis atque ... cultoribus* in n. 84, of *quibus, qui, suarum, suae* and *sua* in n. 85, of *Genitricis Dei et Domini nostri Iesu Christi* and *quorum meritis precibusque* in n. 86 and of *oblationem servitutis nostrae, sed et cunctae familiae tuae* in n. 87. See also the translations of *item* and *aeterni* in n. 90, of *servi* in n. 92, of *haec omnia*

... semper bona creas ...et praestas nobis in n. 97, of *Supplices te rogamus* and of *gloria tua ...satiemur* in n. 113 and 115 and of *erimus* in n. 115.

171. The 2011 text translated *cuncta* literally, as 'all things', and, in parallel with *incarnatus est* in Appendix n. 18, it translated *incarnatum* as 'incarnate'; see the Appendix n. 99. Rather than translating *fons* as the 'fountain' of all holiness, which has the connotation of a particular place, the 2011 text translated it as the 'fount' of all holiness, apparently in order to highlight the twin ideas of source and living water; see the Appendix n. 100. As in the other institution narratives, *aeterni* is translated as 'eternal' in Appendix n. 103. In Appendix n. 105, the verb *ministrare* is translated literally and *eam* is translated as 'her' to reflect the traditionally feminine language used to describe the Church and *caritate* is translated as 'charity', apparently because the emphasis is on growth towards the absolute fullness of 'love' as in n. 2 and n. 117. Also in Appendix n. 105, reflecting the meaning of *mundo* in n. 18 and 117, for example, *ex hoc mundo* is translated as 'from this world' rather than as 'from this life'.

172. In the Appendix, see the translation of *aeterni* as 'eternal' in n. 111. See also the implicit distinction between the pre-consecration 'offering' of bread and wine and the post-consecration 'oblation' of the Body and Blood of Christ when *oblationem Ecclesiae tuae* is translated as 'the oblation of your Church' in n. 113. There seems to be an implicit reference to Christ's self-offering in the self-offering of those who have 'become one body, one spirit' with him when *nos tibi perficiat munus aeternum* is translated as 'make of us an eternal offering to you' and the choice of 'elect' rather than 'saints' as a translation of *electis* in n. 113. In n. 113, *caritate* is translated as 'charity', apparently because the emphasis is on the confirmation of the charity of the pilgrim Church, rather than on 'love' in the absolute sense, as in n. 2 and 117.

173. In the Appendix, see the translation of *sed et ... cuncta fecisti* as 'yet you ... have made all that is' in n. 116, of *imperaret* as 'might have dominion over', of *imperio* as 'domain', of *subvenisti* as 'came ... to the aid of', of *in exspectatione* as 'to look forward to', of *incarnatus* as 'Incarnate' and of *primitias* as 'first fruits' in n. 117, of *aeternum* as 'eternal' in n. 118 and of *hora venisset* as 'the hour had come' in n. 119. See also the translation of *genimine vitis* as 'the fruit of the vine' and of *aeterni* as 'eternal' in n. 120 and of *recolimus* as 'remember', of *exspectantes* as 'as we await', of *parasti* as 'you ... have provided for', of *participabunt* as 'partake of' and of *omnium* as 'all' in n. 122.

174. Pecklers, *The Genius of the Roman Rite*, 107.

175. In the Appendix, see also 1 Corinthians 11:26 (*donec veniat*) and the translation of *donec venias* as 'until you come again' and John 4:42 (*hic est vere Salvator mundi*) and the translation of *Salvator mundi, Salva nos* as 'Save us, Saviour of the world' in n. 91, 104, 112 and 121. On the 'again' in 'until you come again', see Ostdiek, 288.

176. The word *Sabaoth* is a Latin transliteration of the word used in the Greek Septuagint text of Isaiah 6:3 (σαβαωθ) to translate the similarly sounding Hebrew plural noun.

177. See the Appendix n. 83, 99, 107 and 116.

178. See the Appendix n. 90, 92, 111 and 120–121.

179. See the Appendix n. 91.

180. See the following website, consulted on 1 November 2011: http://cin.org/users/james/ebooks/master/trent/tsacr-e.htm.

181. See Jacques Dupuis SJ and Josef Neuner SJ, eds., *The Christian Faith in the Doctrinal Documents of the Catholic Church,* Seventh Revised & Enlarged Edition (New York: Alba House, 2001) at n. 1989/5.

182. See Joachim Jeremias, *The Eucharistic Words of Jesus*, trans. Norman Perrin (London: S.C.M. Press, 1966).

183. See Joseph Pascher, *Eucharistia. Gestalt und Vollzug* (Münster: Aschendorff, 1947).

184. See Norbert Baumert and Maria-Irma Seewann, 'Eucharistie – "für alle" oder "für viele"?' *Gregorianum* 89/3 (2008), 501–32:507, 511.

185. Joseph Ratzinger, *Jesus of Nazareth. Holy Week: From the Entrance into Jerusalem to the Resurrection* (San Francisco: Ignatius Press, 2011), 134.

186. Ibid., 136.

187. See Rudolf Pesch, *Das Abendmahl und Jesu Todesverstaendnis* (Freiburg: Herder, 1978), 99–100; Ulrich Wilckens, *Theologie des Neuen Testaments. Bd. 1/2: Jesu Tod und Auferstehung und die Entstehung der Kirche aus Juden und Heiden* (Neukirchen-Vluyn: Neukirchener Verlag, 2003), 84.

188. Ratzinger, *Jesus of Nazareth. Holy Week*, 136–7.

189. See Pecklers, *The Genius of the Roman Rite*, 107–8.

190. See the Appendix n. 90, 103, 111 and 120.

191. See *Missal* (2011) at 64–5, 77–8, 87–8, 96–7, 106–7, 116–17, 144–5, 154–6, 165, 322–3, 362–4, 366, 369–70, 372–4, 402–25, 436–59, 462–87, 490–9, 641–3, 664–5, 669, 671–2, 676, 683, 701–2, 710–1, 728–9, 732–3, 736–7, 751–2, 775–6, 786–8, 793–4, 818–9, 832–3, 857–8, 870–1, 875, 894–5, 904–5, 909–10, 930–1, 948–9, 952, 1047, 1060, 1064, 1069–70, 1074, 1083–4, 1090–2, 1096–9, 1115–6, 1130, 1134–6, 1177–8, 1237, 1245–9, 1253–4, 1260, 1264–5, 1269.

192. See the translation of *Pater sancte* or *sancte Pater* in the Appendix n. 99, 117 and 119.

193. See the translation of *sancte Pater* in *Missal* (2011) at 488–9, 1127–9.

194. See King, 'Lost, and found, in translation', S11.

195. See the Appendix n. 117.

196. See the Appendix n. 122.

197. The phrase *ad inferos* is used in the *Nova Vulgata Editio* to translate the words Sheol or Hades in many Old Testament texts, cf. Gn 42:38; 44:29, 31; Job 7:9; Prov 5:5; Is 14:11; 57:9; Ezek 31:15; Tob 3:10; 4:19; 13:2; Est 3:13.7. It is also used in one Old Testament text to refer to the shades who inhabit Sheol or Hades; cf. Prov 2:18.

198. See the Appendix n. 117.

199. See King, 'Lost, and found, in translation', S10.

200. King comments that the translators 'have shown sensitivity here to the "target language"' by turning three of the five adjectives into verbs; see ibid., S3.

201. See *Quam oblationem tu, Deus, in omnibus, quaesumus, benedictam, adscriptam, ratam, rationabilem, acceptabilemque facere digneris* in the Appendix n. 88.

202. In the Appendix, see 'In communion with those whose memory we venerate (*Communicantes, et memoriam venerantes*) in n. 86, 'we celebrate the memorial of (*memores*)' in n. 92, 'the offering of (*quod tibi obtulit*)' in n. 93 and 'At the time he was betrayed and entered willingly into his Passion (*Qui cum Passioni voluntarie traderetur*)' in n. 102. See also 'we celebrate the memorial of (*memores*)' in n. 105, 'all you have created (*omnis a te condita creatura*)' in 108, 'we celebrate the memorial of (*memores*)' and 'Listen graciously to (*adesto propitius*)' in n. 113 and 'most holy (*sancte*)' in n. 116. See, in addition, 'most holy (*sancte*)', 'most holy (*sancte*)', 'he shared our human nature in all things but sin (*in nostra condicionis forma est conversatus per omnia absque peccato*)' and 'so that he might sanctify creation to the full (*omnem sanctificationem compleret*)' in n. 117 and 'most holy (*sancte*)' in n. 119.

203. In the Appendix, see 'And with your spirit (*Et cum spiritu tuo*)' in n. 83, 'that you accept and bless (*uti accepta habeas et benedicas*)', 'these gifts, these offerings, these holy and unblemished sacrifices (*haec dona, haec menera, haec sancta sacrificia illibata*)' and 'Be pleased to grant her peace, to guard, unite and govern her (*quam pacificare, custodire, adunare et regere digneris*)' in n. 84, 'whose faith and devotion are known to you (*quorum tibi fides cognita est et nota devotio*)' in n. 85 and 'order our days in your peace (*diesque nostros in tua pace disponas*)' in n. 87. See also 'this offering (*Quam oblationem*)' and 'so that it may become (*ut ... fiat*)' in n. 88, 'looking up to heaven (*elevatis oculis in*)

caelum)', 'giving you thanks he said the blessing (*tibi gratias agens benedixit*)' and 'saying (*dicens*)' in n. 89, 'giving you thanks, he said the blessing (*tibi gratias agens benedixit*)' and 'saying (*dicens*)' in n. 90 and 'this pure victim, this holy victim, this spotless victim (*hostiam puram, hostiam sanctam, hostiam immaculatam*)' in n. 92. See, in addition, 'In humble prayer we ask you … command that these gifts be borne by the hands of your holy Angel (*Supplices te rogamus … iube haec perferri per manus sancti Angeli tui*)', 'so that all of us who receive (*ut, quotquot ... sumpserimus*)' and 'may be filled (*repleamur*)' in n. 94, 'Grant them … a place of refreshment (*Ipsis ...locum refrigerii ... ut indulgeas*)' in n. 95 and 'To us … graciously grant (*Nobis … donare digneris*)' in 96 and 'Through whom (*Per quem*)' in n. 97.

204.In the Appendix, see 'And with your spirit (*Et cum spiritu tuo*)', 'It is truly right and just, our duty and salvation (*Vere dignum et iustum est, aequum et salutare*)', 'Fulfilling (*adimplens*)', 'gaining (*aquirens*)', 'so as to break the bonds of death and manifest the resurrection (*ut mortem solveret et resurrectionem manifestaret*)', 'we declare (*praedicamus*)' and 'we acclaim (*dicentes*)' in n. 99, 'Make holy (*sanctifica*)' in n. 101, 'giving thanks (*gratias agens*)' and 'saying (*dicens*)' in n. 102 and 'giving thanks (*gratias agens*)' and 'saying (*dicens*)' in n. 103. See also 'Chalice of salvation (*calicem salutis*)', 'giving thanks (*gratias agentes*)', 'partaking in (*participes*)', 'be gathered into one (*congregemur in unum*)' [which parallels the translation of *in unum … congregati* in n. 122], 'bring ... to the fullness of (*perficias*)', 'welcome them into the light of your face (*eos in luman vultus tui admitte*)' and 'we may merit to be co-heirs to eternal life and may praise and glorify you (*aeternae vitae mereamus esse consortes, et te laudemus et glorificemus*)' in n. 105.

205.In the Appendix, see 'And with your spirit (*Et cum spiritu tuo*)' in n. 107, 'you give life to all things and make them holy (*vivificas et sanctificas universa*)', 'never cease to (*non desinis*)', 'from the rising of the sun to its setting (*a solis ortu usque ad occasum*)' and 'a pure sacrifice may be offered to your name (*oblatio munda offeratur nomini tuo*)' in n. 108, 'we humbly implore you (*Supplices … deprecamur*)', 'graciously make holy (*sanctificare digneris*)' and 'these mysteries (*haec mysteria*)' in n. 109 and 'giving you thanks he said the blessing (*tibi gratias agens benedixit*)' and 'saying (*dicens*)' in n. 110. See also 'saying (*dicens*)' in n. 111, 'as we look forward to his second coming (*praestolantes alterum eius adventum*)', 'Look … upon the oblation of your Church (*Respice … in oblationem Ecclesiae tuae*)' [compare the translation of *Respice* in n. 122], 'recognising (*agnoscens*)' and 'and filled with his Holy Spirit (*Spiritu eius Sancto repleti*)', 'so that we may obtain (*ut ... consequi valeamus*)', 'Be pleased to confirm in faith and charity (*in fide et caritate firmare digneris*)', 'you have summoned before you (*tibi astare voluisti*)' and 'pleasing to you (*tibi placentes*)' in n. 113 and 'when from the earth he will raise up in the flesh those who have died (*quando mortuos suscitabit in carne de terra*)', 'pleasing to you (*tibi placentes*)', 'you will wipe away every tear (*omnem lacrimam absterges*)' and 'seeing (*videntes*)' in n. 115.

206.In the Appendix, see 'And with your spirit (*Et cum spiritu tuo*)', 'to give you thanks … to give you glory (*tibi gratias agere … te glorificare*)', 'existing before all ages and abiding for all eternity (*qui es ante saecula et permanes in aeternum*)', 'dwelling (*inhabitans*)', 'blessings (*benedictionibus*)', 'so that you might fill (*ut ... adimpleres*)', 'and bring joy to many of them by the glory (*multasque laetificares claritate*)', 'in your presence are … who serve you (*coram te … astant … serviunt tibi*)', 'gazing upon the glory of your face (*vultus tui gloriam contemplantes*)', 'glorify you without ceasing (*te incessanter glorificant*)' and 'confess your name in exultation … as we acclaim (*nomen tuum in exsultatione confidemur canentes*)' in n. 116. See also 'We give you praise … for you are great (*Confitemur tibi … quia magnus es*)', 'you have fashioned all your works in wisdom and in love (*omnia opera tua in sapientia et caritate fecisti*)', 'and entrusted the whole world to his care (*eique commisisti mundi curam universi*)', 'so that ... he might have dominion (*ut ... imperaret*)', 'in serving you alone (*tibi soli Creatori serviens*)', 'through disobedience he had lost (*non oboediens, amisisset*)', 'so that those who seek might mind you (*ut te quærentes invenirent*)', 'covenants (*foedera*)', 'the sorrowful of heart (*maestis corde*)', 'To accomplish your plan (*Ut tuam vero dispensationem impleret*)' and 'bringing to perfection (*perficiens*)' in n. 117. See, in addition, 'that they may become (*ut ... fiant*)' and 'as we celebrate the great mystery (*ad hoc magnum mysterium celebrandum*)' in n. 118, 'having loved (*ac dilexisset*)' in n. 119, 'he loved them to the end (*in finem dilexit eos*)', 'blessed and broke it (*benedixit ac fregit*)', 'and gave (*deditque*)' and 'saying (*dicens*)' in n. 120 and 'as we await (*expectantes*)', 'gathered ... by the Holy Spirit (*a Sancto Spiritu congregati*)', 'we make this offering (*hanc oblationem offerimus*)', 'and those who make this offering (*et offerentium*)', 'those gathered here before you (*circumstantium*)', 'you alone have known (*tu solus cognovisti*)', 'O merciful Father (*clemens Pater*)', 'that we may enter (*consequi valeamus*)' and 'may we glorify you (*te glorificemus*)' in n. 122.

207. See Elich, 327.

208. Three in 588.

209. Four in 701.

210. Six in 676.

211. Two in 437.

212. In the Appendix, see 'be defended by your protecting help (*protectionis tuae muniamur auxilio*)' in n. 86, 'that we be delivered (*nos eripi*)' and 'counted (*numerari*)' in n. 87, 'for the forgiveness of sins (*in remissionem peccatorum*)' in 90 and 'that these gifts be borne by the hands of your holy Angel (*haec perferri per manus sancti Angeli tui*)' in n. 94 and 'and entrusted the whole world to his care (*eique commisisti mundi curam universi*)' in n. 117.

213. See the Appendix n. 105.

214. In the Appendix, see 2 Chronicles 6:12 and the translation of *extendit manus* as 'he stretched out his hands' in n. 99, Romans 6:5 (*Si ... complantati facti sumus similitudini mortis eius, sed et resurrectionis erimus*) and the translation of *complantatus [complantata] fuit similitudini mortis Filii tui* as 'united with your Son in a death like his' and Psalm 89:16 (*in lumine vultus tui*) and the translation of *in lumen vultus tui* as 'into the light of your face' in n. 105.

215. In the Appendix, see Malachi 1:11 (*Ab ortu enim solis usque ad occasum ... et offertur nomini meo oblatio munda*) and the translation of *ut a solis ortu usque ad occasum oblatio munda offeratur nomini tuo* as 'so that from the rising of the sun to its setting a pure sacrifice may be offered to your name' in n. 108 and 1 Peter 2:9 (*populus in acquisitionem*) and the translation of *et omni populo acquisitionis tuae* as 'and the entire people you have gained for your own' in n. 113. See also Romans 6:5 (*Si ... complantati facti sumus similitudini mortis eius, sed et resurrectionis erimus*) and the translation of *complantatus [complantata] fuit similitudini mortis Filii tui* as 'united with your Son in a death like his' and Philippians 3:21 (*transfigurabit corpus humilitatis nostrae, ut illud conforme faciat corpori gloriae suae*), which the Catechism 556 and 999 translated as 'will change our lowly body to be like his glorious body', and the translation of *et corpus humilitatis nostrae configurabit corpori claritatis suae* as 'and transform our lowly body after the pattern of his own glorious body' in n. 115. See, in addition, Revelation 7:17 (*absterget Deus omnem lacrimam ex oculis eorum*) and the translation of *quando omnem lacrimam absterges ab oculis nostris* as 'when you will wipe away every tear from our eyes' in n. 115.

216. In the Appendix, see Genesis 1:26 (*Faciamus hominem ad imaginem et similitudinem nostram*) and the translation of *Hominem ad tuam imaginem condidisti* as 'You formed man in your own image', Romans 8:23 (*primitias spiritus*), which the Catechism n. 735 translates as 'first fruits', and the translation of *misit Spiritum Sanctus primitias credentibus* as 'he sent the Holy Spirit ... as the first fruits for those who believe', Hebrews 4:15 (*per omnia ... absque peccato*) and the translation of *per omnia absque peccato* as 'in all things but sin' and 2 Corinthians 5:15 (*sed ei, qui pro ipsis mortuus est et resurrexit*) and the translation of *sed sibi qui pro nobis mortuus est atque surrexit* as 'but for him who died and rose for us' in n. 117. See also Genesis 17:13 (*in carne vestra in foedus aeternum*) and

the translation of *quod ipse obis reliquit in foedus aeternum* as 'which he himself left us as an eternal covenant' in n. 118. See, in addition, the phrase from John 13:1, *dilexisset suos qui erant in mundo, in finem dilexit eos*, the final words of which the Catechism n. 609, 616, 622, 1380, 1823 and 2843 translates as 'to the end', and the translation 'having loved his own who were in the world, he loved them to the end' in n. 119. Finally, see 1 Corinthians 10:17 (*Quoniam unus panis, unum corpus multi sumus, omnes enim de uno pane participamur*) and the translation of *qui ex hoc uno pane participabunt et calice, ut, in unum corpus a Sancto Spiritu congregati* as 'all who partake of this one Bread and one Chalice that, gathered into one body by the Holy Spirit' and Ephesians 1:12 (*in laudem gloriæ ejus*) and the translation of *in Christo hostia viva perficiantur, ad laudem gloriae tuae* as 'a living sacrifice in Christ to the praise of your glory' in n. 122.

217. Pecklers, *The Genius of the Roman Rite,* 102.

218. In the Appendix, see n. 8, 13, 91–92, 100, 108–109, 112–113, 118, 121–123.

219. In the Appendix, see n. 85, 87, 95, 105, 122. It is not clear if there is a significant distinction between 'O Lord' and 'Lord' just as it is not clear if it is significant that *Pater* is translated as 'O Father' in n. 113 and 122 but as 'Father' in n. 84, 99,116, 117 [three times] and 119.

220. See Pecklers, *The Genius of the Roman Rite*, 103.

221. See the Appendix n. 117.

222. See, for example, Genesis 1:26-27 and Romans 5:12.

223. Pecklers, on the other hand, suspects that the Congregation for Divine Worship did not want the word 'humankind' to appear in the new Missal because it was 'considered to be a neologism'; see Pecklers; *The Genius of the Roman Rite*, 104.

224. Ibid., 103.

225. In the Appendix, see n. 84, where the division is not found at the same point, and the sentence beginning *Fratres nostros* in n. 113, and the sentence in n. 122, where the divisions are found at the same point.

226. See the final sentence of Appendix n. 115.

227. In the Appendix, see nn. 89–90, 92, 94, 96–97; 102, 105 (sentences beginning *Memores igitur* and *Omnium nostrum*); 109–110, 113, 122.

228. In the Appendix, see n. 86, 103, 108, 111 and 116 (first sentence).

229. See the Appendix n. 85.

230. In the Appendix, see the sentences beginning with *Votis huius* and *Omnes filios* in n. 113.

231. In the Appendix, see n. 85, 86, 89, 90, 99, 102, 103, 110, 111, 116, 119 and 120.

232. *See Ratio translationis,* 109–111. See also Appendix n. 86 and 93.

233. In the Appendix, see n. 84, 85, 86, 88, 92, 93, 119 and 120.

234. In the Appendix, see n. 86, 87, and 96.

235. In the Appendix, see n. 89, 90, 94, 96, 99, 102, 103, 110, 111, 113, 116, 119, 120 and 122.

236. In the Appendix, see n. 84 and 85.

237. See the Appendix nn. 89–90, 102, 110–111.

238. See the Appendix nn. 119–120.

239. See King, 'Lost, and found, in translation', S3.

240. In the Appendix, see n. 87, 105, 109, 113 and 118.

241. *Ratio translationis*, 108, 115.

242. In the Appendix, see n. 91, 104, 112 and 121.

243. In the Appendix, see *Papa nostro N. et Antistite nostro N.* in n. 84, *Virginis Mariae, Genetricis* and *Apostolorum … Martyrum … Sanctorum* in n. 86, *Corpus … Sanguis* in n.

88, *Panem ... Calicem* in n. 92, *Angeli ... Corpus et Sanguinem* in n. 94 and *Apostolis ... Martyribus ... Sanctis* in n. 96.

244. In the Appendix, see 'Holy (*Sanctus*)' in n. 100, 'Body and Blood (*Corpus et Sanguis*)' in n. 101, 'Passion (*Passioni*)' in n. 102, 'Body and Blood (*Corporis et Sanguinis*)', 'Bishop (*Episcopo*)', 'Virgin (*Vergine*)', Apostles (*Apostolis*)' and Saints (*Sanctis*) in n. 105.

245. In the Appendix, see 'Body and Blood (*Corpus et Sanguis*)' in n. 109 and 'Body and Blood (*Corpore et Sanguine*)', 'Virgin ... Apostles ... Martyrs ... Saint ... Saints (*Virgine ... Apostolis ... Martyribus ... Sancto ... Sanctis*)' and 'Sacrifice (*Hostia*)' in n. 113.

246. In the Appendix, see 'Creator (*Creatori*)' and 'Only Begotten (*Unigenitum*)' in n. 117, 'Body and Blood (*Corpus et Sanguis*)' in n. 118 and 'Body and Blood (*Corpus et Sanguinem*)', 'Sacrifice (*Hostiam*)', 'Bishops (*Episcoporum*)' and 'Apostles and Saints (*Apostolis et Sanctis*) in n. 122.

247. See the Appendix n. 83, 99, 107 and 116.

248. See the Appendix n. 93.

249. See *Ratio translationis,* 84, 117–19.

250. In the Appendix, see 'Saviour (*Salvator*)' and 'Cross and Resurrection (*crucem et resurrectionem*)' in n. 91, 104, 112 and 121, 'Passion ... Resurrection ... Ascension (*passionis ... resurrectionis ... ascensionis*)' in n. 92, 'Resurrection (*resurrectionis*)' [twice] in n. 105, 'Passion ... Resurrection and Ascension (*passionis ... resurrectionis et ascensionis*)' in n. 113 and 'Angels (*angelorum*)' in n. 116 and 'Resurrection ... Ascension (*resurrectionem ... ascensionem*)' in n. 122.

251. In the Appendix, see 'Order of Bishops (*episcopali ordine*)' in n. 113 and 'Order of Bishops (*Episcoporum ordinis*)' in n. 122.

252. See *Ratio translationis,* n. 120.v. Contrary to these requirements, King recommends changing 'Order of Bishops', which he considers 'too "in your face"' at a time 'when bishops are not the most popular creatures in the world' to 'order of bishops', see King, 'Lost, and found, in translation', S9.

253. In the Appendix, see 'Death (*mortis*)' in n. 105.

254. In the Appendix, see 'Bread (*panem*)' and 'Cup (*calicem*)' in n. 91, 104, 112 and 121, 'Bread of life (*panem vitae*)' and 'Chalice of salvation (*calicem salutis*)' in n. 105 and 'Bread ... Chalice (*pane ... calice*)' in n. 122.

255. See *Ratio translationis,* n. 120.iii.

256. Pecklers, *The Genius of the Roman Rite,* 102. Although he cites 'forever singing to your glory' and 'we sing the hymn of your priase and acclaim without end', the final version of the texts he had in mind would seem to be 'we sing the hymn of your glory as without end we acclaim', 'sing together the unending hymn of your glory, as they acclaim' and 'we sing the hymn of your praise, as without end we acclaim'; see *Missal* (2011) at 402, 404, 406, 412, 414, 426, 428, 430, 432, 434, 436, 438, 440, 442, 446, 456, 462, 466, 474, 478, 490, 496.

257. Pecklers, *The Genius of the Roman Rite*, 101.

258. Paul Turner, 'A New Roman Missal: What to Expect from a New Translation of Liturgical Texts', *America* (26 May–2 June 2008), 14–16.

259. Pecklers, *The Genius of the Roman Rite*, 101–2.

260. See *nobis* in the Appendix n. V. The translation 'dawned' rather than 'dawned for us' may have been chosen to retain the notion of something dawning for humanity as a whole.

261. In the Appendix, see 'For ... by your gracious gift' in n. I, 'and while in this body we not only' in n. IV and 'blessed ... that ... to come. Indeed ... and' in n. V.

262. In the Appendix, see 'we pray' in n. VII, VIII, IX, X, XII, XIV, XV, XVIII, XX, XXIII and XXIV, 'our offerings be worthy ... of the mysteries of the Nativity this day ... and also shone forth

as God' in n. VII, 'grant' in n. VIII and 'in body and mind' in n. IX. See also 'as an example ... causes ... to take flesh ... graciously ... patient' in n. XI, 'Grant' in n. XII, 'May your people exult for ever ... confident' in n. XIII, 'grant ... those you were pleased to renew ... attain in their flesh the incorruptible glory of the resurrection' in n. XIV and 'almighty ... that the splendour of your glory may shine forth upon us ... the bright rays of ... the hearts' in n. XV. See, in addition 'and renewing us with your Sacrament' in n. XVIII, 'graciously grant that ... your divine majesty ... by partaking of the sacred mystery, we may be faithfully ... in mind and heart' in n. XIX, 'to whose suffering we are united' in n. XXI and 'our ... your eternal holy' in n. XXII. Finally, see 'grant us ... that we may always ... the fruits ...in the unity' in n. XXIII and 'Grant ... that we may delight ... in that share in your divine life which is foreshadowed in this present age by our reception of ... precious' in n. XXIV.

263. In the Appendix, see 'one [heavenly Bread]' in n. XVI.

264. See 'we beseech you ... Christ ... the message of' in the Appendix n. VI.

265. In the Appendix, see n. I, V, XI, XIII, XIV, XVIII, XXI, XXII and XXIV.

266. See the Appendix n. VII.

267. In the Appendix, see 'more eagerly intent on ... participating in the mysteries by which they have been reborn' in n. I, 'freed from disordered affections' in n. II, 'bodily fasting ... restrain ... bestow both virtue and its rewards' in n. III, 'even now possess the pledge of life eternal' in n. IV and 'that those saddened by the certainty of dying might be consoled by ... is made ready for them' in n. V.

268. In the Appendix, compare the older and newer translations of *Deus* in n. VII, X, XIII, XV, XVIII and XXIII.

269. In the Appendix, compare the older and newer translations of *Domine* in n. VII and XXIV.

270. Pecklers, *The Genius of the Roman Rite*, 102.

271. In the Appendix, see 'Pour forth ... grace into ... we, to whom ... was made known ... Incarnation ... his Passion and Cross' in n. VI, 'May our offerings be worthy ... of the mysteries of the Nativity this day, that, just as Christ was born a man ... so these earthly gifts may confer on us what is divine' in n. VII, 'O God ... Only Begotten Son has appeared in our very flesh ... that we may be inwardly transformed through him whom we recognise as outwardly like ourselves' in n. VIII and 'sacrifice ... cleanse us of our faults ... paschal festivities' in n. IX. See also 'O God ... illuminate ... with the splendour of your grace, that we may always ponder what is worthy and pleasing to your majesty and love you in all sincerity' in n. X, 'an example ... to follow ... and submit to ... may heed his lesson of patient suffering' in n. XI, 'our reception of ... Sacrament may have a continuing effect' in n. XII and 'to the rejoicing of the day of resurrection ... rejoicing now in the restored glory of our adoption' in n. XIII. See, in addition, 'eternal' in n. XIV, 'born again by your grace' in n. XV, 'Pour on us ... the Spirit of your love' in n. XVI, 'that we may honour you with all our mind, and love everyone in truth of heart' in n. XVII, 'the offerings presented here ... that the sustenance they provide may not fail us' in n. XVIII and 'who give us the gift of true prayer and of peace' in n. XIX. See, finally, 'the workings of this heavenly gift ... take possession of our minds and bodies, so that its effects, and not our own desires, may always prevail in us' in n. XX, 'this heavenly mystery ... that we may be coheirs in glory with ... restore us in mind and body' in n. XXI, 'body and soul ... undivided Unity' in n. XXII, 'this wonderful Sacrament ... Passion ... to revere the sacred mysteries ... in ourselves the fruits of your redemption' in n. XXIII and 'which is foreshadowed in this present age' in n. XXIV.

272. See the Appendix n. IX.

273. See chapter 9 of the eighth Council of Toledo (653 AD) in Giovanni Domenico Mansi, ed., *Sacrorum Conciliorum nova et amplissima collectio*, 31 vols. (Florence & Venice: 1759–98) at 10:1219.

274. See Placide Bruylants, ed., *Les oraisons du missel romain. Texts et Histoire*, ed. Centre de Pastorale Liturgique, 2 vols., Études Liturgiques, 1 (Louvain: Centre de Documentation et

d'Information Litugiques, 1952) at 2:159 n. 581; Daniel McCarthy, 'Act of mature faith', *The Tablet* 16 (February 2008), 16.

275. See the Appendix n. X.

276. Comparing the washing of insensible plates and cups (cf. Mk 7:4) with the Baptismal washing of the sensible 'cup' or container that each person is to constitute, Ambrose comments that Christ's good works should shine there and that the splendour of his grace (*gratiae tuae splendor*) should gleam there; see St Ambrose, *De Mysteriis* 4 (n. 23) in Migne, ed., *PL* at 16:395.

277. See Bruylants, ed., *Les oraisons,* 2:98-99 n. 358; Daniel McCarthy, 'He enlightens all hearts', *The Tablet* 21 (March 2009). See also Alcuin, *Liber sacramentorum*, 3 in Migne, ed., PL, 101:450.

278. In the Appendix, see 'hearts (*mentibus*)' in n. VI, 'minds and hearts (*mentibus*)' in n. XII, 'attain in their flesh the incorruptible glory of the resurrection (*ad incorruptibilem glorificandae carnis resurrectionem pervenire*)' in n. XIV, 'one in mind and heart (*una facias pietate concordes*)' in n. XVI, 'in truth of heart (*rationabili ... affectu*)' in n. XVII, 'united in mind and heart (*sensibus uniamur*)' in n. XIX.

279. See the Appendix n. XIV.

280. See Daniel McCarthy, 'Mystery made personal', *The Tablet* 25 (April 2009), 18.

281. *Ad incorruptibilem glorificandae carnis resurrectionem pervenire,* literally 'attaining to the incorruptible resurrection of the flesh needing to be glorified'.

282. See, for example, the heart's capacity to ponder and to love in the prayer by Alcuin of York in the Appendix n. X.

283. The phrase 'confirm the hearts' would seem to be an intertextual reference to a Latin text of 1 Thessalonians 3:13 where Paul says to the Thessalonians: 'And may he so confirm your hearts in holiness that you may be blameless'.

284. See the Appendix n. X. This prayer is originally found in the *Paduense*, which was complied around 670 to 680 AD, and it is an adaptation of a prayer containing the same phrase in the Gelasian Sacramentary which was compiled between 628 and 715; see Bruylants, ed., *Les oraisons,* 2:242, n. 854.

285. See the Appendix n. XVII. This prayer is found only the *Leonianum*, compiled between 600 and 625; see Daniel McCarthy, 'Two commands, one love', *The Tablet* 27 (January 2007), 15.

286. On this translation see the following website consulted on 30 December 2011: http://knoxlatinmass.net/wdtprs/ordinary4.pdf.

287. See the Appendix n. VI. Slightly different versions of the Collect are found in the *Paduense*, which was complied around 670–680 AD, and in the *Hadrianum* (785–786 AD); see Bruylants, ed., *Les oraisons,* 2:156–57 n. 575; Daniel McCarthy, 'From earth and from heaven', *The Tablet* 16/23 (December 2006), 30–31.

288. See the Appendix n. XII. This prayer is based on a prayer that included the phrase *nostris mentibus* in the Gelasian Sacramentary, which was compiled between 628 and 715; see Bruylants, ed., *Les oraisons,* 2:43–44 n. 133; Daniel McCarthy, 'Grasping after God', *The Tablet* 18 (April 2009), 18.

289. See the Appendix n. XIX. The prayer is found only the Verona Sacramentary (561–574); see Daniel McCarthy, 'In clouds of glory', *The Tablet* 6 (September 2008), 15.

290. See the Appendix n. XX. This prayer comes from the Gelasian Sacramentary (composed 628–715); see Bruylants, ed., *Les oraisons,* 2:189 n. 677; Daniel McCarthy, 'An abiding gift', *The Tablet* 12 (September 2009), 16.

291. See the Appendix n. XXI. This prayer is based on a prayer in the Verona collection of Mass booklets (compiled between 561 and 574) that was incorporated into the Gelasian Sacramentary (compiled between 628 and 715); see Bruylants, ed., *Les oraisons,* 2:308-09 n. 1065; Daniel McCarthy, 'From Suffering to Glory,' *The Tablet* 26 (September 2009), 17.

292. See the Appendix n. IX. A version of this prayer including the phrase in question is found in the *Paduense*, which was complied around 670–680 AD, and in the eighth-century Prague collection; see Bruylants, ed., *Les oraisons*, 2:158-159 n. 580.

293. 'And where is God's image? In your mind, in your intellect!'; see St Augustine, *Homilies on John,* 3.4 in Migne, ed., *PL,* 35:1398.

294. For St Augustine, Christ has 'a complete soul, not the irrational part of the soul only, but the rational part too, which is called the mind'; see St Augustine, *Homilies on John,* 23.6 in ibid., 35:1585. In 434, St Vincent of Lerins described as heretics those who denied that the human soul of Christ was 'endowed with intelligence, possessing mind and reason'; see St Vincent of Lerins, *The Notebooks,* 13 in Migne, ed., *PL,* 50:655. Pope St Leo the Great held that Christ's body was 'under the control of his divinity and of his mind'; see Pope St Leo the Great, *Letters,* 35.3 in Migne, ed., *PL,* 54:809–10.

295. See the translation 'and not our own desires (*non noster sensus in nobis*)' in the Appendix n. XX.

296. See the Appendix n. XVIII. The prayer is taken from the Leonine Sacramentary, a collection of Mass booklets compiled between 561 and 574; see Bruylants, ed., *Les oraisons*, 2:98 n. 353; Daniel McCarthy, 'Food for heart and soul', *The Tablet* 14 (June 2008), 17.

297. St Augustine, *Faith and the Creed,* 10.23; *Continence,* 12.26 in Migne, ed., *PL,* 40:193–4, 367.

298. See Hugh of St Victor, *The Sacraments of the Christian Faith,* 1.6.6; *The Union of Body and Spirit* in ibid., 176:267, 285, 288.

299. See Gilbert of Poitiers, *Commentary on the Book on the Person and the Two Natures Against Eutyches and Nestorius* in ibid., 64:1393.

300. See Peter Lombard, *Commentary on the Psalms,* 145.1; *Sentences II,* 1.10 in ibid., 191:1269, 192:654.

301. Dupuis SJ and Neuner SJ, eds., n. 19, p. 15.

302. In the Appendix, see 'in renewed youthfulness of spirit (*renovata animae iuventute*)' in n. XIII and 'health of body and soul (*salutem corporis et animae*)' in n. XXII.

303. See the Appendix n. XIII.

304. *Populus tuus, quaesumus, Domine, renovata semper exsulted animae iuventute, ut qui ante peccatorum veternoso in mortis venerat senio, nunc laetatur in pristinam se gloriam restitutum;* see Lauren Pristas, 'The Collects at Sunday Mass: An Examination of the Revisions of Vatican II', *Nova et Vetera* 3.1 (Winter, 2005) 5–38 at 20. See also Daniel McCarthy, 'With joy and expectation', *The Tablet* 29 (April 2006), 18.

305. See Leo Cunibert Mohlberg, Leo Eizenhöfer and Petrus Siffrin, eds., *Liber Sacramentorum Romanae Aeclesiae ordinis anni circuli: (Cod. Vat. Reg. Lat. 316/Paris Bibl. nat. 7193, 41/56): (Sacramentarium Gelasianum), Rerum Ecclesiasticarum Documenta*, Series maior, Fontes 4 (Rome: Casa Editrice Herder, 1960) at n. 515.

306. Pristas suggests the translation, 'in renewed youth of soul'; see Pristas, 'The Collects at Sunday Mass: An Examination of the Revisions of Vatican II', 20. See also the translation 'in the youth of their souls having been restored' proposed in the following website, accessed on 30 December 2011: http://romansacristan.blogspot.com.

307. See the Appendix n. XXII. The original prayer was composed by Alcuin of York (c. 735–804), and the phrase 'and undivided unity (*eiusdemque individuae Unitatis*)' was added soon afterwards; see Bruylants, ed., *Les oraisons,* 2:255 n. 897; Daniel McCarthy, 'A spark of majesty', *The Tablet* 6 (June 2009), 16.

308. Dupuis SJ and Neuner SJ, eds., at nn. 614–15, pp. 227–8.

309. Ibid., n. 504, p. 200.

310. See Origen, *Commentaries on Genesis,* 1.13 in Migne, ed., *PG,* 12:155-57.

311. Dupuis SJ and Neuner SJ, eds., at n. 401/1, p. 167.

312. Ibid., n. 402/6, p. 168.

313. In the Appendix, see 'that we may heed his lesson of patient suffering and so merit (*mereamur*) a share in his Resurrection' in n. XI and 'you have nourished (*satiasti*)' in n. XVI.

314. *ut et patientiae ipsius habere documenta, et resurrectionis consortia mereamur*; see the Appendix n. XI.

315. The prayer dates from the *Leonianum,* compiled between 600 and 625; see *Bruylants,* ed., *Les oraisons,* 2:309-310 n. 1069; Daniel McCarthy, 'Feasting together', *The Tablet* 17 (January 2009), 15.

316. *quos uno caelesti pane satiasti, una facias pietate concordes*; see the Appendix n. XVI.

317. See Patrick F. O'Connell, ed., *Thomas Merton: Monastic Observances, Initiation Into the Monastic Tradition,* 5 (Collegeville, Minnesota: Liturgical Press, 2010) at 142 n. 483.

318. On this translation see the following website accessed on 30 December 11: http://wdtprs. com/blog/2006/01/2nd-sunday-of-ordinary-time-post-communion.

319. See Pope Pius XII, *Quoniam Paschalia Sollemnia* (Easter Sunday Homily for 1939) at the following website, consulted on 30 December 2011: http://.vatican.va/holy_father/pius_xii/ homilies/documents/hf_p-xii_hom_19390409_pasqua_lt.html.

320. See Austin Flannery, ed., *Vatican Council II. Constitutions, Decrees, Declarations. A Completely Revised Translation in Inclusive Language* (Dublin: Dominican Publications, 1996), 122.

321. A version of this prayer is found in the eighth-century Prague and Vatican collections; see Bruylants, ed., *Les oraisons*, 2:68, n. 221.

322. 'The origins of both his substances display him as man and as God (*utriusque substantiae ... hominem et Deum exhibuit)*: from the one, born, and from the other, not born; from the one, flesh (*carneum*), and from the other, spiritual.' See Tertullian, *The Flesh of Christ,* 5.7 in Migne, ed., *PL,* 2:761.

323. In the Appendix, see in *substántia nostrae carnis* in n. VIII.

324. See the Appendix n. XI. A version of this prayer is found in the Gelasian Sacramentary, which was compiled between 628 and 715, and in the *Hadrianum* (785–86); see *Bruylants,* ed., *Les oraisons,* 2:222 n. 783; Daniel McCarthy, 'Suffering Shared', *The Tablet* 8 (April 2006), 16.

325. In the Appendix, see *pietátis* in n. IV, *incarnationem* in n. VI, *fidélibus* in n. V and *adoptionis* in n. XIII.

326. In the Appendix, see *ad grátiae filiórum plenitúdinem perducántur* in n. I and *filiis tuis* in n. II.

327. A version of this prayer that includes the phrase *homo génitus* is found in the *Paduense,* which was compiled around 670–80 AD; see Bruylants, ed., *Les oraisons,* 2:194 n. 698.

328. See the Appendix n. VII.

329. In the Appendix, see 'everyone (*omnem hominem*)' in n. X and 'everyone (*omnes homines*)' in n. XVII.

330. In the Appendix, see n. VIII.

331. In the Appendix, see n. I and III.

332. See *Liturgiam authenticam* n. 33 and n. 120.i of the *Ratio translationis* (2007).

333. In the Appendix, see 'Angel (*Angelo*)' in n. VI, 'Only Begotten Son (*Unigénitus*)' in n. VIII and 'Body and Blood (*Corporis et Sanguinis*)' in n. XXIII and XIV.

334. See 'resurrection' in the Appendix n. XIII.

335. See *Ratio translationis,* 84, 117–21.

336. See ibid., n. 120.iii.

337. In the Appendix, see 'Passion and Cross (*passionem ... et crucem*)' and 'Resurrection (*resurrectionis*)' in n. VI, 'Nativity (*nativitátis*)' in n. VII, 'Cross ... Resurrrection (*crucem ...*

resurrectionis)' in n. XI, 'Sacrament (*sacramenti*)' in n. XII, 'Resurrection (*resurrectionis*)' in n. XIII, 'Resurrection (*resurrectionem*)' in n. XIV, 'Bread (*pane*)' in n. XVI, 'Sacrament (*sacramento*)' in n. XVIII, 'Death (*mortem*)' in n. XXI, 'Sacrament (*sacramenti*)' in n. XXII, 'Sacrament (*sacraménto*)' and 'Passion (*passiónis*)' in n. XXIII.

338. The number of paraphrases per 100 Latin words fell from 5.54 to .62 (from 133 to 15 in 2,402 Latin words) in the Eucharistic Prayers and from 6.84 to 1.16 (from 59 to 10 in 863 Latin words) in the other texts listed in sections A–D of the Appendix.

Chapter III. The New Translation and the Tradition of Christian Anthropology

1. *Tota humana familia invenire potest plenissimo modo ac nulli exspectationi obnoxio, ea omnia, quae quasi temptabunda ipsa perquirat de Deo, de homine eiusque sorte futura, de vita et morte, deque veritate.* See *Evangelii nuntiandi* n. 53.

2. See Johannes Pedersen, *Israel: Its Life and Culture*, 2 vols. (Oxford: Oxford University Press, 1946), 2:99.

3. See Georges Pidoux, *L'homme dans l'Ancien Testament*, Cahiers théologiques, 32 (Neucâhtel: Delachaux et Niestlé, 1953), 10.

4. Pedersen, *Israel: Its Life and Culture*, I–II, 171.

5. See also Gn 46:27; Deut 10:22.

6. See Gerrit C. Berkouwer, *Man: The Image of God* (Grand Rapids, Michigan: Wm. B. Eerdmans Publishing Company, 1962), 215.

7. See Charles Hauret, *Beginnings, Genesis and Modern Science* (Dubuque: Priory Press, 1955), 105.

8. Anne Thurston, *Because of her Testimony: The Word in Female Experience* (Dublin: Gill & Macmillan, 1995), 15.

9. See Manfred Hauke, *Women in the Priesthood? A Systematic Analysis in the Light of the Order of Creation and Redemption* (San Francisco: Ignatius Press, 1988), 201; Gerhard Von Rad, *Genesis: A Commentary* (London: SCM, 1963), 82.

10. The collective rather than gender-specific implication of the Hebrew word, *Adam,* is clear from the plural verb ('and let them have dominion') in Genesis 1:26 and from the plural pronouns in Genesis 1:27-28 ('in the image of God he created them; male and female he created them. God blessed them, and God said to them').

11. See Gn 1:26; 5:1-3; 9:6.

12. See Karl Barth, *The Doctrine of Creation: The Work of Creation*, Church Dogmatics, 3/1 (Edinburgh: T & T Clark, 1958), 197, 200; Luis F. Ladaria, *Antropologia Teologica* (Rome: Casale Monferrato, 1986), 92–8; Alan Richardson, *Genesis I-II* (London: SCM, 1953), 54; Gottlieb Söhngen, 'Die biblische Lehre von der Gottesebenbildlichkeit des Menschen', in *Festgabe Erzbischof Jäger*, Bischof Stählin, 'Pro Veritate' (Munster: Aschendorffsche Verlagsbuchhandlung, 1963), 23–57 at 23–4; Bruce Vawter, *On Genesis: A New Reading* (London: Chapman, 1977), 44; Claus Westermann, *Genesis I-II: A Commentary*, trans. John J. Scullion (London: SPCK, 1984), 146–7.

13. See Claus Westermann, *Schöpfung*, Themen der Theologie, 12 (Stuttgart: Kreuz Verlag, 1983), 69; Hans Walter Wolff, *Anthropologie des Alten Testaments* (Munich: Gütersloh, 1973), 145.

14. See St Augustine, *On the Literal Interpretation of Genesis*, 6.25.36 in Migne, ed., *PL*, 34:354.

15. In his 2007 novel, *The Shack,* William Paul Young has Sarayu (the Holy Spirit) comment that the choice of the first man and woman 'to eat of that tree tore the universe apart divorcing the spiritual from the physical. They died, expelling in the breath of their choice the very breath of God.' See William Paul Young, *The Shack* (Newbury Park, California: Windblown Media, 2007), 135.

16. See Gordon J. Wenham, *Genesis 1-15*, ed. David A. Hubbard and Glenn W. Barker, *Word Biblical Commentary*, 1 (Waco, Texas: Word Books, 1987), 142.

17. See Gn 5:8, 11, 14, 17, 20, 27; 6:2; 9:28; 11:10-32; Num 33:29.

18. Daniel Lys, *Nèpèsh. Histoire de l'âme dans la révélation d'Israël* (Paris: Presses Universitaires de France, 1959), 124.

19. See Gn 1:30; 19:17; 32:30; 42:21; Ex 4:19; 21:23; Deut 11:18; Lev 24:17; 1 Sm 19:11; 1 Kgs 17:21-22; 19:10,14; 20:32; Est 7:3; Is 43:4; Jer 4:10; 18:20; 20:13; 31:12; 51:6; Ez 3:19; 18:27; 33:9.

20. See Ps 7:6; 39:15; 53:5; 62:10; 70:10; 85:14; 142:3.

21. See Gn 12:5; Ex 12:4; Lev 16:29; 23:30; 1 Sm 18:1; Ps 41:2-3; 62:2; Wis 7:27; 9:15; 10:16; Is 3:9; 55:3; Jer 38:17, 20; Ez 18:4, 20, 27.

22. See also, for example, 2 Kgs 2:4, 6; 4:30; 1 Sm 25:26.

23. For other texts where 'soul' is equivalent to a reflexive pronoun, see Lev 27:2; Num 30:5; 1 Sm 17:55; Est 4:13; 9:31; Job 16:4; Eccles (Sir) 51:24; Ps 102:1; 103:1,35; Prov 2:10; 19:2; 23:7; 24:14; Jer 26:19. In Amos 6:8, the phrase 'his soul' is used as a reflexive pronoun ('himself') in relation to the Lord.

24. See Jos 10:28, 30, 32, 35, 37, 39; Jer 43:6; Ez 18:4. See also the Greek text of 1 Macc 10:33.

25. The first five books of the Bible: Genesis, Exodus, Leviticus, Numbers and Deuteronomy.

26. On the Septuagint in general, see Karen H. Jobes and Moisés Silva, *Invitation to the Septuagint* (Grand Rapids, Michigan: Baker, 2000).

27. On the dating of the Septuagint, see Raija Sollamo, 'Prolegomena to the Syntax of the Septuagint', in *Helsinki Perspectives on the Translation Technique of the Septuagint*, ed. Raija Sollamo and Sepio Sepilä, *Publications of the Finnish Exegetical Society*, 82 (Göttingen: Vandenhoeck & Ruprecht, 2001), 23–42 at 36.

28. See Juan Luis Ruiz de la Peña, *Immagine di Dio. Antropologia teologica fondamentale*, ed. Carlo Molari, trans. Rossella Del Guerra, Ricerche teologiche (Rome: Borla, 1992), 16.

29. See Albert Gelin, *L'homme selon la Bible*, Foi Vivante, 75 (Paris: Cerf, 1968), 18–22; Gisbert Greshake, *Auferstehung der Toten. Ein Beitrag zur gegenwärtigen theologischen Diskussion über die Zukunft der Geschichte* (Essen: Ludgerus-Verlag Hubert Wingen, 1969); Emil Schürer, *Geschichte des jüdischen Volkes im Zeitalter Jesu Christi*, 3e neu bearb. Aufl. ed., 3 vols. (Leipzig: J. C. Hinrichs Buchhandlung, 1898), III:380–2; Paul Volz, ed., *Die Eschatologie der judischen Gemeinde im neutestamentlichen Zeitalter nach den Quellen der rabbinischen, apokalyptischen und apokryphen Literatur*, Zweite Auflage des Werkes 'Jüdische Eschatologie von Daniel bis Akiba' ed. (Tübingen: J.C.B. Mohr [Paul Siebeck], 1934) at 58–9, 118–19; Georg Ziener, *Die theologische Begriffssprache im Buche des Weisheit* (Bonn: Peter Hanstein, 1956), 88–9.

30. See Hermann Bückers, *Die Unsterblichkeitslehre des Weisheitsbuches. Ihr Ursprung und ihre Bedeutung*, Alttestamentliche Abhandlungen, 13/4 (Münster: Alttestamentliche Abhandlungen, 1938), 141, 143; Pierre Grelot, *De la mort à la vie éternelle*, Études de théologie biblique, Lectio divina, 67 (Paris: Cerf, 1971), 94, 126, 163, 198; Paul Hoffmann, *Die Toten in Christus. Eine religionsgeschichtliche und exegetische Untersuchung zur paulinischen Eschatologie* (Münster: Aschendorff, 1966), 84; C. Larcher, *Études sur le livre de la Sagesse*, Études bibliques (Paris: Gabalda, 1969), 85–103; Wulstan Mork OSB, *The Biblical Meaning of Man*, Impact Books (Milwaukee: The Bruce Publishing Company, 1967), 64; Ruiz de la Peña, *Immagine di Dio. Antropologia teologica fondamentale*, 47–55; Othmar Schilling, *Geist und Materie in biblischer Sicht: ein exegetischer Beitrag zur Diskussion um Teilhard de Chardin*, Stuttgarter Bibelstudien, 25 (Stuttgart: K.B.W., 1967), 56–7; R. J. Taylor, 'The Eschatological Meaning of Life and Death in the Book of Wisdom I–V', *Ephemerides theologicae lovanienses* 42 (1966) 72–137: 85, 101.

31. Ruiz de la Peña, *Immagine di Dio. Antropologia teologica fondamentale*, 52; Taylor, 'The Eschatological Meaning of Life and Death in the Book of Wisdom I–V', 91, 101.

32. See Ruiz de la Peña, *Immagine di Dio. Antropologia teologica fondamentale*, 53.

33. See Wis 3:1-3; 4:14; 14:5, 26.

34. See Ps 9:13; 107:18.

35. See Wis 1:15; 3:4; 4:1; 6:18; 8:13,17; 15:3.

36. See also Wis 2:22, 4:14.

37. See Ruiz de la Peña, *Immagine di Dio. Antropologia teologica fondamentale*, 53.

38. See Wis 1:14; 9:1-3, 9.

39. See Wis 1:4; 2:3; 8:20; 9:15; 18:22.

40. See Taylor, 'The Eschatological Meaning of Life and Death in the Book of Wisdom I–V', 99–100.

41. See Gerhard Dautzenberg, *Sein Leben bewahren. Psyche in den Herrenworten der Evangelien*, SANT, 14 (Munich: Kosel, 1966), 44; Karl Hermann Schelkle, *Theologie des Neuen Testaments*, 4 vols. in 5 vols., Kommentare und Beiträge zum Alten und Neuen Testament (Düsseldorf: Patmos-Verlag, 1968–76), 1:107; Kurt Schubert, 'Die Entwicklung der Auferstehungslehre von der nachexilischen bis frührabbinischen Zeit', *Biblische Zeitschrift* 6 (1962) 177–214: 177, 193; Günter Stemberger, *Der Leib der Auferstehung: Studien zur Anthropologie und Eschatologie des palästinischen Judentums im neutestamentlichen Zeitalter (ca. 170 v. C[h]r.–100 n. Chr.)*, Analecta biblica, 56 (Rome: Biblical Institute Press, 1972), 115; Volz, ed., *Die Eschatologie der judischen Gemeinde im neutestamentlichen Zeitalter nach den Quellen der rabbinischen, apokalyptischen und apokryphen Literatur*, 118.

42. Compare Matthew 11:29 and Jeremiah 6:16, for example. See Mork OSB, *The Biblical Meaning of Man*, 66; Ceslas Spicq OP, *Dio e l'uomo secondo il Nuovo Testamento* (Rome: Edizioni Paoline, 1969), 206–8.

43. See Mt 2:20; 6:25; 11:29; 20:28; Mk 3:4; 10:45; Lk 6:9; 12:22-23; 21:19; Jn 10:11; 13:37-38; 15:13; Acts 2:27,31; 15:26; Phil 2:30; Heb 6:19.

44. See Acts 2:41, 43; 3:23; 7:14; 27:37; 2 Cor 12:15; 1 Pt 2:11, 25; 3:20; 2 Pt 2:14.

45. See Acts 2:43; Rm 2:9; 13:1.

46. See Mt 16:25-26; Lk 14:26; 17:33; Jn 12:24-25. See also Heb 10:39.

47. See Dautzenberg, *Sein Leben bewahren. Psyche in den Herrenworten der Evangelien*, 80–2; Josef Schmid, 'Der Begriff der Seele in Neuen Testament', in *Einsicht und Glaube*, ed. Joseph Ratzinger and Heinrich Fries (Freiburg-im-Breisgau: Herder, 1962), 112–31 at 125.

48. See Werner Georg Kümmel, *Das Bild des Menschen im Neuen Testament* (Zürich: Zwingli, 1948), 16-18.

49. See Dautzenberg, *Sein Leben bewahren. Psyche in den Herrenworten der Evangelien*, 165–6; Ruiz de la Peña, *Immagine di Dio. Antropologia teologica fondamentale*, 59–61.

50. See John A. T. Robinson, *Le corps. Étude sur la théologie de saint Paul*, trans. P. de Saint-Sienne, Collection Parole et Tradition (Lyons: Éditions du Chalet, 1966), 231; Ruiz de la Peña, *Immagine di Dio. Antropologia teologica fondamentale*, 66; Spicq OP, *Dio e l'uomo secondo il Nuovo Testamento*, 228.

51. See Ruiz de la Peña, *Immagine di Dio. Antropologia teologica fondamentale*, 66.

52. See Rm 2:9; 13:1; 16:4; 1 Cor 15:45; 2 Cor 1:23; 12:15; 1 Th 2:8.

53. See Rm 11:3; Ph 2:30.

54. See Jas 3:15; Jude 19.

55. See Gal 6:1.

56. See St Ignatius of Antioch, *Letter to the Smyrnaeans,* 1.1 in Migne, ed., *PG* at 5:708.

57. Justin Martyr, *The Resurrection*, 8 in ibid.; 6:1585.

58. See Justin Martyr, *Dialogue with Trypho the Jew*, 6 and Tatian the Syrian, *Address to the Greeks*, 4, 5, in ibid., 6:489, 492, 813, 817.

59. Tatian the Syrian, *Address to the Greeks*, 13, and Athanagoras of Athens, *The Resurrection of the Dead*, 12, 15, in ibid., 6:834, 997, 1004.

60. Justin Martyr, *The Resurrection*, 10 in ibid., 6:1590.

61. Tertullian, *The Soul*, 22.2 in Migne, ed., *PL*, 2:686.

62. Tertullian, *The Resurrection of the Dead*, 5.8–9, and *Against Marcion* 1.24.5, in ibid., 2:275, 801–2.

63. Tertullian, *The Resurrection of the Dead*, 8.2–3 in ibid., 2:806.

64. Tertullian, *The Soul*, 27.1–3, and *The Resurrection of the Dead*, 40.3; 45.2, 4–5, in ibid., 2:695–6, 850, 865–6.

65. Tertullian, *The Soul*, 9.1; 22.2 in ibid., 2:658–9.

66. Tertullian, *The Resurrection of the Dead*, 8.2-3 in ibid., 2:806.

67. *St Ambrose, The Death of his Brother Satyrus*, 2.87 in ibid., 16:1339.

68. St Augustine, *City of God*, 13.24.2 in ibid., 41:399.

69. St Augustine, *Faith and the Creed*, 10.23 in ibid., 40:193–4.

70. St Augustine, *Sermons*, 174.2 in ibid., 38:941.

71. St Augustine, *Homilies on John*, 23.6 in ibid., 35:1585.

72. See Gilbert of Poitiers, *The Trinity*, I, 10.17 in ibid., 64:1294–5.

73. *Persona est naturae rationalis individua substantia.* Boethius, *Book on the Person and the Two Natures Against Eutyches and Nestorius*, 3 in ibid., 64:1345.

74. Hugh of St Victor, *The Sacraments of the Christian Faith*, 2.1.11 in ibid., 176:411.

75. See Peter Lombard, *Sentences, III*, 5.5 in ibid., 192:767.

76. See Peter Lombard, *Sentences, III*, 22.1 in ibid., 192:803.

77. See Peter Lombard, *Commentary on the Letters of Paul, Eph 4:15-22*, Gilbert of Poitiers, *Commentary on the Book on the Person and the Two Natures Against Eutyches and Nestorius* and Hugh of St Victor, *The Sacraments of the Christian Faith*, 1.6.6 in ibid., 192:204, 64:1393, 176:267.

78. See Peter Lombard, *Commentary on the Psalms*, 141.10 in ibid., 191:1216.

79. See William of Auxerre, *Summa aurea* or *Golden Compendium* (1215–20), cited in Richard Heinzmann, *Die Unsterblichkeit der Seele und die Auferstehung des Leibes. Eine Problemgeschichtliche Untersuchung der Frühscholastischen Sentenzen und Summenliteratur von Anselm von Laon bis Wilhelm von Auxerre*, Beiträge zur Geschichte der Philosophie und Theologie des Mittelalters, 40/3 (Münster in Westfalen: Aschendorffsche Verlagsbuchhandlung, 1965), 145.

80. ... *anima humana esse suum in quo subsistit corpori communicat.* St Thomas Aquinas, *Quaestiones disputate de Anima*, 14 ad 11.

81. ... *manifestum est quod homo non est anima tantum, sed est aliquid compositum ex anima et corpore.* St Thomas Aquinas, *Summa theologiae*, 1.75.4.

82. Dupuis SJ and Neuner SJ, eds., *The Christian Faith* at n. 405, 169–70.

83. Rejecting any distinction between the state of the body and soul after death, he is later recorded as saying: 'Now, if one should say that Abraham's soul lives with God but his body is dead, this distinction is rubbish. I will attack it.'; see Martin Luther, Table Talk, 5534 in Jaroslav Pelikan and Helmut T. Lehmann, eds, *Luther's Works* (Saint Louis – Philadelphia: Concordia Publishing House – Fortress Press, 1955–) at 54:447.

84. See Martin Luther, *An Answer to Several Questions on Monastic Vows* in ibid., 46:146.

85. See Martin Luther, *Genesis*, 2:7 in ibid., 1:84, 86.

86. See Martin Luther, *Letter to Nicholas von Amsdorf* (1522), in ibid., 48:360–1.

87. See Martin Luther, *Genesis*, 25:7–10 and 26:24, 25 in ibid., 4:309 and 5:75. See also Mt 9:24; Jn 11:11; 1 Th 4:13.

88. Martin Luther, *Genesis*, 25:17 in ibid., 4:329.

89. Martin Luther, *Ecclesiastes*, 9:5 in ibid., 15:147. Luther's view of death is interpreted by Moltmann 'as a deep, dreamless sleep, removed from time and space, without consciousness and without feeling'; see Jürgen Moltmann, 'Is There Life After Death?' in *The End of the World and the Ends of God: Science and Theology on Eschatology,* ed. John Polkinghorne and Michael Welker (Harrisburg, PA: Continuum, 2000), 238–55 at 248.

90. See Dupuis SJ and Neuner SJ, eds, *The Christian Faith* at n. 512, p. 203.

91. See St Teresa of Avila, *The Interior Castle,* 1.1.1 in Kieran Kavanaugh OCD and Otilio Rodriguez OCD, eds, *The Collected Works of Saint Teresa of Avila*, 2nd revised ed., 3 vols. (Washington: ICS Publications, 1987), 2:283.

92. See St Teresa of Avila, *The Interior Castle*, 1.1.2 in ibid., 2:284.

93. See St Teresa of Avila, *The Way of Perfection*, 31.2 in ibid., 2:153.

94. See Steven Payne OCD, *John of the Cross and the Cognitive Value of Mysticism. An analysis of Sanjuanist Teaching and its Philosophical Implications for Contemporary Discussions of Mystical Experience*, Synthese Historical Library 37 (Dordrecht – Boston – London: Kluwer Academic Publishers, 1990), 17–18.

95. See ibid., 45 n. 4.

96. See St John of the Cross, *The Spiritual Canticle,* 19.2 in Kieran Kavanaugh OCD and Otilio Rodriguez OCD, eds., *The Collected Works of St John of the Cross* (Washington, DC: ICS Publications, 1991), 549.

97. See St John of the Cross, *The Living Flame of Love*, 4.14 in ibid, 713.

98. *hómine ad imáginem tuam facto, inseparábile viro mulíeris adiutórium condidísti*; see Books, ed., *Missal* (1974), 768. See also 'You formed man in your own likeness and set him over the whole world to serve you (*Hominem ad tuam imaginem condidisti, eique commisisti mundi curam universi)'* in the Appendix n. 117.

99. *qui omnes homines vis salvos fieri*; see ibid., 815.

100. *Et cum amicitiam tuam, non oboediens, amisisset, non eum dereliquisti in mortis imperio*, see the Appendix n. 117.

101. See 'share his victory (*huius vitae mortalitáte devícta)'* in *Missal* (1974), 884.

102. *Deus, qui illuminas omnem hominem venientem in hanc mundum*, see the Appendix n. IV.

103. *humanae salutis amator*; see *Missal* (1974), 904.

104. *qui Unigénitum tuum ex homínibus nasci voluísti, ut hómines ex te mirábili mystério renasceréntur*; see ibid.,597.

105. *qui humano generi ad imitandum humilitatis exemplum, Salvatorem nostrum carnem sumere, et crucem subire fecisti*; see the Appendix n. XI.

106. *imáginem bonitátis tuae inter hómines referámus*; see *Missal* (1974), 664.

107. *humána singulórum perficiátur persóna*; see ibid., 822.

108. *hominibus bonae voluntatis*; see the Appendix n. 8.

109. *Qui propter nos homines et propter nostram salutem descendit de caelis ... et homo factus est*; see the Appendix n. 18.

110. *Verbum tuum in útero Vírginis Maríæ veritátem carnis humánæ suscípere voluísti*; see *Missal* (1974), 546.

111. *nosmetípsos exhibeámus hóstiam sanctam, tibi placéntem*; see ibid., 697.

112. *qui ex eádem Vírgine carnem dignátus est suscípere*; see ibid., 624.

113. *Deum et hóminem*; see ibid., 546. See also 'who became man and lived among us (*sicut homo génitus idem præfúlsit et Deus*)' in the Appendix n. VII.

114. *qui tibi oblatiónem seípsum in cruce óbtulit immaculátam*; see ibid., 616.

115. *nobis succúrrat humánitas*; see ibid., 616, 624.

116. *divinitatis tuae sempiterna fruitione repleri: quam ... perceptio praefigurat*; see the Appendix n. XXIV.

117. *Fílii tui divinitátis partícipes nos semper effíciant*; see *Missal* (1974), 696.

118. *ut divínae consórtes natúrae éffici mereámur*; see ibid.,739.

119. See *ánimam suam pro óvibus pósuit ... eodem Spiritu moti ... animam nostram pro fratribus ponere non vereamur*; see ibid., 662.

120. See *ad animárum salútem, ánimas quaerere tibíque soli servíre valeámus, desidério salútis hóminum ... pro animárum salúte, gratiámque et glóriam aetérnam consequámur animárum, animórum communióne ... Ecclésia ... véluti ánima societátis humánae ... semper exsístat, animas fratrum lucrari Christo, ánima ... N., ánimae fámuli tui N.*, communiónem obtíneat animórum, *animábus famulórum tuórum, pro quibus tuam deprecámur cleméntiam, Animábus famulórum tuórum ... profíciat, fidélis remunerátor animárum ... ánimam fámuli tui Papae N., immortális pastor animárum ... ánimam fámuli tui Papae N. ... ánima fámuli tui Papae N., ut ánima ... N. epíscopi ... gáudia Dómini sui ingrediátur aetérna, ut ánima ... N., tibi pro animábus famulórum tuórum offérimus, pro ánimae N. ... salúte ... pro ánima N. ... ánima N. ... semper exsúltet, Concéde ... ánimae ... felicitátis aetérnae consórtium ... ut ... N. ... cum iis qui bene ministravérunt partem recípere, ut ánima ... N. ... ánima fámuli tui N. ... ánima fámuli tui N., ánima fámuli tui N. ... ánimam fámuli tui N.* and *animábus ... cunctórum remissiónem tríbue peccatórum ... ut ánimae ... a peccátis ómnibus expiátae* in ibid., 526, 529, 670, 734, 777, 791, 816, 836, 883, 884, 885, 887, 888, 889, 891, 892, 893, 894, 895, 896, 897, 898, 904. See also *renováta ánimae iuventúte* in the Appendix n. XIII.

121. See 'which burned in the gentle heart Frances de Sales (*mitíssimum beáti Francísci ánimum mirabíliter inflammásti*)' in ibid., 526.

122. See 'and give them freedom of mind and heart for ever (*et ánimae perpétua gáudeant libertáte*)' in ibid., 837.

123. See 'fill us with your strength (*cor unum simus et ánima una, tua caritáte firmáti*)' in ibid., 583.

124. *cor unum et ánimam unam*; see ibid., 848.

125. See 'unite in one heart and spirit (*cor unum et ánima una esse persevérent*)' in ibid., 647.

126. *ad salútem córporis et ánimae*; see the Appendix n. XXII.

127. *sospitátem córporum gratiámque et glóriam aetérnam consequámur animárum*; see *Missal* (1974), 734.

128. *córpore et ánima ad caeléstem glóriam assumpsísti*, see ibid., 611. See also *Ecclésiae tuae consummándae inítium et imágo* in *Missal* (1974), 462.

129. *vobis fíeri templum suum et habitáculum Spíritus Sancti*; see *Missal* (1974), 689. This same Latin phrase is translated elsewhere as 'you build your temple of living stones'; see *Missal* (1974), 455.

130. *dissolúta terréstris huius incolátus domo, aetérna in caelis habitátio comparátur;* see the Appendix n. V.

131. *Domine, non sum dignus ut intres sub tectum meum: sed tantum dic verbo, et sanabitur anima mea*; see the Appendix n. 132.

132. *hómine ad imáginem tuam facto, inseparábile viro mulíeris adiutórium condidísti*; see *Missal* (2011), 1092. See also 'You formed man in your own image and entrusted the whole world to his care (*Hominem ad tuam imaginem condidisti, eique commisisti mundi curam universi*)' in the Appendix n. 117.

133. *qui omnes homines vis salvos fieri*, see ibid., 1182.

134. *Et cum amicitiam tuam, non oboediens, amisisset, non eum dereliquisti in mortis imperio*; see the Appendix n. 117.

135. See 'to sustain our mortal life (*mortális vitae subsídium cónferat*)' in *Missal* (2011), 986. See also 'with the mortality of this life overcome (*huius vitae mortalitáte devícta*)' in *Missal* (2011), 899, 1297.

136. *Deus, qui illuminas omnem hominem venientem in hanc mundum*; see the Appendix n. IV.

137. *humanae salutis amator*; see *Missal* (2011), 1318.

138. *qui Unigénitum tuum ex homínibus nasci voluísti, ut hómines ex te mirábili mystério renasceréntur*; see ibid., 810.

139. *Qui propter nos homines et propter nostram salutem descendit de caelis ... et homo factus est*; see the Appendix n. 18.

140. *Verbum tuum in útero Vírginis Maríæ veritátem carnis humánæ suscípere voluísti*; see *Missal* (2011), 735. See also 'who from her was pleased to take flesh (*qui ex eádem Vírgine carnem dignátus est suscípere*)' in *Missal* (2011), 850.

141. *hominibus bonae voluntatis*; see the Appendix n. 8.

142. *humánam famíliam*; see *Missal* (2011), 643.

143. See ibid. at 644, 646, 659, 660, 666, 674, 680.

144. *qui humano generi ad imitandum humilitatis exemplum, Salvatorem nostrum carnem sumere, et crucem subire fecisti*; see the Appendix n. XI.

145. See the Appendix n. 88, 108, 122.

146. See the Appendis n. 87, 113. See also 'Look with favour on the oblation of your Church, in which we show forth the paschal Sacrifice of Christ that has been handed on to us (*In oblatiónem Ecclésiae tuae, in qua paschále Christi sacrifícium nobis tráditum exhibémus, réspice propítius*)' in *Missal* (2011), 662.

147. *Deum et hóminem*, see ibid., 735. See also 'just as Christ was born a man and also shone forth as God (*sicut homo génitus idem præfúlsit et Deus*)' in the Appendix n. VII.

148. *ut eius nobis succúrrat humánitas, qui tibi oblatiónem seípsum in cruce óbtulit immaculátam*; see ibid., 839.

149. *nobis succúrrat humánitas*; see ibid., 850.

150. *nosmetípsos exhibeámus hóstiam sanctam, tibi placéntem*; see ibid., 960.

151. *divinitatis tuae sempiterna fruitione repleri: quam ... perceptio praefigurat*; see ibid., 367.

152. *humána singulórum perficiátur persóna*; see ibid., 1199.

153. *Fílii tui divinitátis partícipes nos semper effíciant*; see ibid., 965.

154. *ut divínae consórtes natúrae éffici mereámur*; see ibid., 1011. See 'may merit to become partakers even in his divine nature (*ipsíus étiam divínæ natúræmereámur esse consórtes*)' in *Missal* (2011), 735.

155. *humanitátis novae in dilectióne caritátis tibi reconciliátae*; see *Missal* (2011), 717. See also 'to create in Bridget the New Man in your image, the old having passed away' and 'the likeness of the New Man' in *Missal* (2011), 807.

156. *imáginem bonitátis tuae inter hómines referámus*; see *Missal* (2011), 916.

157. See 'you wonderfully inflamed the most gentle soul of Saint Frances de Sales (*mitíssimum beáti Francísci ánimum mirabíliter inflammásti*)' in ibid., 695.

158. See 'for the salvation of souls (*ad animárum salútem*)', 'for the salvation of souls' (*desidério salútis hóminum*)', 'for the salvation of souls' (*pro animárum salúte*)' and 'and grace and eternal glory for our souls (*gratiámque et glóriam aetérnam consequámur animárum*)' in ibid., 695, 926, 927, 1006.

159. See 'we may seek out souls and serve you alone (*ánimas quaerere tibíque soli servíre valeámus*)' and 'with zeal for souls (*animárum zelo*)' in ibid., 699, 829.

160. See ibid., 1293, 1294, 1295, 1296, 1297, 1298, 1300, 1306, 1308, 1309, 1311, 1312, 1313, 1314, 1318.

161. *animas fratrum lucrari Christo;* see ibid., 816.

162. *ánimam suam pro óvibus pósuit ... eodem Spiritu moti ... animam nostram pro fratribus ponere non vereamur;* see ibid., 914.

163. See 'may bring about a communion of minds and hearts (*communiónem obtíneat animórum*)' in ibid., 1205.

164. *salútem córporis et ánimae;* see ibid., 364, 1232.

165. See 'and rejoice in lasting freedom of soul (*et ánimae perpétua gáudeant libertáte*)' in ibid., 1216.

166. See 'in renewed youthfulness of spirit (*renováta ánimae iuventúte*)' in the Appendix n. XIII and 'to sustain them in communion of spirit (*animórum communióne ... sustentáre*)' in ibid., 1164. Something like 'in renewed youthfulness of soul' and 'to sustain the communion of their souls' might be more appropriate translations.

167. *quem discórdans ánimus non capit, quem mens cruénta non récipit;* see ibid., 1202.

168. See 'that your Church ... may ... always be ... the soul of human society (*Ecclésia ... véluti ánima societátis humánae ... semper exsístat*)' in ibid., 1142.

169. See 'we may be one heart and one soul (*cor unum simus et ánima una*)' and 'persevere as one heart and one soul (*cor unum et ánima una esse persevérent*)' in ibid., 795, 887.

170. *cor unum et ánimam unam;* see ibid., 1172.

171. *ad salútem córporis et ánimae;* see ibid., 364, 1232.

172. *sospitátem córporum gratiámque et glóriam aetérnam consequámur animárum;* see ibid., 1006.

173. *Corpus tuum custódiat et ánimam tuam salvet;* see ibid., 1043.

174. See the *Catechism of the Catholic Church* (1992), n. 1386.

175. *Domine, non sum dignus ut intres sub tectum meum: sed tantum dic verbo, et sanabitur anima mea;* see the Appendix n. 132.

176. *in hoc córpore and in corpore;* see *Missal* (2011), 450, 1309.

177. *vobis fieri templum suum et habitáculum Spíritus Sancti;* see ibid., 950, 952–3, 1132.

178. *dissolúta terréstris huius incolátus domo, aetérna in caelis habitátio comparátur;* see the Appendix n. V.

179. *córpore et ánima ad caeléstem glóriam assumpsísti ... Ecclésiae tuae consummándae inítium et imágo;* see *Missal* (2011), 831, 833.

180. See Gn 17:11,13-14, 24; Exod 4:7; Lev 19:28; 21:5; Num 8:7; Judg 8:7; Neh 5:5; Job 13:14; Ez 44:7.

181. See Ps 56:4, 11; 77:39; Is 31:3; 40:6; Jer 17:5; 32:27; Job 10:4.

182. See Deut 12:23, 27; Lev 17:11; Sir 14:18.

183. For the equivalent term in Greek, see also Sir 14:17; 18:13; 41:4. Ruiz de la Peña notes that, in the Wisdom literature, the Greek term *sarx* coincides with, and frequently translates, the Hebrew term *bashar;* see Ruiz de la Peña, *Immagine di Dio. Antropologia teologica fondamentale*, 48.

184. See Gn 6:12, 19; 7:15-16, 21; 8:17; 9:11, 15, 17; Lev 17:14; Num 16:22; 27:16; Deut 5:26; Job 34:15.

185. See Ps 55:5, 12; Is 58:7; Jer 17:5.

186. See Job 12:10; 34:15; Ps 64:3; 136:25; 144:21; Is 40:5; 66:16, 23-24; Jer 25:31; 45:5; Ez 21:4; Joel 2:28.

187. Qoheleth describes making a vow that one might not be able to fulfil as allowing one's mouth to cause one's flesh to sin (cf. Qoh 5:5).

188. See Ps 16:9; 73:26; 84:2; Qoh 5:2.

189. See Ruiz de la Peña, *Immagine di Dio. Antropologia teologica fondamentale*, 15.

190. See 2 Cor 10:3; Gal 2:20; Phil 1:22.

191. See Mt 24:22; Lk 3:6; Jn 17:2; Acts 2:17; Rm 3:20; 1 Cor 1:29; Gal 2:16. Compare Ps 64:3; 136:25; 145:21; Is 40:5; 66:16,23-24; Jer 25:31; 45:5; Ez 21:4; Jl 2:28.

192. See Rm 1:3; 4:1; 9:3; 1 Cor 10:18; Gal 4:23, 29.

193. See 1 Cor 1:26; 2 Cor 1:17; 10:2-3; Col 3:22; Eph 6:5.

194. See Jn 3:6; 6:63.

195. See Jn 3:5: 6:63.

196. See Rm 6:19.

197. See 1 Pt 2:11, 25; 2 Pt 2:9-10; 1 Jn 2:15-16.

198. See Rm 7:5; 13:14; Eph 2:3; 1 Pt 2:11.

199. See Rm 6:17, 20; 7:25.

200. See Herrade Mehl-Koehnlein, *L'homme selon l'apôtre Paul,* Cahiers théologiques, 28 (Neuchâtel: Delachaux & Niestlé, 1951), 12–17; Alexander Sand, *Der Begfiff 'Fleisch' in den paulinischen Hauptbriefen,* Biblische Untersuchungen, 2 (Regensburg: Pustet, 1967); Spicq OP, *Dio e l'uomo secondo il Nuovo Testamento,* 257–8.

201. See Rm 1:24; 4:19; 1 Cor 5:3; 6:13, 16, 18; 7:4; 9:27; 13:3; 2 Cor 5;6, 8; 10:10; 12:2-3; Gal 6:17.

202. See Robert H. Gundry, *Sôma in Biblical Theology, with Emphasis on Pauline Anthropology,* Society for New Testament Studies, Monograph Series, 29 (Cambridge: Cambridge University Press, 1976); Ruiz de la Peña, *Immagine di Dio. Antropologia teologica fondamentale,* 81–5.

203. See Hans Conzelmann, *Théologie du Nouveau Testament* (Geneva: Labor et Fides, 1969), 189; Rodolphe Morissette, 'L'expression sôma in 1 Co 15 et dans la littérature paulinienne', *Révue des sciences philosophiques et théologiques* 56 (1972) 223–39: 230; Robinson, *Le corps,* 48, 52 n. 32.

204. James D. G. Dunn, *The Theology of Paul the Apostle* (Grand Rapids, Michigan: Wm. B. Eerdmans, 1998), 56.

205. See Rm 12:4; 1 Cor 12:12-26.

206. See Rm 6:13; 12:1-2; 1 Cor 7:4-5.

207. See Rm 12:5; 1 Cor 3:16-17. See also Col 1:18; Eph 1:23; 5:23, 30.

208. See also Rm 12:1-2.

209. See Maximiliano García Cordero OP, 'La esperanza del más allá en el Nuevo Testamento', *Ciencia tomista* 114 (1987), 209–64: 223–3.

210. See also Phil 1:20.

211. See 1 Cor 12:12-27.

212. See 1 Cor 6:14-20.

213. Matthew uses the word fourteen times and Luke thirteen, significantly more frequently than other sections of the New Testament (six times in John, five times in both Hebrews and James, and four times in Mark); see Morissette, 'L'expression sôma in 1 Co 15 et dans la littérature paulinienne', 234 n. 38.

214. See Mt 5:29-30; 6:23–23.

215. See Mt 6:25; Lk 12:22-23.

216. See Spicq OP, *Dio e l'uomo secondo il Nuovo Testamento*, 223 n. 172. See also Mt 5:29-30; 18:8-9; 27:53-53.

217. See Bo Reicke, 'Body and Soul in the New Testament', *Studia theologica* 19 (1965), 200–12 at 204.

218. Athanagoras of Athens, *The Resurrection of the Dead*, 12 in Migne, ed., *PG* at 6:1000.

219. St Irenaeus, *Against Heresies*, 5.7.1 in ibid., 7:1140.

220. St Irenaeus, *Against Heresies*, 5.2.2, 3 in ibid., 7:1124, 1125–6.

221. St Irenaeus, *Against Heresies*, 5.31.2 in ibid., 7:1209.

222. St Clement of Alexandria, *The Instructor of Children*, 3.1.1.5-2.1 in Der Kirchenväter-commission der königl. preussischen Akademie der Wissenschaften, ed., *Die griechischen christlichen Schriftsteller der ersten drei Jahrhunderte*, 53 vols. (Leipzig – Berlin: J. C. Hinrichs, 1897–1971), 236–7.

223. St Clement of Alexandria, *Miscellanies*, 4.26 [4.163.1-2] in ibid., 52:320.

224. St Clement of Alexandria, *Miscellanies*, 3.5 in *Migne*, ed., *PG*, 8:1143–4.

225. Origen, *The Fundamental Doctrines*, 4.4.10 [4.4.37] in Wissenschaften, ed., *GCS* at 22:363.

226. Origen, *The Fundamental Doctrines*, 4.2.4 [4.11] in ibid., 22:313.

227. Origen, *The Fundamental Doctrines*, 3.6.6 in ibid., 22:288.

228. St Augustine, *Continence*, 12.26 in Migne, ed., *PL*, 40:367.

229. St Augustine, *City of God*, 21.10.1 in ibid., 41:725.

230. St Augustine, *The Morality of the Catholic Church*, 1.27.52 in ibid., 32:1332.

231. St Augustine, *Sermons*, 154.10.15 in ibid., 38:839.

232. See St Augustine, *Confessions*, 10.34.53, *The True Religion*, 39.72, *Explanations of the Psalms*, 41.7-8, and *Sermons*, 96.2.2, in ibid., 32.801, 34.154, 36.468-89, 38.585.

233. *commúnem illam cum céteris córporis formam*, see *Missal* (1974), 453.

234. *quae Fílium tuum … ineffabíliter de se génuit incarnátum*, see ibid., 462.

235. See the Appendix n. 122.

236. *in totíus Ecclésiae córpore declaráret impléndum quod eius mirabíliter praefúlsit in cápite*, see *Missal* (1974), 453.

237. *et Ecclésiam per orbem diffúsam in domínici compágem córporis facis augéri*, see ibid., 455.

238. See the Appendix n. 19, 115.

239. Despite the implicit citation of 2 Corinthians 4:10, Christians who have been baptised are described as 'accepting in our lives a share in the sufferings of Jesus Christ (*mortificatiónem Iesu in córpore nostro circumferéntes*)' and 'sharing in Christ's suffering (*Christi mortificatiónem feréntes*)' in *Missal* (1974), 731, 669. See also 'Each day (*in hoc córpore*)' in the Appendix IV and 'the courage to endure torture and death for the Gospel (*ómnia córporis torménta devícit*)', 'that your Church may live in harmony (*ut Ecclésiae tuae corpus concórdia vígeat*)' and 'during his life (*in corpore*)' in *Missal* (1974), 525, 848, 892.

240. See 'our observance of Lent (*corporáli ieiúnio*)' and 'may we give ourselves once more to your service (*quod … corporáli servítio exhíbuit*)' in *Missal* (1974), 414, 687.

241. See *incarnatum* in the Appendix n. 99 and *Verbum caro factum*, see ibid., 681.

242. See 'the privilege of being the mother of your Son (*ex ipsa secúndum carnem nascerétur*)', 'who brought the dawn of hope and salvation to the world (*Fílii tui … humánitas, qui ex eádem Vírgine carnem dignátus est suscípere*)' and 'joined (*ut iam non duo essent, sed una caro*)' in ibid., 609, 624, 771. See also 'share his resurrection (*quando mortuos suscitabit in carne de terra*)' and 'bring us to the glory of the resurrection (*ad incorruptíbilem glorificándae carnis resurrectiónem perveníre*)' in the Appendix n. 115 and XIV.

243. See 'became man for us and was presented in the temple (*nostrae carnis substántia in templo est praesentátus)*', 'became man and was born (*veritátem carnis humánae suscípere)*', 'whom we proclaim to be God and man (*vitam Iesu in carne nostra mortáli manifestémus)*', 'joined as husband and wife in union of body and heart (*inseparábile viro mulieris adiutórium condidísti, ut iam non duo essent, sed una caro)*' and 'in human weakness (*per fragilitátem carnis*) while they lived on earth' in ibid., 533, 546, 698, 771, 901. See also 'was born (*incarnatus est)*', 'was conceived (*incarnatus)*', coming ... as man (*incarnationem)*', 'your only Son revealed himself to us by becoming man (*in substántia nostrae carnis appáruit)*' and 'by becoming man (*nustrum carnem sumere)*' in the Appendix n. 18, 117, VI, VIII and XI.

244. *vir et múlier, in carnis et cordis unitáte coniúncti*; see ibid., 771.

245. *qui sunt generatióne terréni, fiant regeneratióne caeléstes*; see ibid., 753.

246. *ex aqua et Spíritu Sancto renátos*; see ibid., 760.

247. *unum in Christo corpus et unus spíritus*; see ibid., 870. See also the Appendix n. 113.

248. *vir et múlier, in carnis et cordis unitáte coniúncti*; see ibid., 771.

249. *salútem mentis et córporis*; see ibid., 850. See also 'health in mind and body (*tutamentum mentis et corporis)*', 'you give us food for body and spirit ... bring us health of mind and body (*corpóribus nostris subsídium non desit et méntibus)*' in the Appendix n. 131 and XVIII and 'you provide food for strength ... bring us health of mind and body (*corpóribus nostris subsídium non desit et méntibus)*' in *Missal* (1974), 829.

250. *nos córpore páriter et mente puríficet*; see *Missal* (1974), 737.

251. Compare the paraphrases 'May this eucharist take away our sins (*fidélium tuórum córpora mentésque sanctíficet)*', 'May the eucharist ... influence our thoughts and actions (*Mentes nostras et córpora possídeat)*' and 'bring us salvation (*reparátio mentis et córporis)*' in the Appendix n. IX, XX and XXI and 'influence our thoughts and actions (*subsídium mentis et córporis)*' in ibid., 842.

252. *Corporis et Sanguinis*, see ibid., 539. See also the Appendix nn. 88–89, 94, 101–102, 105, 109–110, 113, 118–119, 122, 131 (twice), 133, XXIII and XXIV.

253. *usque ad sánguinem;* see ibid., 571.

254. See ibid., 622, 662, 704.

255. See 'a martyr's death (*fuso sánguine)*', 'martyrdom (*sánguine)*' and 'martyrdom (*sánguinis effusióne)*' in ibid., 464, 596, 648.

256. In the Appendix, see *fructum terrae et operis manuum hominum* in n. 23 and *fructum vitis et operis manuum hominum* in n. 25.

257. *See* 'the faith we profess with our lips (*fidem, quam ore profitémur)*' in *Missal* (1974), 682.

258. See 'spread the faith by his teaching (*fidem, quam ore dócuit)*' and 'give us the courage to proclaim our faith (*fidem tuam, quam lingua nostra lóquitur)*' in ibid., 571, 576.

259. See the Appendix n. IV.

260. *commúnem illam cum céteris córporis formam*; see *Missal* (2011), 819.

261. *quae Fílium tuum ... ineffabíliter de se génuit incarnátum;* see ibid., 833.

262. *ex ipsa secúndum carnem nascerétur*; see ibid., 830.

263. *qui sunt generatióne terréni, fiant regeneratióne caeléstes*; see ibid., 1031.

264. *ex aqua et Spíritu Sancto renátos*; see ibid., 1040.

265. See the Appendix n. 122.

266. *Fílii tui membra*; see *Missal* (2011), 662, 669, 676, 683.

267. *unum in Christo corpus et unus spíritus*; see ibid., 1274. See also the Appendix n. 113.

268. *in totíus Ecclésiae córpore declaráret impléndum quod eius mirabíliter praefúlsit in cápite*; see ibid., 819.

269. *et Ecclésiam per orbem diffúsam in domínici compágem córporis facis augéri*; see ibid., 949. See also 'gathered into one Body in Christ (*in unum corpus congregéntur in Christo*)' in *Missal* (2011), 646.

270. *ut Ecclésiae tuae corpus concórdia vígeat*; see *Missal* (2011), 1172.

271. See the Appendix n. 19, 115.

272. *Verbum caro factum*; see *Missal* (2011), 941. See also 'the same Word made flesh (*Verbum ... caro factum*)' in *Missal* (2011), 673.

273. In the Appendix, see *incarnatus/incarnatum de Spiritu Sancto* in n. 18, 99 and 117 and 'the Incarnation of Christ (*Christi ... incarnationem*)' in n. VI.

274. *veritátem carnis humánae suscípere*; see *Missal* (2011), 735. See also 'appeared in our very flesh (*in substantia nostrae carnis apparuit*)' and 'to take flesh (*nostrum carnem sumere*)' in the Appendix n. VIII and XI.

275. See 'the humanity of your son, who from her was pleased to take flesh (*Fílii tui ... humánitas, qui ex eádem Vírgine carnem dignátus est suscípere*)' in ibid., 850.

276. See 'your Only Begotten Son was presented ... in the Temple in the substance of our flesh (*nostrae carnis substántia in templo est praesentátus*)' in ibid., 709.

277. See 'may show forth in our mortal flesh the life of Jesus (*vitam Iesu in carne nostra mortáli manifestémus*)' in ibid., 966.

278. See 'through the frailty of the flesh (*per fragilitátem carnis*) during their earthly lives' in ibid., 1304.

279. *reflóreat cor et caro nostra vigóre pudicítiae et castimóniae novitáte*; see ibid., 1212.

280. See 'whose Only Begotten Son has appeared in our very flesh (*in substántia nostrae carnis appáruit*)' in the Appendix n. VIII.

281. *uscitabit in carne;* see the Appendix n. 115.

282. *ad incorruptíbilem glorificándae carnis resurrectiónem perveníre*; see the Appendix n. XIV.

283. *quod ... corporáli servítio exhíbuit*; see *Missal* (2011), 950.

284. *ómnia córporis torménta devícit;* see ibid., 694.

285. *mortificatiónem Iesu in córpore nostro circumferéntes* and *Christi mortificatiónem feréntes*; see ibid., 1004, 925.

286. *casto córpore ... mundo corde ... reflóreat cor et caro nostra vigóre pudicítiae et castimóniae novitáte*; see ibid., 1212.

287. *uni, thoro iuncti*; see ibid., 1087. See also 'no longer two, but one flesh (*ut iam non duo essent, sed una caro*)' in *Missal* (2011), 1086.

288. *vir et múlier, in carnis et cordis unitáte coniúncti*; see *Missal* (2011), 1092.

289. See *corporáli ieiúnio* in ibid., 420.

290. *salútem mentis et córporis*; see ibid., 1214, 1226.

291. See 'protection in mind and body (*tutamentum mentis et corporis*)', 'sanctify your faithful in mind and body (*fidélium tuórum córpora mentésque sanctíficet*)', 'take possession of our minds and bodies (*Mentes nostras et córpora possídeat*)', 'restore us in mind and body (*reparátio mentis et córporis*)' in the Appendix n. 131, IX, XX and XXI. See also 'may purify us both in body and in mind (*nos córpore páriter et mente puríficet*)' and 'help in mind and body (*subsídium mentis et córporis*)', ibid., 1008, 1224.

292. See the Appendix n. XVIII.

293. See the Appendix n. XVIII and *Missal* (2011), 1193, 1224.

294. *Corporis et Sanguinis*; see ibid., 720, 815. See also the Appendix nn. 88–89, 94, 101–102, 105, 109–110, 113, 118–119, 122, 131 (twice), 133, XXIII and XXIV.

295. *usque ad sánguinem*; see ibid., 772.

296. *sanguine*; see ibid., 809.

297. See ibid., 845–846, 888, 914, 922, 974.

298. In the Appendix, see *fructum terrae et operis manuum hominum* in n. 23 *and fructum vitis et operis manuum hominum* in n. 25.

299. *adversárii manus coniúngant*; see *Missal* (2011), 651.

300. See 'so that what has passed our lips as food', ibid., 1212.

301. See 'the faith he taught with his lips', 'the faith we profess with our lips' and 'the faith in you which we confess with our lips' in ibid., 772, 783, 942.

302. See also Eccl (Qo) 7:9; 10:4.

303. See 1 Chr 5:26; 2 Chr 21:16; Jer 51:11; Ezra 1:1, 5; Hg 1:14.

304. See Eccl (Qo) 7:8; Ps 76:13; Prov 29:23.

305. See also Is 57:15.

306. See also Job 32:18; Ps 77:8.

307. See also Deut 5:20.

308. See Jn 3:8; Heb 1:7.

309. See Lk 8:55; 23:46; Jn 20:22; 2 Th 2:8; Heb 12:23.

310. See Mt 27:50; Jn 19:30; Acts 7:59; Jas 2:26; Rv 11:11.

311. See 2 Tm 1:7; Eph 4:17, 23. See also the 'gentle and quiet spirit' mentioned in 1 Pt 3:4.

312. See Mk 8:12.

313. See Acts 17:16.

314. See 1 Cor 4:21.

315. See Jn 11:33.

316. See Jn 13:21.

317. See H. Wheeler Robinson, *The Christian Doctrine of Man* (Edinburgh: T. and T. Clark, 1947), 109.

318. See Conzelmann, *Théologie du Nouveau Testament*, 187; Ruiz de la Peña, *Immagine di Dio. Antropologia teologica fondamentale*, 67; Spicq OP, *Dio e l'uomo secondo il Nuovo Testamento*, 239.

319. See 1 Cor 12:13; Gal 3:28. See also Eph 4:3.

320. See 2 Cor 4:13.

321. See 1 Cor 3:1; 9:11. See also Col 2:5.

322. See Eph 4:23.

323. See Acts 16:14; 2 Cor 3:15; Eph 1:18.

324. See 1 Cor 7:37; 2 Cor 9:7.

325. See Rm 10:1. See also Col 3:22; Eph 6:5.

326. See Mt 22:37; Mk 12:30; Lk 10:27; Rm 5:5.

327. See Jn 16:6,22; Acts 2:6, 37; Rm 9:2; 2 Cor 2:4; 8:16; Ph 1:7-8.

328. See Mk 2:6, 8; Lk 3:15; 9:47; 24:25; Rm 6:17; 10:9-10.

329. See Rm 8:27; Rv 2:23.

330. On Paul's understanding of mind and heart, see Dunn, *The Theology of Paul the Apostle*, 73–5.

331. See Jn 1:33.

332. See Jn 10:10.

333. Justin Martyr, *The Resurrection*, 10 in Migne, ed., *PG*, 6:1590.

334. Tatian the Syrian, *Address to the Greeks*, 13, 15 in ibid., 6:833, 836, 837, 840.

335. St Clement of Alexandria, *The Instructor of Children*, 3.1.1.5–2.1 in Wissenschaften, ed., GCS, 236–7.

336. Origen, *The Fundamental Doctrines*, 4.2.4 [4.11] in ibid., 22:313.

337. He notes that, for some thinkers, the body is 'dead and utterly devoid of life' until it is given life by the soul and that it is also considered, as such 'inimical to the spirit' in the sense that 'we are drawn and enticed to those evils that are agreeable to the body'. Origen, *The Fundamental Doctrines*, 3.4.1 in ibid., 22:264.

338. See Theodoret of Cyr, *The Theology of the Trinity and the Divine Incarnation,* 18 in Migne, ed., *PG,* 75:1448.

339. See St Gregory of Nazianz, *Letters*, 101 in ibid., 37:184.

340. St Augustine, *Confessions,* 1.1 *in Migne*, ed., *PL*, 32:661.

341. St Augustine, *Confessions,* 8.12 [29] in ibid., 32:762.

342. See St Augustine, *Confessions*, 7.1 [1] in ibid., 32:734.

343. See St Augustine, *Confessions*, 7.10 [16] in ibid., 32:742.

344. *Dicitur spiritus et ipsa mens rationalis, ubi est quidam tamquam oculus animae, ad quem pertinet imago et agnitio Dei;* see St Augustine, *The Literal Translation of Genesis*, 12.7 [18] in ibid., 34:460.

345. The term 'spirit (*spiritus*)' can also be applied to the wind (cf. Ps 148:8) and to the breath of animals (cf. Eccl (Qo) 3:21); see St Augustine, *The Literal Translation of Genesis*, 12.7 [18] in ibid.

346. *quia omnis mens spiritus est, non autem omnis spiritus mens est ... Dicitur etiam spiritus in homine, qui mens non sit, ad quem pertinent imaginationes similes corporum ... Si autem oravero lingua, spiritus meus orat, mens autem mea infructuosa est ... quia nec dici potest, nisi corporalium vocum imagines sonum oris spiritus cogitatione praeveniant;* see St Augustine, *The Trinity*, 14:16 [22] in ibid., 42:1053.

347. See St Augustine, *City of God*, 8.6 in ibid., 41:231.

348. *anima intellectualis;* see St Augustine, *City of God*, 10.2, 9, 27 in ibid., 41:280, 287, 305.

349. *anima rationalis;* see St Augustine, *City of God,* 10.2, 9 and *The Trinity*, 15.1 in ibid., 41:279–80, 287, 42:1037.

350. *anima spiritalis*; see St Augustine, *City of God,* 10.9, 27 in ibid., 41:287, 305.

351. *quod excellit in anima;* see St Augustine, *The Trinity*, 15:7 [11] in ibid., 42:1065.

352. See St Augustine, *On the Immortality of the Soul*, 16 [25] in ibid., 32:1034.

353. See St Augustine, *City of God*, 5.11 in ibid., 41:154.

354. *animo tamen corporales imagines intuemur, seu veras, sicut ipsa corpora vidimus, et memoria retinemus; seu fictas, sicut cogitatio formare potuerit;* see St Augustine, *The Literal Translation of Genesis*, 12.6 [15] in ibid., 34:458.

355. *animo ac mente sentiuntur;* see St Augustine, *City of God*, 11.3 in ibid., 41:318.

356. St Augustine, *Homilies on John*, 32.5 in ibid., 35:1644.

357. St Augustine, *Sermons*, 174.2 in ibid., 38:941.

358. St Augustine, *Homilies on John*, 23.6 in ibid., 35:1585.

359. St Augustine, *Homilies on John*, 3.4 in ibid., 35:1398.

360. St Augustine, *The Lord's Sermon on the Mount in Matthew*, 2.6 [23] in ibid., 34:1279.

361. St Augustine, *City of God*, 15.1; 19:17 in ibid., 41:437–8, 645–6.

362. 'And where is God's image? In your mind, in your intellect!'; see St Augustine, *Homilies on John*, 3.4 in ibid., 35:1398.

363. For St Augustine, Christ has 'a complete soul, not the irrational part of the soul only, but the rational part too, which is called the mind'; see St Augustine, *Homilies on John*, 23.6

in ibid., 35:1585. In 434, St Vincent of Lerins described as heretics those who denied that the human soul of Christ was 'endowed with intelligence, possessing mind and reason; see St Vincent of Lerins, *The Notebooks*, 13 in Migne, ed., *PL* at 50:655. Pope St Leo the Great held that Christ's body was 'under the control of his divinity and of his mind'; see Pope St Leo the Great, *Letters*, 35.3 in Migne, ed., *PL*, 54:809-10.

364. Dupuis SJ and Neuner SJ, eds., *The Christian Faith* at nn. 614–15, pp. 227–8.

365. Ibid., n. 504, p. 200.

366. Ibid., n. 401/1, p. 167.

367. Ibid., n. 402/6, p. 168.

368. See the prayers asking that the Lord be 'in your heart and on your lips (*in corde tuo et in labiis tuis*)' or asking God to 'cleanse my heart and my lips (*Munda cor meum ac labia mea*)' in the Appendix n. 14.

369. See 'Give us purity of heart (*sincéro nos corde pérfice*)' in *Missal* (1974), 723. See also 'You give us strength to purify our hearts (*ad reparándam méntium puritátem*)' in the Appendix n. II.

370. *Sursum corda. Habemus ad Dominum.* See the Appendix n. 83, 99, 107, 116.

371. *in Corde beátae Maríae Vírginis dignum Sancti Spíritus habitáculum praeparásti;* see *Missal* (1974), 567.

372. See 'free our hearts to serve you (*líbera tibi mente servíre*)' in ibid., 647.

373. *súbdito tibi semper afféctu;* see ibid., 458.

374. See 'one in simplicity of heart (*cum ... simplicitáte cordis*)' in ibid., 866.

375. See 'with all their hearts (*toto corde*)', 'with all our hearts (*toto corde*)' and 'with all our hearts (*sincéro corde*)' in ibid., 634, 799, 819, 847.

376. See 'pure of heart (*mundos corde*)', 'with pure hearts (*mundo corde*)' and 'with undivided (*sincéro corde*)' in ibid., 478, 545, 807.

377. *corde sincero;* see the Appendix n. 122.

378. See also 'make our hearts steadfast in faith (*in córdibus nostris sacrae fídei semper exérceat firmitátem*)', in *Missal* (1974), 608.

379. *córdibus infúnde fidélium perpétui lúminis claritátem;* see ibid., 531.

380. *illúmina, ... corda nostra grátiae tuae splendóre;* see the Appendix n. X and see also ibid, 641, 803, 862.

381. *da córdibus nostris tuae doctrínae verba percípere;* see ibid., 537. See also *Missal* (1974), 636.

382. See 'By the power of the Holy Spirit establish his teaching in our hearts (*quod ille divíno affátus spíritu dócuit, nostris iúgiter stabiliátur in córdibus*)' in *Missal* (1974), 728.

383. See 'fill our hearts with your love (*corda nostra tui amóris igne iúgiter inflámmet*)' in ibid., 704. See also *Missal* (1974), 23, 526, 556, 601, 709, 760, 822, 862.

384. See *Missal* (1974), 833.

385. *una fáciat caritáte concórdes*' and *in mútuo vos servet amóre concórdes* and *in ... cordis unitáte coniúncti;* see ibid., 768–9.

386. *ad Cor apértum Salvatóris attrácti;* see ibid., 448.

387. See 'May this sacifice unite the hearts of all men in peace (*haec pacífica oblátio communiónem obtíneat animórum*)' in ibid., 836.

388. See 'open our hearts to your truth (*ut cordi dulce sápiant quae nobis credénda mandásti*)' and 'fill our hearts with the gentle love of your Spirit (*suavitátem Spíritus tui penetrálibus nostri cordis infúnde*)' in ibid., 551, 861.

389. See 'that they may serve you with carefree hearts (*líbero ac secúro corde tibi váleant deservíre*)' in ibid., 834. See also *Missal* (1974), 647, 686, 827.

390. See 'You were sent to heal the contrite', 'and to those in sorrow, joy', 'and fill us with your light', 'He revealed his glory to the disciples to strengthen them for the scandal of the cross', 'strengthen us in your love', 'how to live in your service', 'to live in your love', 'bring light into our darkness', 'lived to perfection', 'She asks your blessing' and 'hear the prayers of those who call to you' in the Appendix n. 6, 117 and XV and *Missal* (1974), 453, 525, 590, 612, 664, 742, 768, 846.

391. *cor unum et ánima una esse persevérent*; see ibid., 647.

392. *cor unum et ánimam unam;* see ibid., 848.

393. *cor unum simus et ánima una* in ibid., 585.

394. See the Appendix n. 4 and 113.

395. *nos córpore páriter et mente puríficet*, see *Missal* (1974), 737.

396. *salútem mentis et córporis*; see ibid., 850. See also 'health in mind and body (*tutamentum mentis et corporis*)' and 'bring us health of mind and body (*corporibus nostris subsidium non desit et mentibus*)' in the Appendix n. 131 and XVIII and 'you provide food for strength ... bring us health of mind and body (*corpóribus nostris subsídium non desit et méntibus*)' in *Missal* (1974), 829.

397. See *corporáli ieiúnio ... mentem élevas, Mentes nostras et corpora possideat* and *salutem corporis et animae* in the Appendix n. III, XX and XXII.

398. See the translations of *corpora mentesque sanctificet* and of *reparatio mentis et corporis* in the Appendix n. IX and XXII and of *pura mente ac férvido corde* in *Missal* (1974), 738.

399. See 'you give us food for body and spirit ... bring us health of mind and body (*corpóribus nostris subsídium non desit et méntibus*)' in the Appendix n. XVIII.

400. *purífica per infusiónem Spíritus Sancti cogitatiónes cordis nostri*; see *Missal* (1974), 861. See also 'Strengthen us with your Holy Spirit and fill us with your light' in the Appendix n. XV.

401. *offeréntium mentes ad Fílii tui confórma imáginem*; see ibid., 788.

402. *mente ab inordinátis afféctibus expedíta*; see ibid., 412.

403. In the last chapter, we have already noted that the paraphrase 'heart' is anachronistic as a translation for *mente*.

404. *ut tota mente veneremur, et omnes homines rationabili diligamus affectu*; see the Appendix n. XVII.

405. *quem mens cruénta non récipit*; see *Missal* (1974), 825.

406. *ad te semper corda mentésque érigant*; see ibid., 784.

407. See 'in purity of heart (*pura mente*)', 'with mind and heart renewed (*purificátis méntibus*)', 'fill our hearts (*mentibus nostris infunde*)' and 'live for ever in our minds and hearts (*contínua in nostris méntibus persevéret*)' in the Appendix n. 137, I, VI and XII and 'May he free our hearts from sin (*purificátis ... méntibus*)' in ibid., 533.

408. See 'in liberty (*líberis méntibus*)', 'guide those who believe in you into the way of salvation and peace (*ómnium fidélium mentes dírige in viam salútis et pacis*)', 'keep us free from sin (*puris ... méntibus*)' and 'May we keep before us the loving sacrifice of your Son (*caritátis et passiónis Fílii tui in méntibus nostris signa ferámus*)' in ibid., 522, 578, 591, 711.

409. See 'with our heart set (*inhaerérent*)' in the Appendix n. II and 'give us holiness of mind and body (*nos salvet*)' in ibid., 739.

410. See the Appendix n. VI and XII.

411. See the Appendix n. 137. This prayer is first recorded in an eighth-century collection from Prague; see Bruylants, ed., *Les oraisons*, n. 952, 2:274.

412. See the Appendix n. I and Henry Ashworth, '*Praefationum fontes novarum liturgici, biblici et patristici*', *Ephemerides Liturgicae* 82 (1968), 430–4: 435–6; Louis Soubigou, *Les préfaces de la liturgie étudiées, prêchées, méditées. II. Huit nouvelles préfacfes – Anaphores – Pater* (Paris: P. Lethielleux, 1969), 59, 64.

413. *purificatis mentibus atque corporibus*; see St Leo the Great, *Sermons*, 55.5 in Ashworth, 436; Antoine Dumas, 'Les nouvelles préfaces du Missel Romain', *La Maison Dieu* 94 (1968), 159–72: 162; Antoine Dumas, 'Les préfaces du nouveau missel', *Ephemerides Liturgicae* 85 (1971), 16–28: 22; Cuthbert Johnson and Anthony Ward, 'Fontes Liturgici. The Sources of the Roman Missal (1975) II: Prefaces', *Notitiae* 252–4 (1987), 409–1010: 507–13; Cuthbert Johnson and Anthony Ward, 'The Sources of the Eucharistic Prefaces of the Roman Rite', *Ephemerides Liturgicae* 107 (1993), 359–83: 363; Cuthbert Johnson and Anthony Ward, 'The Sources of the Roman Missal (1975)', *Notitiae* 32 (1996), 7–179: 164; Migne, ed., *PL*, 54:325. For the phrases *pietatis officia, paschalia sacramenta and opera charitatis,* see St Leo the Great, Sermons, 42.1 *(pietatis officia),* 45.2 *(sacramentorum paschalium)* and 55.5 *(charitatis opere)* in Migne, ed., *PL ,* 54:275, 290, 325.

414. See St Leo the Great, *Sermons,* 42.1 in Migne, ed., *PL,* 54:275. See also Johnson and Ward, 'Fontes Liturgici. The Sources of the Roman Missal (1975) II: Prefaces', 493–7; Johnson and Ward, 'The Sources of the Eucharistic Prefaces of the Roman Rite', 362–3; Johnson and Ward, 'The Sources of the Roman Missal (1975)', 164. Dumas initially cited *Sermons* 91.2 and 42.2 as sources; see Dumas, 'Les préfaces du nouveau missel,' 22. He later cited *Sermons*, 42.1 as the source; see Antoine Dumas, 'Les sources du nouveau Missel romain,' *Notitiae* 7 (1971), 37–42, 74–7, 94–5, 134–6, 276–80: 279.

415. St Leo the Great refers to a purified mind (*mentis ... puritati*), a mind that has been recalled from wrong-doing (*mens ab iniquitate revocetur*) and that carries out a holy and spiritual fast (*mens sanctum agit atque spiritale jejunium*) in pursuit of spiritual understanding (*spiritali intellectu*). He says that the one whose heart is not defiled by any infidelity has prepared himself by a true and rational purification (*is vera et rationabili purificatione se praeparat, cujus cor nulla infidelitate polluitur*) and he invites his people to embrace the wondrous mystery of their salvation with purified minds and bodies (*Amplectamur itaque, dilectissimi, purificatis mentibus atque corporibus, salutis nostrae mirabile sacramentum*). He also writes that the minds (*mentes*) of the faithful, ought indeed always to be occupied with wonder at God's works and their capacities for rational deliberation (*rationales animos*) devoted particularly to those reflections (*cogitationibus*) by which they may gain increase of faith; see St Leo the Great, *Sermons*, 42.2; 46.1, 2; 55.5; 67.1 in Migne, ed., *PL*, 54:276, 292–3, 325, 368.

416. See the Appendix n. I and II.

417. See the paraphrase of *affectus* in 'your saints guide us when in our weakness we tend to go astray (*illum pietátis afféctum, quem Sanctis tuis infudísti*)' in *Missal* (1974), 738. On this prayer, see Bruylants, ed., *Les oraisons*, n. 614, 2:168.

418. See the paraphrases of *animus* in 'humble and contrite hearts (*spiritu humilitatis et ... animo contrito*)' in the Appendix n. 26, which comes from the Liturgy of the Eucharist, and 'Give his zeal for the faith to all who believe in you (*da, ut fidélium ánimi eódem fídei zelo férveant*)', which comes from a prayer that was newly composed for the 1969 Missal; see Johnson and Ward, 'The Sources of the Roman Missal (1975)', n. 858, p. 157. See also the following texts taken from Ritual Masses and Masses for Special Occasions: 'with loving hearts (*corde magno et ánimo volénti*)', 'keep them united in brotherly love (*fratérno semper ánimo uniántur*)' and 'violence and cruelty can have no part with you (*quem discórdans ánimus non capit*) in *Missal* (1974), 670, 757, 824, 825.

419. See the paraphrase of *pectus* in 'help your servants to serve the Church and mankind in the spirit of your love (*concéde propítius, ut gemínátum devotiónis munus famulórum tuórum péctora in Ecclésiae hominúmque servítium veheménti caritáte compéllat*)' in *Missal* (1974), 787.

420. See the paraphrase of *unanimes* in 'with all who have served you (*tibi unánimes serviéntes*)' in ibid., 850.

421. See the paraphrase of *una fácias pietáte concórdes* as 'one in peace and love' in the Appendix n. XVI, a prayer that dates from the late fifth-century *Sacramentarium Veronese*; see Johnson and Ward, 'The Sources of the Roman Missal (1975)', n. 422, p. 85. See also the translation of this phrase as 'one in faith and peace' and 'in love and peace' in *Missal*

(1974), 763, 813. See also the paraphrase of *concordes* in 'those who are at peace with one another (*qui concórdes sunt*)' in *Missal* (1974), 825.

422. See the paraphrase of *sensibus* in 'make us one with (*fideliter sensibus uniamur*)' in the Appendix n. XIX, which is taken from a prayer that dates from the late fifth-century *Sacramentarium Veronese*; see Johnson and Ward, 'The Sources of the Roman Missal (1975)', n. 484, p. 96.

423. ... *quos si animadverterint esse concordes, tunc eos oderunt et persequuntur*; see St Augustine, *Rudimentary Catechesis*, 16 [25] in Migne, ed., *PL*, 40:329.

424. *animo ac mente sentiuntur*; see St Augustine, *City of God*, 11.3 in ibid., 41:318.

425. *Recedat a nostris sensibus tam periculosa persuasio*; see the appendix to the works of St Augustine, *Sermons*, 176.3 in ibid., 39:2082.

426. See St Augustine, *On the Immortality of the Soul,* 16 [25] in ibid., 32:1034.

427. See St Augustine, *City of God*, 5.11 in ibid., 41:154.

428. ... *semper se intelligentium sensibus inferat salutiferum mysterium per insigne miraculum*; see Pope St Leo the Great, *Sermons*, 35.1 in ibid., 54:249–50.

429. *quibus temporáliter enutríti, spiritálibus quoque profíciant increméntis*; see *Missal* (1974) at 832.

430. *unum corpus et unus spiritus inveniamur in Christo*; see the Appendix n. 113. See also *unum in Christo corpus et unus spíritus* in ibid., 870.

431. See the Appendix n. 2, 3, 15, 83, 99, 107, 116, 127 and 141.

432. See 'humble and contrite hearts (*spiritu humilitatis et in animo contrito*)' in the Appendix n. 26 and 'Help us to be zealous in continuing his work (*eódem spíritu fervéntes*)', 'inspire us with your grace (*spíritum nobis tuae dilectiónis infúnde*)' and 'with joyful hearts (*spíritu gaudéntes*)' in *Missal* (1974), 633, 687, 743.

433. See 'may we give ourselves once more to your service (*spiritáliter se retulísse cognóscat*)' and 'and anointed ... with the oil of salvation (*spiritalíque sunt unctióne signáti*)' in ibid., 591, 761.

434. See 'food for body and spirit (*et alimento vegetas et renovas sacramento*)' in the Appendix n. XVIII.

435. See 'keep us faithful to the Spirit [*sic*] we have received, who makes us your children (*spíritum adoptiónis, quo fílii tuinominámur et sumus, fidéliter custodiámus*)', 'fill us with the Spirit [*sic*] who makes us your children (*adoptiónis spíritu ... sanctífices*)', 'your Spirit of courage and peace (*Spíritum ... fortitúdinis etpacis*)' and 'Fill with the Spirit [*sic*] of Christ (*spíritu christiáno fervéntes*)' in *Missal* (1974), 536, 597, 662, 809.

436. See 'an offering in spirit and truth (*oblationem ... benedictam, adscriptam, ratam, rationabilem*)' in the Appendix n. 88 and 'May we worship you in spirit and truth (*da fámulis tuis spíritum rectum*)' in ibid., 861.

437. See 'in the spirit of Saint Paul (*spíritu Pauli apóstoli*)' in ibid., 588.

438. See 'Give your Church joy in spirit (*da pópulis tuis spiritálium grátiam gaudiórum*)' in ibid., 578.

439. See 'may we always be alive with the spirit of your love (*spíritus nos semper tuae dilectiónis accéndat*)' and 'a spirit of love' in ibid., 561, 780. See also 'a spirit of humility and love (*spíritu humilitátis et diligéntiae*)' and 'the spirit of patience and love (*spíritum patiéntiae et caritátis*)' in *Missal* (1974), 805, 818.

440. See 'follow Christ in poverty of spirit (*in paupertáte spíritus Christum sequéntes*)' and 'in the spirit of poverty (*in spíritu paupertátis*)' in *Missal* (1974), 608, 807.

441. See 'give the spirit of wisdom (*spíritum sapiéntiae*)' and 'the spirit of your wisdom (*spíritum tuae sapiéntiae cleménter*)' in ibid., 623, 822.

442. See 'may we be filled with his spirit of zeal (*eódem spíritu fervéntes*)' in ibid., 614.

443. See 'fill the world with the spirit of Christ (*mundum spíritu ímbuant Christi*)' and 'May we bring the spirit of Christ to all our efforts (*opéribus nostris christiáno spíritu inténti*)' in ibid., 810, 830.

444. See 'Fill all men with the spirit of the sons of God (*omnes hómines spíritu filiórum Dei repleántur*)' in ibid., 823. See 'keep us faithful to the Spirit [*sic*] we have received, who makes us your children (*spíritum adoptiónis, quo fílii tuinominámur et sumus, fidéliter custodiámus*)' in *Missal* (1974), 536.

445. See 'You give us a spirit of loving reverence for you (*pietatis officia ... propensius exsequentes*)' in the Appendix n. I.

446. See 'Increase the spiritual gifts you have given to your Church (*spíritum grátiae, quem dedísti*)' in *Missal* (1974), 688.

447. See 'offering ourselves as a spiritual sacrifice (*nosmetípsos in spiritálem hóstiam offeréntes*)' in ibid., 805. See also 'May I who share in his priesthood always be a spiritual offering pleasing to you (*oblatiónem spiritálem me tibi semper exhíbeam placéntem*)' and 'Accept our spiritual sacrifice (*hóstiae spiritális oblatióne suscépta*)' in *Missal* (1974), 803, 847.

448. *potus spiritalis*, see the Appendix 25.

449. See 'give them spiritual freedom (*concéde ... spiritálem libertátem*)' in *Missal* (1974), 808.

450. *Sursum corda. Habemus ad Dominum.* See the Appendix n. 83, 99, 107, 116.

451. *fraternitátis caritátem et lumen veritátis in corde exhibeámus et ópere*; see *Missal* (2011), 1021.

452. See the prayers asking that the Lord be 'in your heart and on your lips (*in corde tuo et in labiis tuis*)' or asking God to 'cleanse my heart and my lips (*Munda cor meum ac labia mea*)' in the Appendix n. 14.

453. *sincéro nos corde pérfice*; see *Missal* (2011), 697. See also 'a sincere heart (*corde sincéro*)' in *Missal* (2011), 1066, 1072, 1076, 1111, 1118, 1120.

454. *in Corde beátae Maríae Vírginis dignum Sancti Spíritus habitáculum praeparásti;* see *Missal* (2011), 767.

455. *sanare contritos corde;* see the Appendix n. 6.

456. Given the implied reference to 'the meditation of my heart' in Psalm 19:14, 'thoughts of our heart' should, perhaps, have been translated as 'meditations of our hearts (*cogitationes cordis nostri*)' here.

457. *purífica per infusiónem Spíritus Sancti cogitatiónes cordis nostri*; see *Missal* (2011), 1247. See also 'by the bright rays of the Holy Spirit, the light of your light may confirm the hearts of those born again by your grace (*lux tuae lucis corda eórum, qui per tuam grátiam sunt renáti, Sancti Spíritus illustratióne confírmet*)' in the Appendix n. XV and 'cleanse the hearts (*corda ... emúndet*)' in *Missal* (2011), 1134.

458. *et tibi sincéro corde servíre*; see *Missal* (2011) at 1211. See also 'with a sincere heart (*corde sincero*)' in the Appendix, n. 122.

459. *cum ... simplicitáte cordis*; see ibid., 1267.

460. *toto corde*; see ibid., 868, 1013, 1152, 1187.

461. *puro et húmili corde*; see ibid., 1015. See also *Missal* (2011), 700, 703, 731, 835, 1013, 1116, 1167, 1212, 1226.

462. See the translation of *confóveat* as 'give us new heart in *Missal* (2011), 935.

463. *educ de cordis nostri durítia lácrimas compunctiónis*; see ibid., 1211.

464. *ómnium fidélium mentes dírige in viam salútis et pacis*; see ibid., 785. See also *Missal* (2011), 770, 827, 1101, 1105.

465. *cordis nostri ténebras cleménter illústra*; see *Missal* (2011), 916. See also *Missal* (2011), 706, 1043.

466. *illúmina, ... corda nostra grátiae tuae splendóre*; see the Appendix n. X. See also *Missal* (2011), 879, 1157, 1250.

467. *et lux tuae lucis corda eorum, qui per tuam gratiam sunt renati ... confirmet*; see the Appendix n. XV.

468. *da córdibus nostris tuae doctrínae verba percípere*; see *Missal* (2011), 717. See also *Missal* (2011), 852, 872.

469. See *Missal* (2011), 835, 958. See also the prayer asking that, in the light of the Transfiguration, 'the scandal of the Cross might be removed from the hearts' of Christ's disciples (*de córdibus discipulórum crucis scándalum tollerétur*)' in *Missal* (2011), 819.

470. See 'what he taught when moved by the divine Spirit may always stay firm in our hearts (*quod ille divíno affátus spíritu dócuit, nostris iúgiter stabiliátur in córdibus*)' in *Missal (*2011), 987, 1000.

471. *Per Spíritum namque tuum pérmoves hóminum corda, ut inimíci íterum in collóquia véniant*; see ibid., 651.

472. See 'pour your love into their hearts (*caritáte tua in córdibus eórum diffúsa*) that they may remain faithful in the Marriage covenant' in ibid., 1087. See also 'Pour forth ... your grace into our hearts (*Gratiam tuam ... mentibus nostris infunde*)' in the Appendix n. VI and 'cherishing in our hearts the signs of your love (*caritátis tuae in córdibus nostris testimónia geréntes*)'. in *Missal* (2011), 753.

473. See 'constantly kindle in our hearts the fire of your love (*corda nostra tui amóris igne iúgiter inflámmet*)' in *Missal* (2011), 972. See also *Missal* (2011), 695, 814, 831, 926, 978, 1040, 1123, 1199, 1250.

474. See *Missal* (2011), 936, 1197.

475. See ibid., 887, 1168, 1202.

476. See ibid., 701, 826, 1035, 1205.

477. *ad Cor apértum Salvatóris attrácti*; see ibid., 1244.

478. See ibid., 694, 981, 1214.

479. See ibid., 702, 743, 1249. Jesus is described as proclaiming joy to 'the sorrowful of heart (*maestis corde*)'; see the Appendix n. 117.

480. See 'that they may have strength to serve you with free and untroubled hearts (*líbero ac secúro corde tibi váleant deservíre*)' in ibid., 1206. See also *Missal* (2011), 887, 1102, 1106, 1126, 1204.

481. *una fáciat caritáte concórdes, in mútuo vos servet amóre concórdes* and *in ... cordis unitáte coniúncti*; see *Missal* (2011), 1086, 1088, 1092.

482. *una fácias pietáte concórdes*; see the Appendix n. XVI and ibid., 1042, 1180.

483. See ibid, 1214, 1226.

484. See the Appendix n. 131, IX, XVIII, XX and XXI and ibid., 1011.

485. *mentem élevas*; see the Appendix n. III.

486. *mente consímili ... copuléntur*; see *Missal* (2011), 1095.

487. See 'have a continuing effect in our minds and hearts (*contínua in nostris méntibus persevéret*)' in the Appendix n. XII.

488. See *Comme le prévoit*, n. 13.

489. *offeréntium mentes ad Fílii tui confórma imáginem*; see *Missal* (2011), 1124. See also 'grant that we may be conformed to the image of your Son (*imágini Fílii tui confórmes fíeri concéde*)' in Missal (2011), 676.

490. See 'minds made pure' and 'a pure mind' in the Appendix n. I and *Missal* (2011), 709, 803, 1212.

491. *tota mente;* see the Appendix n. XVII.

492. We have already noted that the paraphrase 'heart' is anachronistic in the prayers from the late patristic period listed in the Appendix as n. 137, II, VI, XVII and XIX. It is also anachronistic in the Prayer over the Offerings for St Luke (18 October) first recorded in an eighth- or ninth-century Paris collection; see Bruylants, ed., *Les oraisons*, n. 514, 2:514; *Missal* (2011), 887.

493. See 'in purity of heart', 'for the renewing and purifying of their hearts ... freed from disordered affections', 'Pour forth ... into our hearts', 'in truth of heart' and 'united in mind and heart' in the Appendix n. 137, II, VI, XVII and XIX and 'serve you in freedom of heart' in *Missal* (2011), 887. The texts in question might be better translated as 'in purity of mind (*pura mente*)', 'and love everyone with rational good will (*et omnes hómines rationábili diligámus afféctu*)', 'Pour ... into our minds (*mentibus nostris infunde*)', 'united in [our] reasonings (*sénsibus uniámur*)', 'for the renewal and purifying of their minds, that, freed from disordered affections (*ad reparándam méntium puritátem ... mente ab inordinátis afféctibus expedíta*)' and 'serve you in freedom of mind (*líbera tibi mente servíre*)'.

494. See 'contrite heart' in Appendix n. 26 and 'you change our hearts to prepare them for reconciliation' and 'a heart always subject' in ibid., 650, 1249. The texts in question might be better translated as 'contrite disposition (*animo contrito*)', 'you change our dispositions to prepare them for reconciliation (*te ánimos fléctere, ut sint ad reconciliatiónem paráti*)' and 'with a disposition of mind that is always subject to you (*súbdito tibi semper afféctu*)'.

495. See 'and, as they turn back to you in spirit', 'that spirit of devotion which you instilled in your Saints', 'a willing spirit' and 'always be united by a fraternal spirit' in ibid., 643, 1009, 1035, 1201. The texts in question might be better translated as 'and, as their disposition is turned back to you (*eíque ad te ánimum converténti*)', 'that disposition of devotion which you instilled in your Saints (*illum pietátis afféctum, quem Sanctis tuis infudísti*)', 'a willing disposition (*ánimo volénti*)' and 'always be united by a fraternal disposition (*fratérno semper ánimo uniántur*)'.

496. *ad te semper corda mentésque érigant;* see ibid., 1117.

497. See 'sanctify our minds and hearts (*mentes et corda nostra sanctíficent*)' in ibid., 1011. See also 'whose mind and heart became a throne of rest for the Holy Spirit' in *Missal* (2011), 703.

498. *pura mente ac férvido corde*; see *Missal* (2011), 1009.

499. In the Proper for Ireland, the Prayer after Communion for St Columba (June 9) prays that the healing power of the holy gifts we receive in the Eucharist 'may work within us in body, mind and spirit'; see ibid., 777.

500. See 'make it spiritual and acceptable (*rationabilem, acceptabilemque facere*)' in the Appendix n. 88.

501. See the Appendix n. 2, 3, 15, 83, 99, 107, 116, 127 and 141.

502. See 'and worship you in spirit and truth' (cf. Jn 4:24) in *Missal* (2011), 735.

503. *quod ... corporáli servítio exhíbuit, spiritáliter se retulísse cognóscat*; see ibid.,950.

504. *potus spiritalis*; see the Appendix n. 25.

505. *corpóribus nostris subsídium non desit et méntibus*; see the Appendix n. XVIII.

506. *unum in Christo corpus et unus spíritus*; see *Missal* (2011), 1274. See also 'may become one body, one spirit in Christ (*unum corpus et unus spiritus inveniamur in Christo*)' in the Appendix n. 113.

507. See 'may redound upon them as a spiritual gift (*spiritáliter se retulísse cognóscat*)' in ibid., 950.

508. See 'a spirit of counsel and fortitude (*spíritum consílii et fortitúdinis*)' in ibid., 805.

509. See 'a spirit of fortitude and peace (*Spíritum ... fortitúdinis etpacis*)' in ibid., 914.

510. See 'in freedom of spirit (*líberis méntibus*)' and 'grant ... spiritual freedom (*concéde ... spiritálem libertátem*)' in ibid., 689, 1170.

511. See 'a generous spirit' in ibid., 700.

512. *spiritu humilitatis;* see the Appendix n. 26.

513. See 'a spirit of humility and zeal (*spíritu humilitátis et diligéntiae*)' in *Missal* (2011), 1068, 1074, 1078.

514. See 'give your people … the grace of spiritual joys (*da pópulis tuis spiritálium grátiam gaudiórum*)' and 'with joyful spirit (*spíritu gaudéntes*)' in ibid., 785, 1018.

515. 'be set aflame with the spirit of your love (*spíritus nos semper tuae dilectiónis accéndat*)' and 'pour out upon us … a spirit of love for you (*spíritum nobis tuae dilectiónis infúnde*)' in ibid., 761, 803.

516. See 'a spirit of perfect charity (*spíritum perféctae caritátis*)' and 'a spirit of patience and charity (*spíritum patiéntiae et caritátis*)' in ibid., 1169, 1185.

517. See 'the spirit of penance and prayer' in ibid., 892.

518. See 'following Christ in poverty of spirit (*in paupertáte spíritus Christum sequéntes*)' and 'in a spirit of poverty (*in spíritu paupertátis*)' in ibid., 825, 1167.

519. 'with a spirit of wisdom (*spíritum sapiéntiae*)' and 'the spirit of your wisdom (*spíritum tuae sapiéntiae cleménter*)' in ibid., 848, 1190.

520. See 'in the spirit of the Apostle Paul we may pursue (*spíritu Pauli apóstoli prosequámur*)' in ibid., 798.

521. *eódem spíritu fervéntes*; see ibid., 867. See also 'following the same spiritual path (*eándem spiritálem viam sectántes*)' and 'on fire with the same spirit (*eódem spíritu fervéntes*)' in *Missal* (2011), 747, 837.

522. See 'nourished by these in the present age, they may also grow in spiritual things (*quibus temporáliter enutríti, spiritálibus quoque profíciant increméntis*)' in *Missal* (2011), 1196.

523. See 'offering ourselves as a spiritual sacrifice (*nosmetípsos in spiritálem hóstiam offeréntes*)' in ibid., 1074, 1078. See also 'may always offer myself as a spiritual sacrifice pleasing to you (*oblatiónem spiritálem me tibi semper exhíbeam placéntem*)' and 'accepting the oblation of the spiritual sacrifice (*hóstiae spiritális oblatióne suscépta*)' in *Missal* (2011), 1157, 1213.

524. See 'may imbue the world with the spirit of Christ (*mundum spíritu ímbuant Christi*)' in *Missal* (2011), 1161.

525. See 'give your servants a right spirit (*da fámulis tuis spíritum rectum*)' in ibid., 1247. See also 'restore your spirit within us' in *Missal* (2011), 901.

526. See 'may be fervent with the Christian spirit (*spíritu christiáno fervéntes*)' and 'undertaking in a Christian spirit what we are to do (*opéribus nostris christiáno spíritu inténti*)' in *Missal* (2011), 1161, 1194.

527. See 'the spirit of grace you have bestowed (*spíritum grátiae, quem dedísti*)' in ibid., 908.

528. See 'preserve faithfully the spirit of adoption (*spíritum adoptiónis, quo fílii tuinominámur et sumus, fidéliter custodiámus*)' and 'you may sanctify by the spirit of adoption (*adoptiónis spíritu … sanctífices*)' in ibid., 714, 810. To avoid confusion with the divine Spirit of divine sonship and to reflect the Latin plural, the phrase 'all may be filled with the spirit of divine sonship (*omnes hómines spíritu filiórum Dei repleántur*)' might have been better translated as 'spirit of God's children'; see *Missal* (2011), 1199. See also 'strengthened by the Spirit [*sic*] of adoption to sonship' in *Missal* (2011), 714, 876.

529. *eius cruce spiritalíque sunt unctióne signáti*; see *Missal* (2011), 1041.

Conclusion

1. Arthur J. Serratelli, 'Address to the 2008 National Meeting of Diocesan Liturgical Commissions', *Newsletter: United States Conference of Catholic Bishops Committee on Divine Worship*, October 2008. The text is cited in Pecklers, *The Genius of the Roman Rite*, 113–14.

2. See *Liturgiam authenticam*, n. 6.

Appendix

1. See *Missal* (1974). A version of this text may be found on the following website, consulted on 26 September 2011: http://clerus.org/bibliaclerusonline/en/t4.htm. See also the following website, consulted on 18 October 2011: http://ssecdn.net/stcharlesgreece/new_roman_missal/ThreeColumnedRomanRiteLiturgy.pdf.

2. See *Missal* (2011). A version of this text may be found on the following website, consulted on 27 September 2011: http://catholicliturgy.com/index.cfm/FuseAction/TextContents/Index/4/SubIndex/67/TextIndex/9.

3. See ibid.

4. Apparently as an error, the word *Quia* is given as *Qui* in the following website, consulted on 27 September 2011: http://catholicliturgy.com/index.cfm/FuseAction/TextContents/

Bibliography

Ashworth, Henry, 'Praefationum fontes novarum liturgici, biblici et patristici.' *Ephemerides Liturgicae* 82 (1968): 430–44.

Baldovin, John F., 'History of the Latin Text and Rite.' In *A Commentary on the Order of Mass of the Roman Missal*, ed. Edward Foley et al. Collegeville, Minnesota: Liturgical Press, 2011, 247–54, 311–16, 401–06, 593–600.

Barba, Maurizio, 'Le formule alternative per il congedo della messa.' *Rivista Liturgica* 96 (2009): 147–159.

Barth, Karl, *The Doctrine of Creation: The Work of Creation Church Dogmatics*, 3/1. Edinburgh: T & T Clark, 1958.

Baumert, Norbert and Maria-Irma Seewann, 'Eucharistie – "für alle" ode "für viele"?' *Gregorianum* 89 (2008) 3: 501–32.

Berkouwer, Gerrit C., *Man: The Image of God*. Grand Rapids, Michigan: Wm. B. Eerdmans Publishing Company, 1962.

Borden, Sarah R., *Edith Stein* Outstanding Christian thinkers. London; New York: Continuum, 2003.

Botte, Bernard, ed. *Hippolyte de Rome: La tradition apostolique d'après les anciennes versions*, Sources chrétiennes 11 bis. Paris: Les éditions du Cerf, 1968.

Bruylants, Placide, ed. *Les oraisons du Missel romain. Texts et Histoire*. Edited by Centre de Pastorale Liturgique, Études Liturgiques, 1. Louvain: Centre de Documentation et d'Information Litugiques, 1952.

Bückers, Hermann, *Die Unsterblichkeitslehre des Weisheitsbuches. Ihr Ursprung und ihre Bedeutung* Alttestamentliche Abhandlungen, 13/4. Münster: Alttestamentliche Abhandlungen, 1938.

Butterworth, Charles C., *The English Primers (1529–1545)*. New York: Octagon, 1971.

Catechism of the Catholic Church. Dublin: Veritas, 1994.

Chupungco, Anscar J., 'The Translation of Liturgical Texts.' In *Handbook for Liturgical Studies: Introduction to the Liturgy*, ed. Anscar J. Chupungco. Collegeville: Liturgical Press, 1997, 381–397.

—, 'Excursus on Translating OM2008.' In *A Commentary on the Order of Mass of the Roman Missal*, ed. Edward Foley et al. Collegeville, Minnesota: Liturgical Press, 2011, 133–141.

—, 'The ICEL2010 Translation.' In *A Commentary on the Order of Mass of the Roman Missal*, ed. Edward Foley et al. Collegeville, Minnesota: Liturgical Press, 2011, 137–141, 181–185, 219–220.

Congregation for Divine Worship and the Discipline of the Sacraments, 'Instruction Liturgiam authenticam, on the use of vernacular languages in the publication of the liturgical books of the Roman Rite.' Acta Apostolicae Sedis 93 (2001): 91–134.

—, 'Instruction Varietates legitimae, on Inculturation in the Roman Liturgy.' Acta Apostolica Sedis 87 (1995): 288–314.

—, ed. Ratio translationis for the English Language. Vatican City: Congregation for Divine Worship and the Discipline of the Sacraments, 2007.

Conzelmann, Hans, Théologie du Nouveau Testament. Geneva: Labor et fides, 1969.

Dautzenberg, Gerhard, Sein Leben bewahren. Psyche in den Herrenworten der Evangelien SANT, 14. Munich: Kosel, 1966.

Der Kirchenväter–commission der königl. preussischen Akademie der Wissenschaften, ed. Die griechischen christlichen Schriftsteller der ersten drei Jahrhunderte. Leipzig – Berlin: J. C. Hinrichs, 1897–1971.

Dumas, Antoine, 'Les nouvelles préfaces du Missel Romain.' La Maison Dieu 94 (1968): 159–172.

—, 'Les préfaces du nouveau missel.' Ephemerides Liturgicae 85 (1971): 16–28.

—, 'Les sources du nouveau Missel romain.' Notitiae 7 (1971): 37–42, 74–77, 94–95, 134–136, 276–280.

Dunn, James D. G., The Theology of Paul the Apostle. Grand Rapids, Michigan: Wm. B. Eerdmans, 1998.

Dupuis SJ, Jacques and Josef Neuner SJ, eds. The Christian Faith in the Doctrinal Documents of the Catholic Church. New York: Alba House, 2001.

Elich, Tom., 'The ICEL2010 Translation.' In A Commentary on the Order of Mass of the Roman Missal, ed. Edward Foley et al. Collegeville, Minnesota: Liturgical Press, 2011, 327–33, 375–82, 607–14, 639–44.

Flannery, Austin, ed. Vatican Council II. Constitutions, Decrees, Declarations. A Completely Revised Translation in Inclusive Language. Dublin: Dominican Publications, 1996.

Foley, Edward, John Baldovin, Anscar Chupungco, Mary Collins, Keith Pecklers, David Power and Joyce Ann Zimmerman, eds. A Commentary on the Order of Mass of 'The Roman Missal'. Collegeville, Minnesota: Liturgical Press, 2011.

García Cordero OP, Maximiliano, 'La esperanza del más allá en el Nuevo Testamento.' Ciencia tomista 114 (1987): 209–264.

Gelin, Albert, L'homme selon la Bible, Foi Vivante, 75. Paris: Cerf, 1968.

Gember, Klaus, The Modern Rite: Collected Essays on the Reform of the Liturgy. Farnborough: St Michael's Abbey Press, 2002.

Grelot, Pierre, De la mort à la vie éternelle. Études de théologie biblique Lectio divina, 67. Paris: Cerf, 1971.

Greshake, Gisbert, Auferstehung der Toten. Ein Beitrag zur gegenwärtigen theologischen Diskussion über die Zukunft der Geschichte. Essen: Ludgerus–Verlag Hubert Wingen, 1969.

Gundry, Robert H, Sôma in Biblical Theology, with Emphasis on Pauline Anthropology. Society for New Testament Studies, Monograph Series, 29. Cambridge: University Press, 1976.

Hauke, Manfred, *Women in the Priesthood? A Systematic Analysis in the Light of the Order of Creation and Redemption*. San Francisco: Ignatius Press, 1988.

Hauret, Charles, *Beginnings, Genesis and Modern Science*. Dubuque: Priory Press, 1955.

Heinzmann, Richard, *Die Unsterblichkeit der Seele und die Auferstehung des Leibes. Eine Problemgeschichtliche Untersuchung der Frühscholastischen Sentenzen und Summenliteratur von Anselm von Laon bis Wilhelm von Auxerre* Beiträge zur Geschichte der Philosophie und Theologie des Mittelalters, 40/3. Münster in Westfalen: Aschendorffsche Verlagsbuchhandlung, 1965.

Hoffmann, Paul, *Die Toten in Christus. Eine religionsgeschichtliche und exegetische Untersuchung zur paulinischen Eschatologie*. Münster: Aschendorff, 1966.

Conference, Irish Catholic Bishops' Conference, ed., *Introducing the New Missal*. Dublin: Veritas, 2011.

Jeffery, Peter, *Translating Tradition: A Chant Historian Reads Liturgiam Authenticam*. Collegeville: Liturgical Press, 2005.

Jeremias, Joachim. *The Eucharistic Words of Jesus*. Translated by Norman Perrin. London: S.C.M. Press, 1966.

Jobes, Karen H. and Moíses Silva. *Invitation to the Septuagint*. Grand Rapids: Baker, 2000.

Johnson, Cuthbert and Anthony Ward, 'Fontes Liturgici. The Sources of the Roman Missal (1975) II: Prefaces.' *Notitiae* 252–253–254 (1987): 409–1010.

—, 'The Sources of the Eucharistic Prefaces of the Roman Rite.' *Ephemerides Liturgicae* 107 (1993): 359–383.

—, 'The Sources of the Roman Missal (1975).' *Notitiae* 32 (1996): 7–179.

Johnson, Samuel, *A Dictionary of the English Language*. 2 vols. London, 1755.

Jungmann, Joseph A., The *Mass of the Roman Rite: its Origins and Development*. Translated by F. A. Brunner. Westminster, MD: Christian Classics, 1986.

Kavanaugh OCD, Kieran and Otilio Rodriguez OCD, eds, *The Collected Works of Saint Teresa of Avila*. Washington: ICS Publications, 1987.

—, eds, *The Collected Works of St John of the Cross*. Washington, DC: ICS Publications, 1991.

King, Nicholas, 'Lost, and found, in translation.' *The Tablet,* 19 November 2011.

Knox, Ronald, *The Mass in Show Motion*. London: Sheed and Ward, 1948.

—, *On Englishing the Bible*. London: Burns and Oates, 1949.

Kümmel, Werner Georg, *Das Bild des Menschen im Neuen Testament*. Zürich: Zwingli, 1948.

Ladaria, Luis F., *Antropologia Teologica*. Rome: Casale Monferrato, 1986.

Larcher, C., *Études sur le livre de la Sagesse Études bibliques*. Paris: Gabalda, 1969.

Lewis, Charlton T., *A Latin Dictionary*. Oxford: Clarendon Press, 1987.

The National Centre for Liturgy, ed., *The New Missal. Explaining the Changes*. Dublin: Veritas, 2011.

Lys, Daniel, Nèpèsh. *Histoire de l'âme dans la révélation d'Israël*. Paris: Presses Universitaires de France, 1959.

Mabillon, Jean, *Museum Italicum*. 2 vols. Paris: Montalant, 1724.

Magee, Michael K., 'The Liturgical Translation of the Response Et cum spiritu tuo.' *Communio* 29 (Spring 2002): 152–171.

Mansi, Giovanni Domenico, ed., *Sacrorum Conciliorum nova et amplissima collectio*. Florence & Venice, 1759–1798.

McCarthy, Daniel, 'An abiding gift.' *The Tablet* 12 (September 2009): 16.

—, 'Act of mature faith.' *The Tablet* 16 (February 2008): 16.

—, 'Feasting together.' *The Tablet* 17 (January 2009): 15.

—, 'Food for heart and soul.' *The Tablet* 14 (June 2008): 17.

—, 'From earth and from heaven.' *The Tablet* 16/23 (December 2006): 30–31.

—, 'From Suffering to Glory.' *The Tablet* 26 (September 2009): 17.

—, 'Grasping after God.' *The Tablet* 18 (April 2009): 18.

—, 'He enlightens all hearts.' *The Tablet* 21 (March 2009).

—, 'In clouds of glory.' *The Tablet* 6 (September 2008): 15.

—, 'Mystery made personal.' *The Tablet* 25 (April 2009): 18.

—, 'A spark of majesty.' *The Tablet* 6 (June 2009): 16.

—, 'Suffering Shared.' *The Tablet* 8 (April 2006): 16.

—, 'Two commands, one love.' *The Tablet* 27 (January 2007): 15.

—, 'With joy and expectation.' *The Tablet* 29 (April 2006): 18.

Mehl-Koehnlein, Herrade, *L'homme selon l'apôtre Paul Cahiers théologiques*, 28. Neuchâtel: Delachaux & Niestlé, 1951.

Migne, Jacques-Paul, ed., *Patrologia Latina*. Paris: Vrayet, 1844–1891.

—, ed., *Patrologia Graeca*. Paris: Vrayet, 1857–1866.

Mohlberg, Leo Cunibert, Leo Eizenhöfer and Petrus Siffrin, eds., *Liber Sacramentorum Romanae Aeclesiae ordinis anni circuli: (Cod. Vat. Reg. Lat. 316/Paris Bibl. nat. 7193, 41/56): (Sacramentarium Gelasianum)*, Rerum Ecclesiasticarum Documenta, Series maior, Fontes 4. Rome: Casa Editrice Herder, 1960.

Moloney, Raymond, *The Eucharistic Prayers in Worship, Preaching and Study*. Dublin: Dominican Publications, 1985.

Moltmann, Jürgen, 'Is There Life After Death?' In *The End of the World and the Ends of God: Science and Theology on Eschatology*, John Polkinghorne and Michael Welker eds., Harrisburg, PA: Continuum, 2000, 238–255.

Morissette, Rodolphe, 'L'expression sôma in 1 Co 15 et dans la littérature paulinienne.' *Révue des sciences philosophiques et théologiques* 56 (1972): 223–239.

Mork OSB, Wulstan, *The Biblical Meaning of Man*. Impact Books, Milwaukee: The Bruce Publishing Company, 1967.

Nida, Eugene, 'Principles of Correspondence.' In *The Translation Studies Reader*, ed. Lawrence Venuti. New York: Routledge, 2004, 153–167.

O'Connell, Patrick F., ed., *Thomas Merton: Monastic Observances, Initiation Into the Monastic Tradition*, 5. Collegeville, Minnesota: Liturgical Press, 2010.

Ostdiek, Gilbert. 'The ICEL2010 Translation.' In *A Commentary on the Order of Mass of the Roman Missal*, ed. Edward Foley et al. Collegeville, Minnesota: Liturgical Press, 2011, 279–292, 417–423.

Pascher, Joseph, *Eucharistia. Gestalt und Vollzug*. Münster: Aschendorff, 1947.

Paul VI, Pope, 'Allocutio Summi Pontificis ad participantes "Conventum de popularibus interpretationibus textuum liturgicorum" (Address to translators of liturgical texts into vernacular languages).' *Notitiae* 1 (1965): 377–381.

Payne OCD, Steven, *John of the Cross and the Cognitive Value of Mysticism. An analysis of Sanjuanist Teaching and its Philosophical Implications for Contemporary Discussions of Mystical Experience*. Synthese Historical Library 37. Dordrecht – Boston – London: Kluwer Academic Publishers, 1990.

Pecklers, Keith, *The Genius of the Roman Rite. The Reception and Implementation of the New Missal*. London: Burns & Oates, 2009.

Pecklers, Keith and Gilbert Ostdiek, 'The History of Vernaculars and Role of Translation.' In *A Commentary on the Order of Mass of the Roman Missal*, ed. Edward Foley et al. Collegeville, Minnesota: Liturgical Press, 2011, 35–72.

Pedersen, Johannes, *Israel: Its Life and Culture*, 2 vols. Oxford: Oxford University Press, 1946.

Pelikan, Jaroslav and Helmut T. Lehmann, eds, *Luther's Works*. Saint Louis – Philadelphia: Concordia Publishing House – Fortress Press, 1955–.

Pesch, Rudolf. *Das Abendmahl und Jesu Todesverstaendnis*. Freiburg: Herder, 1978.

Pidoux, Georges, *L'homme dans l'Ancien Testament Cahiers théologiques*, 32. Neucâhtel: Delachaux et Niestlé, 1953.

Posselt OCD, Sr Teresia de Spiritu Sancto, *Edith Stein*. Translated by Cecily Hastings and Donald Nicholl. London and New York: Sheed and Ward, 1952.

Pristas, Lauren, 'The Collects at Sunday Mass: An Examination of the Revisions of Vatican II.' *Nova et Vetera* 3.1 (Winter, 2005): 5–38.

Ratzinger, Joseph, *Jesus of Nazareth. Holy Week: From the Entrance into Jerusalem to the Resurrection*. San Francisco: Ignatius Press, 2011.

Regan, Patrick. 'Theology of the Latin Text and Rite.' In *A Commentary on the Order of Mass of the Roman Missal*, ed. Edward Foley et al. Collegeville, Minnesota: Liturgical Press, 2011, 211–217.

Reicke, Bo, 'Body and Soul in the New Testament.' *Studia theologica* 19 (1965): 200–12.

Richardson, Alan. *Genesis I–II*. London: SCM, 1953.

Robinson, John A. T. *Le corps. Étude sur la théologie de saint Paul*. Translated by P. de Saint-Sienne Collection Parole et Tradition. Lyons: Éditions du Chalet, 1966.

Roguet, A. M. and Lancelot Sheppard. 'Translation of the Roman Canon.' In *The New Liturgy*, Lancelot Sheppard ed. London: Darton, Longman & Todd, 1970, 161–173.

Ruiz de la Peña, Juan Luis, *Immagine di Dio. Antropologia teologica fondamentale.* Translated by Rossella Del Guerra Ricerche teologiche, Carlo Molari ed., Rome: Borla, 1992.

Sand, Alexander. *Der Begfiff 'Fleisch' in den paulinischen Hauptbriefen,* Biblische Untersuchungen, 2. Regensburg: Pustet, 1967.

Schelkle, Karl Hermann, *Theologie des Neuen Testaments.* 4 vols. in 5 vols. Kommentare und Beiträge zum Alten und Neuen Testament. Düsseldorf: Patmos–Verlag, 1968–76.

Schilling, Othmar. *Geist und Materie in biblischer Sicht: ein exegetischer Beitrag zur Diskussion um Teilhard de Chardin,* Stuttgarter Bibelstudien, 25. Stuttgart: K.B.W., 1967.

Schmid, Josef, 'Der Begriff der Seele in Neuen Testament.' In *Einsicht und Glaube,* Joseph Ratzinger and Heinrich Fries, eds. Freiburg-im-Breisgau: Herder, 1962, 112–31.

Schubert, Kurt, 'Die Entwicklung der Auferstehungslehre von der nachexilischen bis frührabbinischen Zeit.' *Biblische Zeitschrift* 6 (1962): 177–214.

Schürer, Emil, *Geschichte des jüdischen Volkes im Zeitalter Jesu Christi.* 3 vols. 3e neu bearb. Aufl. ed. Leipzig: J. C. Hinrichs, 1898.

Serratelli, Arthur J., 'Address to the 2008 National Meeting of Diocesan Liturgical Commissions.' *Newsletter: United States Conference of Catholic Bishops Committee on Divine Worship,* October 2008, 37.

Söhngen, Gottlieb, 'Die biblische Lehre von der Gottesebenbildlichkeit des Menschen.' In *Festgabe Erzbischof Jäger, Bischof Stählin, 'Pro Veritate',* Munster: Aschendorffsche Verlagsbuchhandlung, 1963, 23–57.

Sollamo, Reija, 'Prolegomena to the Syntax of the Septuagint.' In *Helsinki Perspectives on the Translation Technique of the Septuagint,* Raija Sollamo and Sepio Sepilä, eds. Göttingen: Vandenhoeck & Ruprecht, 2001, 23–42.

Soubigou, Louis, *Les préfaces de la liturgie étudiées, prêchées, méditées.* II. Huit nouvelles préfacfes – Anaphores – Pater. Paris: P. Lethielleux, 1969.

Spicq OP, Ceslas, *Dio e l'uomo secondo il Nuovo Testamento.* Roma: Edizioni Paoline, 1969.

Stein, Edith, Übersetzungen II. *John Henry Newman, Briefe und Texte zur ersten Lebenshälfte (1801–1846). Einführung, Bearbeitung und Anmerkungen von H.–B. Gerl–Falkovitz* Gesamtausgabe, 22. Freiburg: Herder, 2002.

—, *Übersetzungen V. Alexandre Koyré, Descartes und die Scholastik. Einführung, Bearbeitung und Anmerkungen von H.–B. Gerl–Falkovitz* Gesamtausgabe, 25. Freiburg: Herder, 2002.

—, *Selbstbildnis in Briefen III: Briefe an Roman Ingarden.* 2 ed. Edith Stein Gesamtausgabe, 4. Freiburg: Herder, 2004.

—, *Übersetzungen I. John Henry Newman, Die Idee der Universität. Einführung, Bearbeitung und Anmerkungen von H.–B. Gerl–Falkovitz* Gesamtausgabe, 21. Freiburg: Herder, 2004.

—, *Übersetzungen III–IV. Thomas von Aquin, Über die Wahrheit 1–2* Gesamtausgabe, 23–24. Freiburg: Herder, 2008.

—, *Übersetzungen VI. Thomas von Aquin, Über das Seiende und das Wesen* Gesamtausgabe, 26. Freiburg: Herder, 2010.

Stemberger, Günter, *Der Leib der Auferstehung: Studien zur Anthropologie und Eschatologie des palastinischen Judentums im neutestamentlichen Zeitalter* (ca. 170 v. C[h]r.–100 n. Chr.) Analecta biblica, 56. Rome: Biblical Institute Press, 1972.

Taft, Robert F., 'Translating Liturgically.' *Jogos: A Journal of Eastern Christian Studies* 39/2–4 (1988): 155–190.

Taylor, R. J., 'The Eschatological Meaning of Life and Death in the Book of Wisdom I–V.' *Ephemerides theologicae lovanienses* 42 (1966): 72–137.

The Roman Missal. Dublin: Veritas, 2011.

The Roman Missal. Dublin: Liturgical Books, 1974.

Teixeira de Cunha, Jorge, 'A Eucaristia e a Missao da Igreja: Uma reflexao subre a Sacramentum caritatis de Bento XVI.' *Didaskalia* 38 (2008), no. 2: 311–326.

Thurston, Anne, *Because of her Testimony: The Word in Female Experience*. Dublin: Gill & Macmillan, 1995.

Thurston, Herbert, *Familiar Prayers: Their Origins and History*. London: Burns & Oates, 1953.

Turner, Paul, 'A New Roman Missal: What to Expect from a New Translation of Liturgical Texts.' *America* 26, 2 May June 2008: 14–6.

Vagaggini, Cipriano, *The Canon of the Mass and Liturgical Reform*. London: Chapman, 1967.

Van Unnik, W.C., 'Dominus Vobiscum: The Background of a Liturgical Formula.' In *New Testament Essays*, A. J. B. Higgins, ed. Manchester: University Press, 1959, 270–305.

Vawter, Bruce, *On Genesis: A New Reading*. London: Chapman, 1977.

Vincie, Catherine, 'The Mystagogical Implications.' In *A Commentary on the Order of Mass of the Roman Missal*, ed. Edward Foley et al. Collegeville, Minnesota: Liturgical Press, 2011, 143–150, 187–194, 221–27.

Volz, Paul, ed., *Die Eschatologie der judischen Gemeinde im neutestamentlichen Zeitalter nach den Quellen der rabbinischen, apokalyptischen und apokryphen Literatur*. Tübingen: J.C.B. Mohr [Paul Siebeck], 1934.

Von Rad, Gerhard, *Genesis: A Commentary*. London: SCM, 1963.

Wedig, Mark E. 'The Mystagogical Implications.' In *A Commentary on the Order of Mass of the Roman Missal*, ed. Edward Foley et al. Collegeville, Minnesota: Liturgical Press, 2011, 293–300, 425–30, 575–82.

Wenham, Gordon J. *Genesis 1–15* Word Biblical Commentary, 1, David A. Hubbard and Glenn W. Barker, eds. Waco, Texas: Word Books, 1987.

Westermann, Claus. *Schöpfung* Themen der Theologie, 12. Stuttgart: Kreuz Verlag, 1983.

—, *Genesis 1–11: A Commentary*. Translated by John J. Scullion. London: SPCK, 1984.

Wheeler Robinson, H., *The Christian Doctrine of Man*. Edinburgh: T. and T. Clark, 1947.

Wilckens, Ulrich. *Theologie des Neuen Testaments. Bd. 1/2: Jesu Tod und Auferstehung und die Entstehung der Kirche aus Juden und Heiden*. Neukirchen–Vluyn: Neukirchener Verlag, 2003.

Witczak, Michael, 'History of the Latin Text and Rite.' In *A Commentary on the Order of Mass of the Roman Missal*, ed. Edward Foley et al. Collegeville, Minnesota: Liturgical Press, 2011, 161–170.

Wolff, Hans Walter, *Anthropologie des Alten Testaments*. Munich: Gütersloh, 1973.

Young, William Paul, *The Shack*. Newbury Park, California: Windblown Media, 2007.

Ziener, Georg, *Die theologische Begriffssprache im Buche des Weisheit*. Bonn: Peter Hanstein, 1956.

Zimmerman, Joyce Ann, 'The Mystagogical Implications.' In *A Commentary on the Order of Mass of the Roman Missal*, ed. Edward Foley et al. Collegeville, Minnesota: Liturgical Press, 2011, 335–39, 383–388, 615–20, 645–50.